Going off the Rails

Global Capital and
the Crisis of Legitimacy

John Plender

WILEY

Published by John Wiley & Sons Ltd, The Atrium, Southern Gate, Chichester,
West Sussex PO19 8SQ, England

Telephone (+44) 1243 779777

Email (for orders and customer service enquiries): cs-books@wiley.co.uk
Visit our Home Page on www.wileyeurope.com or www.wiley.com

Other Wiley Editorial Offices

John Wiley & Sons Inc., 111 River Street, Hoboken, NJ 07030, USA

Jossey-Bass, 989 Market Street, San Francisco, CA 94103-1741, USA

Wiley-VCH Verlag GmbH, Boschstr. 12, D-69469 Weinheim, Germany

John Wiley & Sons Australia Ltd, 33 Park Road, Milton, Queensland 4064, Australia

John Wiley & Sons (Asia) Pte Ltd, 2 Clementi Loop #02-01, Jin Xing Distripark, Singapore
129809

John Wiley & Sons Canada Ltd, 22 Worcester Road, Etobicoke, Ontario, Canada M9W 1L1

Wiley also publishes its books in a variety of electronic formats. Some content that appears in
print may not be available in electronic books.

British Library Cataloguing in Publication Data

A catalogue record for this book is available from the British Library

ISBN 0-470-85314-X

Project management by Originator, Gt Yarmouth, Norfolk (typeset in 11/15pt Goudy)
Printed and bound in Great Britain by Antony Rowe Ltd, Chippenham, Wiltshire
This book is printed on acid-free paper responsibly manufactured from sustainable forestry
in which at least two trees are planted for each one used for paper production.

Contents

About the author   vii

Preface   ix

Part 1   IMPATIENT CAPITAL   1

1   The turn of the global tide   3
2   The Third World ghetto   25
3   Dr Pangloss comes to Wall Street   53
4   Europe pulls up a drawbridge   81

Part 2   DOUBLE STANDARDS   107

5   Uncreative destruction   109
6   The just-in-time CEO   137
7   Enron, alas   161

Part 3   THE LIMITS OF CONVERGENCE   183

8   Apocalypse later   185
9   The semi-detached samurai   201

Part 4   BEYOND SHAREHOLDER VALUE   217

10   The legitimacy crisis   219
11   Putting the world to rights   243

Index   275

About the author

After completing a modern languages degree at Oxford University, John Plender joined Deloitte, Plender, Griffiths & Co. in the City of London in 1967, qualifying as a chartered accountant in 1970.

John subsequently moved into journalism and was appointed Financial Editor of *The Economist* in 1974, where he remained until taking up a governmental appointment in the Foreign Office policy-planning staff in 1980.

On leaving the Foreign Office, John took up his current position at the *Financial Times* where he has been a senior editorial writer and columnist. In addition to this he has been a regular current affairs broadcaster for both the BBC and Channel Four.

Formerly a member of the London Stock Exchange's Quality of Markets Advisory Committee and a past chairman of Pensions and Investment Research Consultants (PIRC), a corporate governance consultancy, John is currently a non-executive director of Quintain PLC. He chairs the Advisory Council of the Centre for the Study of Financial Innovation, a London-based think tank and is a member of the advisory board of the Association of Corporate Treasurers.

John served on the UK government's Company Law Review Steering Group and has consulted on corporate governance for the International Finance Corporation, the private sector lending and investing arm of the World Bank.

In 1994 John received the Wincott Award, Britain's premier prize for financial journalism. Previous works by the author include: *That's the Way the Money Goes*, Andre Deutsch, 1981, on the rise of British pension funds; *The Square Mile* (with Paul Wallace), Hutchison, 1985, based on a six-part documentary television series covering the Big Bang in the City of London's markets; *A Stake in the Future*, Nicholas Brealey Publishing, 1997, outlining a left-of-centre economic agenda before the election that brought Tony Blair to power in the UK.

Preface

A striking feature of the English-speaking countries at the turn of the millennium was that they seemed to be doing better economically than just about everyone else. As a group they had grown faster for a decade than most of the other developed countries. They had provided a vital source of demand in a world economy where Japan was stagnating and continental Europe was advancing at a painfully slow pace. And they appeared, with the US very much in the lead, to be more flexible than others in adapting to the forces of globalization and technological change. This performance bred a conviction among policy-makers and business people in the English-speaking world that their model of capitalism was inherently superior because of its ability to deploy capital more efficiently. That in turn led to the belief that the world would and should converge on the Anglo-American model, with its emphasis on free capital markets and the primacy of the shareholder.

When I started this book, which was written between September 2001 and June 2002, with some subsequent revisions, my aim was to explore this assumption about the systemic superiority of the Anglo-American model, which had a suspiciously triumphalist ring about it. Since the Asian crisis, private portfolio capital flows, which were substantially managed by the Americans and the British, appeared highly unstable. The US stock market had been through a period of wild euphoria, which had prompted much wasteful investment both in high technology and the more mundane areas of the economy. It also seemed odd, if the model was so efficient, that its advocates had so signally failed to persuade anti-globalization protesters, as well as many politicians in the non-Anglophone world, of its merits.

The standard response of mainstream policy-makers and economists to the wave of anti-globalization protests has been dismissive. They argue bluntly that we need more globalization, not less. I certainly share the view that the best hope for the world's poor lies in economic growth and that too little private capital currently flows to the emerging market economies. Many well-meaning protesters fail to appreciate that in advocating policies that entail lower economic growth they seriously damage the interests of developing countries. Yet advocates of the Anglo-American model have also shown a patronizing complacency in downplaying the problems of free capital flows. They have succeeded in conveying the impression to those who worry about the impact of liberal economic policies on global inequality or the environment that the real agenda is to create a world fit for business moguls and investment bankers. Small wonder that the anti-globalization protesters remain vocal. Though a far-from-coherent group, they rightly sense a lack of legitimacy in the workings of capital.

Since Enron, WorldCom and all the other corporate scandals, the issue of legitimacy has moved to the forefront of attention. The American model has been shown to be much less impressive than its cheerleaders in Washington had thought. Too many companies in the 1990s pursued a corrupted concept of shareholder value in which managers who were heavily rewarded with stock options became obsessed with pushing up the stock price at the expense of all else. Accountancy, a vital part of the plumbing of the capitalist system, turned out to be weak, and the independence of the auditor had been eroded thanks to the aggressive commercialization of the accountancy profession. Non-executive directors had failed to do their job in monitoring the executives, as had the big institutional shareholders. The checks and balances of the American system were exposed as hopelessly ineffective.

In the UK the story was more one of incompetence than crookery.

Yet the catastrophic decline of Marconi was one of many examples of directors and managers who worked under a warped system of accountability being driven time and again into injudicious takeovers. Here and elsewhere the takeover mechanism was failing to deliver on its promise of facilitating the kind of creative destruction that was supposed to be capitalism's great strength. As in the US, the system had become hostage to the short-term movement of share prices and the values of investment bankers. The obsession with financial activity and corporate deal-making distracted managers from the basic job of minding the shop.

After Enron, confidence in the integrity of the system has been severely dented. Yet a central theme of this book is that the Anglo-American system is in fact very different from the one conventionally described in the speeches of politicians, bankers and business people. The risks and rewards in the system have been so heavily manipulated by central bankers and corporate managers that many aspects of the model are no longer determined by the market. And the corruption of the shareholder value concept partly reflects a difficulty in adapting a 19th century capitalist model to the economic realities of the modern world.

Over the past decade and a half I have been involved in various ways in trying to make the UK model work more effectively. Pensions & Investment Research Consultants (PIRC), a corporate governance consultancy which I chaired until recently, helped promote shareholder activism in the UK. Then as a member of the UK Company Law Steering Group I spent three years pondering the question of how to adapt a company law framework that still bore a heavy imprint from the Gladstonian era to the demands of the 21st century. Latterly I have had some involvement with the Organization for Economic Cooperation and Development (OECD) – World Bank-backed Global Corporate Governance Forum, which has given me the opportunity to explore the same issues in the context of developing country needs.

Among the conclusions I have drawn from these experiences is that the Anglo-American model has been stretched to its limits in trying to cope with the transition to an economy in which human and social capital are of far greater importance than physical capital. Legal frameworks, traditional corporate governance disciplines and long-standing accountancy conventions have been struggling to address the growing importance of intangible values in the economy. The great stock market bubble that reached its climax at the turn of the millennium was, I believe, symptomatic in part of that strain. Vastly inflated boardroom pay awards in the form of stock options were likewise not just a matter of bubble-fed greed, but a symptom of this difficult transition. The distribution of the rewards between the different stakeholders in the knowledge economy was becoming messy and inequitable, not least because the heavy emphasis on the primacy of the shareholder in Anglo-American capital markets was increasingly at odds with the thrust of technological development.

Against that background the policy response to corporate scandals is addressing only the obvious and superficial systemic flaws, instead of looking at the more subtle distortions in the incentive structure of the capital markets that affect the behaviour of all the actors in the economic drama, along with the financial well-being and livelihoods of millions of ordinary people. I have tried in this book to explain to the intelligent general reader how the system works and to explore these distorted incentives in so far as they influence both the pattern of global capital flows around the world and the behaviour of corporations. It amounts to a set of perspectives, all of which look at the world through the narrow, but revealing focus of capital. This helps us understand such things as why developing countries end up financing the world's richest economy, the US, instead of the other way round; how markets have come to appear so unstable; and why the legitimacy of the wealth creation process is being eroded by business scandals. I approach these questions from the position that the globalization of capital flows has enormous potential for good, but that we will have to make the liberal capital regime work a great deal better for that potential to be realized.

The debate about the relative merits of the many different models of capitalism has, I believe, been greatly overblown. All the developed

country models have advantages and disadvantages. It is possible that
the English-speaking countries' models – in the plural, because they
all have their differences – may be better suited than most in adapting
to the challenges of globalization, the requirements of the knowledge
economy and the ageing of populations. But it is not self-evident. And
if the rest of the world moves closer to the Anglo-American model, it
is unlikely to converge on it, not least because the model suffers from
a lack of legitimacy relating specifically to the way the corrupted
shareholder value concept works. The risk is that, while the malfunctioning of the capital markets may not be an economic disaster, it may
nonetheless strengthen the constituency for anti-market policies and
more specifically for protectionism. The odds are against a full-scale
retreat from globalization of the kind that took place in the Slump of
the 1930s, but the risk is nonetheless there and it needs to be
managed.

In writing this book I have been grateful for the sympathetic
support of Richard Lambert and Andrew Gowers, successive editors
of the *Financial Times*, and colleagues on the paper too numerous to
mention. But I have to acknowledge a specific debt to Martin Wolf,
who is an unfailing stimulus. Among countless others who have
influenced the content of the book I would like to express my particular gratitude to my old friend Brian Reading and his colleagues
Tim Congdon and Charles Dumas at Lombard Street Research, to
Michael Brett, David Hale, Andrew Smithers, Anne Simpson, Ira
Millstein, Jonathan Charkham, Robert Monks, Allen Sykes, Geoffrey
Owen, David Marsh, Philip Augar, Jonathan Rickford, Andrew
Hilton, David Lascelles, Paul Coombes, Ariyoshi Okumura, Gabriele
Pantucci, Robert Lenzner, Adrian Wyatt and to all the colleagues
with whom I worked at PIRC. None of them, I hasten to add, will
agree with all my arguments. I am also grateful for the helpful com-
ments of John Wiley's anonymous referee. It is a great sadness to me
that my friend and colleague Peter Martin, an inspired commentator
on many of the issues here, did not live long enough to read the book.

The generous contributions of others will be apparent to readers at
every point in the text. Much helpful input has come from seminars at

the London School of Economics, the Yale School of Management, the World Bank, the Royal Institute of International Affairs, the German-British Forum, and the Centre for the Study of Financial Innovation. I am enormously grateful for the enthusiastic support of my agent, Leslie Gardner. Also to the super-efficient Julia Hubbard at the *Financial Times*, without whose help my day-to-day journalism would have been more seriously derailed. The greatest encouragement throughout has been my beloved wife Stephanie, for whose generosity I am forever grateful. All errors are, of course, my own.

Part 1

Impatient Capital

1

The turn of the global tide

"America," said the British historian Arnold Toynbee, "is a large friendly dog in a very small room. Every time it wags its tail it knocks over a chair." During the Cold War a few broken chairs seemed a small price to pay for a very large friend. But with the demise of the Soviet Union and the rising tide of globalization many of America's friends started to feel that the room was growing smaller and the dog more threatening. That feeling reached a peak of intensity when George W. Bush graduated in 2001 from the governorship of Texas to the presidency of the United States.

Suspicious non-Americans took fright at the unilateralist streak in the new Bush administration, as it retreated from environmental and missile treaty commitments. And they worried that globalization was becoming synonymous with Americanization, which many equated with a litany of perceived horrors that included the death penalty, inner city violence, genetically modified "Frankenfoods", brutal labour markets and chronically volatile capital flows.

These concerns went into abeyance after the terrorist assault on the World Trade Center in September 2001 and the Bush Administration's apparent conversion to a less parochial foreign policy. But they quickly returned following moves such as America's unilateral imposition of curbs on steel imports and George W. Bush's denunciation of Iraq, Iran and North Korea as part of an "axis of evil" in the world. So there remains in continental Europe and much of Asia a sense of unease over the thrust of US policy, along with a profound fear that the world has become less tolerant of differing ways of organizing capital and labour. Many have felt that a Darwinian process of competition between the 57 different varieties of capitalism is leading to global convergence on a single Rotweiler version that emphasizes the primacy of shareholder rights against those of other stakeholders such as employees and the wider community.

Such fears, originally voiced by the French businessman Michel Albert in his book *Capitalisme contre Capitalisme*,[1] have given rise to a charged debate and a big literature. They have also played a part in the numerous anti-globalization protests around the world since the riots at the World Trade Organization meeting in Seattle in 1999. Yet the US policy-making establishment appears deaf to the anxieties of those outside America on what amounts to a central policy challenge of the century, namely, how to manage economic interdependence or, in plain language, the fact that one country's policies invariably have fallout for others in the context of the increasing globalization of trade and capital flows.

Since the turn of the millennium much triumphalist rhetoric has emanated from the US political and financial community claiming that the market-oriented American system is endowed with innate economic and technological advantages. The succession of corporate scandals at Enron, Global Crossing, Tyco, WorldCom and the rest has modestly dented the confidence of American policy-makers. Yet George W. Bush maintained, in the face of these excesses, that "the American economy is the most creative and enterprising and productive system ever devised." His response to the scandals was based on the premise that there was nothing much wrong with the model and that the problem was down to a few bad apples in the barrel.

Economic triumphalism is not, of course, a vice exclusive to America. In 1958 when the Cold War was notably tense, the Soviet leader Nikita Khrushchev famously declared that Soviet eco-

---

[1] Le Seuil, 1991. The English language version, *Capitalism against Capitalism*, Whurr Publishers, 1993.

nomic strength would bury the Americans. And in the 1980s visitors to Tokyo like myself were often assured by Japanese businessmen that America and Europe were finished as players in the world economy – a view that overlooked the fact that economics is not a zero-sum game like chess, where the victory of one player inevitably entails the defeat of another. But people more plausibly sought to explain the extra-ordinary success of the Japanese and German economies at that time by reference to innate national advantages in culture and in the wider political, economic and social institutions that provided the frame-work for their markets. Their particular models of capitalism were held to be in special harmony with the thrust of contemporary technological innovation, notably in areas such as manufacturing and consumer electronics where the Germans and Japanese were dominant.

New Age-ism

The American claim to systemic economic superiority that emerged at the turn of the millennium was similarly predicated on the assumption that economic and technological change was playing to US strengths. The extreme form of the argument is admittedly no longer much heard. This was the assertion that the country had arrived at a new paradigm in which information and communications technology was transforming the US economy in a way and on a scale quite different from earlier, enabling technologies such as steam, rail or electricity. Many Americans convinced themselves in the second half of the 1990s that the US had embarked on a new era in which all the conventional rules of economics and finance had become redun-dant and the business cycle, the bane of economic life since Adam, had been abolished. Anyone who dared to question this prevailing wisdom of the late 1990s, or the astonishing values placed on loss-making high-technology companies, was curtly told by the super-optimists of Wall Street and Silicon Valley that they "simply didn't get it".

Economic history tells us that new-era psychology of this kind usually leads to a stock market bubble followed by a crash, which in turn precipitates a recession. Events in the US at the start of the new century followed this time-honoured pattern. It was true that the US enjoyed a productivity spurt in the second half of the 1990s on the basis of heavy investment by American business in the new information and communications technologies. The spurt was not matched in Europe or Japan. It remains true that those technologies will continue to yield great benefits over future decades. But since the investment boom proved unsustainable, much of the supposed miracle was probably little more than a cyclical fluctuation. And the business cycle, far from disappearing, produced at the start of the decade one of the most savage inventory corrections in living memory, as managers reduced the amount of goods they held in stock to confront a lower level of demand from customers.

A proper assessment of the underlying productivity trend will not be possible until the end of the current economic cycle. It is nonetheless clear that the growth in productivity achieved in those five years, however impressive in relation to Europe and Japan, did not match the productivity growth of the 1960s. If there was something historically unusual in the boom and bust, it lay rather in the fact that production in the industries most affected by these technological innovations was organized on a global basis. So when American business stopped investing in the new technologies, the economic and stock market fallout caused an unexpected degree of pain across the world.[2]

The more enduring argument for the superiority of the American model, which continues to echo around the world in the new millennium, rests on the way capital is deployed within the system. It applies with equal force to the economies of the other English-speaking countries, which with America outperformed most other developed countries in the 1990s in terms of their growth in gross domestic

---

[2] For an extended discussion, see *World Economic Outlook*, October 2001 (International Monetary Fund).

product, or output, per person. The striking feature they all share in common is that their capital markets play a very large role in the economy when compared with others in the developed world, most notably in continental Europe.

No-one has put the case more cogently or with greater authority than Lawrence Summers, former US Treasury Secretary, Dean of Harvard University and an economist of world repute. In a lecture delivered at the London Stock Exchange in June 2001 Summers confessed to his audience that he had once been sympathetic to the notion that Anglo-American markets were speculative and too short-term in focus, while German and Japanese companies enjoyed closer and more constructive relationships with the providers of capital. The ability of the Germans and Japanese to take a long-run view of investment was generally reckoned in the 1980s to be of great benefit to the wider economy and society.

This, Summers now felt, was entirely wrong. Most of the investments carried out in the name of long-termism in Japan and Germany had shown poor returns. "It was," he said, "impatient, value-focused shareholders who did America a great favour by forcing capital out of its traditional companies, and thereby making it available to fund the venture capitalists and the Ciscos and the Microsofts that are now in a position to propel our economy very rapidly forward." Summers heaped especial praise on the venture capital market. "The most important reason why the United States has been uniquely successful in technology," he added, "is that the United States is the only country where you can raise your first $100m before you buy your first suit . . ."

Financial innovation, a particular strength of the US, had been a boon because, among other things, it allowed high-tech firms with no profits to use stock options as remuneration for their employees. The existence of sophisticated stock markets allowed venture capitalists to take risks backing fledgling high-tech companies in the knowledge that they could sell these early stage investments in very big public markets. Moreover, said Summers, the balance of advantage had shifted from large companies like General Motors and IBM that had operated in their heyday on a command-and-control model of management toward a less crude system of motivation and incentive. That is, the new US economy worked with a more refined set of sticks and carrots and favoured a high degree of decentralization. The UK, with its extensive financial infrastructure, enjoyed similar advantages.

Summers concluded that "if you are looking for reasons why some countries succeed and why other countries do not succeed in the new global economy, a very large part of it goes to the greater success of the successful countries in channelling capital into the right places and then making sure that it is used in a disciplined and functioning way ... Indeed prudent budget policies that make large amounts of capital available and well-functioning financial markets that use that capital well are two crucial requisites for national economic success in the global economy." For those who equated the financial sophistication of the Anglo-American system with financial instability he had nothing but scorn. That belief, he suggested, "is observed in inverse proportion to knowledge of these matters."

Liberals on top

Summers' encapsulation of the argument about the efficacy of Anglo-American capital is now firmly embedded in the Washington consensus, the set of political and economic tenets associated with successive US administrations, the US Federal Reserve and with the big Washington-based financial institutions, the International Monetary Fund and the World Bank. This view emphasizes financial deregulation, tight budgetary discipline, the promotion of international trade and investment, privatization and other market-oriented policies. Under George W. Bush the US has become less committed to budgetary rectitude and open trade. But in terms of what the US preaches to the rest of the world on economic policy, the difference between President Bush and his predecessor Bill Clinton is only a matter of degree.

As with much else in the Washington mindset, the belief in the efficient use of capital harks back to 19th century liberalism, which the historian of economic thought Eric Roll has called "the philosophy of triumphant capitalism".[3] At a time when capital flowed freely around the world economic liberals believed in individualism, limited government, free markets and enforceable property rights. They saw the shareholder as the ultimate risk-taker in the economy, who consequently enjoyed a legitimate right to the residual profits of enterprise after all the contractual claims of other stakeholders such as customers, employees, creditors and society had been settled. Business people were assumed to discharge their wider obligations to society simply by pursuing the narrow objective of profit in the interests of the owners of the corporation, the shareholders. For 19th century liberals, an economy organized on this basis promised accelerating moral as well as material progress and a suitable distribution of rewards in society.

Modern economic liberals have seen in the lifting of national controls on the flow of capital an opportunity to allocate capital more efficiently around the globe. Part of the justification for such liberalization was the belief that if investors were able to diversify their risks through globalization, the global economy and global markets would be more stable. And in fact capital now drives the process of globalization far more than trade. In the 15 years to 2000, the outstanding stock of cross-border bank-lending rose from less than $1 trillion to $6.5 trillion, a factor of around seven compared with a factor of three for the growth in world trade over the same period. Other cross-border flows into equities, or stocks and shares, and bonds – the capital market term for IOUs – are reckoned to have risen even faster.[4]

Many also see the globalization of capital flows as a potential solution to the developed world's demographic problems. Common to all long-term economic forecasts is the recognition that in Europe

---

[3] Eric Roll, A History of Economic Thought, Faber & Faber, 1938.

[4] Figures from the Bank for International Settlements, quoted by Alastair Clark, a director of the Bank of England, in his contribution to Developing Countries and the Global Financial System, edited by Stephany Griffith-Jones and Amar Bhattacharya, Commonwealth Secretariat, 2001.

and Japan a diminishing pool of workers is going to have to support an expanding number of retired people. Yet if the surplus savings of mature economies in these regions can be transferred to younger economies in the developing world where profit opportunities are greater and returns on capital higher, it will be easier to finance more generous retirement incomes in the developed world. This is the most ambitious element of the globalization project since it requires people in countries with very much lower living standards and hugely different institutions to share the underlying assumptions of the Anglo-American capital market model and to accept an exceptional degree of financial interdependence.

In domestic markets, economic liberals also emphasize the importance of a critical change in the way Anglo-American capitalism works – the dramatic increase in takeover activity. Mergers and acquisitions have long been a feature of the corporate world and an instrument of rationalization in mature industries. But it is only recently that they have become a central discipline of the capital markets because of the growing number and size of hostile takeover bids. In American corporate life these have become one of the main engines of creative destruction, the competitive process identified by the economist Joseph Schumpeter as the ultimate dynamic of capitalism. It involves the continuous scrapping of old technologies or, as the chairman of the Federal Reserve Alan Greenspan puts it, "a continuous churning of an economy in which the new displaces the old".[5] The same discipline applies in the UK, Australia and New Zealand. In fact the contested takeover is one of the more extreme expressions of the English-speaking countries' common adversarial culture. It allows professional investors who dominate the modern capital markets a powerful say in who manages companies and how. The robust logic of the hostile takeover increasingly affects the employment prospects of millions around the world.

There is no doubt that what the Continental Europeans inaccur-

[5] Robert P. Maxon lecture on globalization at George Washington University, 3 December 2001.

ately refer to as the "Anglo-Saxon" way of corporate life does indeed have the potential for great economic efficiency. It also helps explain a significant difference between the US and leading Continental European economies. While the Americans and Europeans now have broadly similar levels of labour productivity, or output per hour of work, America uses much less capital to achieve that output. In other words it has a significant advantage in the productivity of its capital. That advantage is also apparent *vis-à-vis* Japan. Many economists also claim that financial systems in which companies rely more heavily on the use of equity capital rather than bank finance are better suited to the needs of high technology. This is because banks are said to lend less readily to knowledge-based industries where the assets are intangible than to those with physical assets such as plant and machinery that provide hard collateral. By contrast, sophisticated capital markets with vibrant venture capital activity are thought to be better at financing companies where the competitive advantage lies in intellectual creativity.[6] So the triumphalist thesis seems, at first sight, to accord with economic reality in suggesting that the Anglo-American way of recycling capital from old to new industries works more efficiently. In which case it would appear that Europe is in trouble.

Capitalism without capital

The peculiar nature of the versions of capitalism adhered to by the big continental European economies of Germany, France and Italy is that stock markets have traditionally been small in relation to the countries' economic output and shareholders have been of only marginal importance. This is partly because the Germans, French and Italians finance their retirement mainly through pay-as-you-go state pensions, where retirement benefits of the older generation are paid mainly out

---

[6] For a review of the arguments, see Raghuram G. Rajan and Luigi Zingales of Chicago University, "Financial systems, industrial structure and growth", in the *Oxford Review of Economic Policy*, Vol. 17, No. 4, Winter 2001.

of taxes and pension contributions of those in work. It is a legacy of the innovative social insurance put in place in the late 19th century by the German Chancellor Bismarck. Pay-as-you-go has provided far more generous pensions to the mass of the Continental European population than the Americans and British have enjoyed. And it does not require the support of sophisticated financial markets because the people's pension contributions have not been invested in the stock market. The security of retirement incomes depends more heavily on the state's implicit guarantee rather than on the build-up of independent investment funds. The outcome has been a rare example of brilliantly successful public sector financial-engineering, leading to a form of capitalism without capital. Higher levels of benefit have been paid at an earlier stage than would have been possible with a pension system that relied on advance funding. Meantime the role played by the stock markets in the Anglo-American system in financing industry and commerce has been filled in much of Continental Europe by banks.

Yet, if the new conventional wisdom about the Anglo-American model of capitalism is right, the Continental European economies are at a disadvantage in recycling capital from old industrial sectors to new high-tech industries. Despite the notable advances resulting from the arrival of Europe's single market and the introduction of the euro, capital markets are still much less developed than those of the US or UK. Since hostile takeovers remain a relative rarity in continental Europe and attract growing political antipathy, creative destruction in mature industries is inhibited – especially against the background of employment legislation that makes it difficult and expensive to fire people.

Much the same applies to Japan. Although the Japanese stock market is large in relation to the size of the economy, the main purpose of the Japanese corporation is to serve the interests of managers and employees, not shareholders. Hostile takeovers remain anathema there and equity capital serves a very different function. It exists to cement relationships between members of the loosely knit industrial groups known as *keiretsu*. Members of these groups have traditionally maintained cross-shareholdings in each other as an indication of their mutual commitment and as a protection against hostile takeover by predators from outside the group. As in Germany, Japanese industrialists have traditionally regarded outside share-holders as a source of unwelcome pressure for short-term performance.

The message implicit in American capital market triumphalism and in countless research documents produced by investment bankers around the world is that these countries will have to change their ways. If they fail to converge on the Anglo-American capital market model, the argument runs, they will incur a heavy and lasting eco-nomic penalty in the shape of much lower living standards than in the US. They will also forgo the opportunity to mitigate the problems associated with the ageing of their populations. Yet it remains worth asking whether these arguments are any more plausible than earlier assertions of the superiority of the German or Japanese models. For the modern conventional wisdom on capital, as enunciated by the former US Treasury Secretary, can be challenged on almost every point.

Dissecting Larry Summers

For a start, the suggestion that efficient financial markets are the key to the ranking achieved by countries in the global economic race is at odds with the logic of globalization. If companies in the developed world suffer from deficient capital markets at home, they can and do now look for capital abroad. NASDAQ, the US stock exchange on which countless high-tech companies are quoted, actively scours the world for prospective candidates for its market. The same is true of other exchanges. The venture capital market is similarly global. Continental European and Asian economies have not excelled in the financing of new companies in high-technology areas. Yet the American venture capital boom of the 1990s spilled over into the rest of the world, providing finance for both fledgling companies and management buyouts from mature companies. And the larger European countries set up their own imitations of NASDAQ with a view to encouraging the development of local high-tech companies. If Europe had a problem in this area, it was lack of entrepreneurship rather than a shortage of capital.

There is, admittedly, academic evidence to suggest that developing countries that are reluctant to accept foreign capital inflows and that have underdeveloped financial systems may be disadvantaged.[7] Yet this sits oddly with experience in China, where real growth in gross domestic product has been cautiously estimated at an average $7\frac{1}{2}$ per cent a year between 1978 and 1995 despite the burden of a ramshackle and largely state-owned financial system that is in a state of near-collapse.[8] That is a phenomenal rate of growth by any historic standard. China has also been reluctant to give foreign capital an easy entrée. The argument works rather better for the transition economies in Eastern Europe where those that opted for rapid development of well-regulated capital markets appear to have enjoyed a big relative advantage.[9]

The Summers argument also makes sense in relation to Japan, which is imperfectly integrated into the global capital markets. In the Japanese bubble of the 1980s capital was seriously misallocated as a result of absurdly inflated stock prices. The banking system was also poor at allocating credit. Having been used to taking instructions on lending priorities from bureaucrats in the Ministry of International Trade and Industry (MITI), banks had little expertise in making independent judgements about the creditworthiness of corporations in free markets. The resulting and continuing misallocation of resources provides part of the explanation for the poor performance of the Japanese economy since 1990. That no doubt helps explain why

---

[7] Geert Bekaert and Campbell R. Harvey, "Economic growth and financial liberalisation", *NEBR Reporter*, Spring 2001 (National Bureau of Economic Research).

[8] See *Chinese Economic Performance in the Long Run* by Angus Maddison, OECD, 1998.

[9] See Glaeser, Johnson and Shleifer in "Coase versus the Coasians" in the *Quarterly Journal of Economics*, vol. 116, No. 3, 2001, where they compare the successful development of capital markets in Poland with a dismal outcome in the Czech Republic.

arguments about the productivity of US capital have proved more durable than those about the so-called new paradigm.

What casts the Summers case in a more curious light is its application to the UK. For the UK shares with the US a flexible model that is well designed for the efficient recycling of capital. Yet despite this, Britain's productivity growth did not show any comparable spurt with that of the US in the late 1990s. There was no information technology revolution in the UK. Yet perhaps the most bizarre feature of the Summers case is that it should have been made so soon after the peak of the greatest stock market bubble of all time. This market malfunctioning was not confined to the dotcom boom. On conventional yardsticks relating to the valuation of corporate earnings and assets, the US stock market set off from the mid-1990s into unprecedented and stratospheric territory, with serious consequences for the wider economy. Because a rise in stock prices causes the cost of capital to fall, the bubble led to capital costs being artificially depressed. With capital markets now being closely linked regardless of geography, industrialists around the world were confronted with misleading price signals for capital that encouraged them to engage in wasteful over-investment. And since the value of high-tech companies was wildly overestimated in this period, the waste was greatest in the areas of information technology and telecommunications.

Whatever else impatient shareholders may have been doing, they were not concentrating single-mindedly on the pursuit of value. With their enthusiasm for productivity miracles and the new-era economy, they ignored the fact that there has been no historical correlation between productivity growth and growth in corporate earnings. Even the Chairman of the Federal Reserve Alan Greenspan became increasingly impressed with the productivity prospects for the economy, retreating from his much-quoted statement in 1996 that the stock market was prey to "irrational exuberance". In fact, it can be argued that the thinking behind US monetary policy – the setting of interest rates and credit conditions to stabilize the economy – was deeply flawed in this period. Many of the policy mistakes of the 1980s

Japanese bubble were repeated in the US in the 1990s, but with an impact outside the US that was greatly magnified by globalization.

What a waste!

Nowhere was the misallocation of resources greater than in the market for venture capital. By the time Summers was lauding the US venture capitalists this market was already experiencing one of its worst manic depressive swings in years and it was well nigh impossible for a young high-tech business to raise $100m. In the preceding boom two-thirds of all venture capital funding between 1980 and 2000 took place in just two years, 1999 and 2000. By 2001 some in the market were estimating that nine-tenths of the venture capital committed in the bubble period of the late 1990s had been squandered, as too much capital beat a path to all the wrong places.[10] In the fevered atmosphere of the time, venture capitalists had given up conventional appraisal of business plans and had been investing by the seat of their pants for fear of missing out on the next Microsoft or Cisco Systems.[11] The resulting famine after the earlier feast was hardly a great advertisement for American capital efficiency.

The dotcom bubble also reflected a huge failure of corporate governance, the system of incentives and checks that encourages managers to drive the business forward within a framework of proper accountability. Instead of having a majority of independent non-executive directors, high-tech company boards were stuffed with service providers, venture capitalists and consultants. Because of their own business relationship with the company these people lacked objectivity. Many took payment in stock options, which impaired their ability to make dispassionate judgements. So this market

---

[10] *The Economist*, "The new-economy vultures", 8 December, 2001, p. 81.

[11] See Michael Lewis's highly entertaining account of the collapse of standards among Silicon Valley's venture capitalists in *The New New Thing*, Hodder & Stoughton, 1999 in the UK, W.W. Norton in the US.

could hardly be said to have operated in a disciplined and functioning way.

It has to be said that Europe was not immune from technology fever. While the Americans were betting furiously on Internet-related technologies, the Europeans were pumping money into scores of telecommunications companies that quickly foundered in the harsher economic climate of the new millennium. They also backed plenty of shaky information technology companies on markets such as Germany's Neuer Markt, which saw a catastrophic collapse. From the peak in March 2000 to the trough in September 2001 this market for fledgling companies shed 94 per cent of its value. The decision was taken to close it down in 2002. The question, then, is not so much about superior Anglo-American efficiency in deploying capital, but about which continent has been managing capital less badly than the other and how important that is for their respective economic performance.

There is no obvious answer. Euphoria prevailed on both sides of the Atlantic, with the main difference being that the bad judgements were perpetrated in the US mainly through markets and in Europe more by banks, whose credit judgements in sectors such as telecommunications were heavily influenced by what was happening in the markets. What can be said with reasonable certainty, in the light of the bursting of the bubble, is that if the US enjoyed a comparative advantage in the productivity of its capital, it did not lie exclusively in the way impatient shareholders promoted the recycling of capital from mature to new industries at the end of the 1990s. Work by McKinsey Global Institute, the research arm of the management consulting group, has shown that the recent advance in US productivity reflected incremental improvements in the way businesses were managed in conventional sectors of the economy such as retailing and whole-saling, as well as in information technology and telecoms. Moreover, other English-speaking countries such as Australia, which outper-formed the US in the 1990s in terms of growth in gross domestic product per person, were clearly not outperforming exclusively on the basis of recycling capital from old to new high-tech industries.

This underlines the dangers of explaining the sources of a country's economic strength by reference to a single characteristic of the economy. It is the economist's version of one-club golfing.

It follows that the conventional wisdom in the English-speaking countries about capital reflects a top-of-the-cycle complacency, just as German and Japanese triumphalism did a decade before. The reality is that capital markets have become increasingly accident-prone and unstable. Indeed, the globalization of capital flows has been accompanied by an unprecedented rise in the incidence of financial crises. And in the recent case of Argentina, the crisis came despite the country having been the star pupil of the Washington consensus school of economic thinking. The consensus is looking increasingly tarnished. In industry and commerce, meantime, Anglo-American shareholders and managers have been working in a system where incentives and accountability have become severely distorted. They preside over a takeover-based process of creative destruction that all too often turns out to be more destructive and less creative than the Washington prospectus proclaims.

Scandals and scams

Yet the most devastating indictment of the US model lies in the spate of corporate scandals that commenced with the collapse of the Houston-based energy-trader Enron in 2001. This raised the suspicion that much recycling of capital in the US system had more to do with shunting liabilities off the balance sheet and lining the managers' pockets than with the efficient allocation of resources. What drove the people at Enron was the urge to raise the price of the company's stock at any cost and thus enhance the value of their stock options. Like everyone else in the Anglo-American system they were pursuing a narrowly financial view of shareholder value, but they went to a dishonest extreme that caused employees to lose much of their pension entitlements. The means used by Enron's Kenneth Lay, Jeffrey Skilling, Andrew Fastow and others in pursuit of this goal included making large donations to the politicians on Capitol Hill and to George W. Bush's presidential campaign.

While Enron was the most extreme of the scandals, the nature of the scam was not unique. As one corporate disaster followed another in 2002 it became clear that many heroes of the bull market at companies like Global Crossing and Qwest Communications had acquired a mountainous pile of stock options during the bubble and cashed in many millions-worth before their companies hit trouble. All of this cast the shareholder revolution in an unexpected new light. America, it appeared, was no more immune from crony capitalism than the emerging economies of Asia. And the auditors, the ultimate guardians of the capitalist system, were also paying off the politicians and failing, at companies like Enron and WorldCom, to act as effective watchdogs.

WorldCom, under Chief Executive Bernie Ebbers and Chief Financial Officer Scott Sullivan, was driven by much the same imperative as Enron into cooking the books. Between 1999 and 2002 the giant telecoms group fraudulently treated billions of operating expenses as capital investment. The removal of this cost from the profit and loss account to the balance sheet meant that WorldCom's net income was vastly inflated, when it would otherwise have recorded losses. This was a much simpler accounting scam than at Enron and it was uncovered in the course of a routine internal audit. But the simplicity of the fraud also makes the failure of the external auditors all the more inexplicable. The auditor at WorldCom, as at Enron, was Andersen. The verdict of Lynn Turner, a former chief accountant at the Securities and Exchange Commission, on the initial revelation of fraud was damning: "The numbers are so big it has got to the point where the public wonders if you can depend on the auditors. If you can't find $3.8bn then what can you find?"[12] The numbers subsequently grew bigger still, rising to $9bn by the time WorldCom settled its fraud case with the SEC late in 2002. The disclosure on which the capital markets depended turned out to be more fallible than even seasoned

---

[12] *Financial Times*, 27 June 2002.

Wall Street watchers had feared. As the protracted post-mortem into Enron continued into 2002 and corporate scandals multiplied, the accounting practices of such leading companies as General Electric and IBM attracted hostile comment.

Meantime the integrity of investment bankers, who play a central role in the US and UK capital market model, was shown to have wilted under the pressure of conflicts of interest. In particular, the assessments of high-tech companies made by Wall Street analysts were devoid of independence. Those that were employed by investment banks were expected to curry favour with companies to help generate fees for the bank through issues of fresh capital, or mergers and acquisitions. And they were rewarded with bonuses that reflected the flow of such deals rather the quality of their analysis. So the scribes of Wall Street, with Henry Blodget of Merrill Lynch and Jack Grubman of Citigroup's Salomon Smith Barney to the fore, peddled absurdly favourable judgements of loss-making companies during the boom years.

As the investigation by New York State Attorney General Eliot Spitzer subsequently revealed, some were rubbishing companies in internal emails while enthusiastically promoting them in public. The conflict of interest inherent in the analysts' position close to the heart of the capital market system was systematically abused. At the same time Wall Street's big investment banks offered stock in "hot" initial public offerings to top corporate executives who were in a position to bring their company's business to the bank. In the euphoria of the bubble, the stock would often double or treble in value when trading began, giving the executive the opportunity to dump the stock at a large, instant profit. According to Eliot Spitzer, this was "commercial bribery", whereby chief executives were being bought off by the investment banks.

A breakdown of trust

The outcome of all this was that trust, which is essential to the smooth workings of markets, evaporated. Small investors all over

America felt they had been cynically exploited by the investment banks. A decline in the quantity and quality of corporate earnings contributed to a protracted bear market in which stocks and shares sank inexorably. Somehow the people in the investment banks and their clients in corporate America had succeeded in doing the unthinkable. They had turned the most optimistic nation on earth into a poorer, gloomier, miserably uncertain place. So the Anglo-American capital market model was beset by a crisis of legitimacy. While leading politicians, business people and economists continued to declare their unwavering belief in the superiority of the shareholder-value-based model of capitalism, there was a progressive erosion of public confidence. And not without reason. Enron, a messianic advocate of deregulation and a pioneer of financial innovation, had appeared to represent everything that was most dynamic about the American system. Yet it was a sham. Companies like Tyco and WorldCom exploited the takeover mechanism to the full, yet ended up revealing huge losses on their acquisitions and firing thousands of employees.

Many of these business chiefs who destroyed value on a grand scale were richly rewarded. Typical of the rewards-for-failure culture was the acquisitive British telecom group Vodafone where the chief executive, Sir Christopher Gent, was awarded a multi-million pound compensation package after recording the biggest loss in UK corporate history. Somehow the relationship between risk and reward in the capitalist system seemed to have gone completely haywire. And the extent to which the notion of shareholder value had become corrupted was perfectly illustrated by WorldCom's Bernie Ebbers in responding to a *Financial Times* reporter's question about the company's low return on capital before it all turned sour. "Investors," he replied, "do not care if a company's return on capital is 6 or 60 per cent. They only care that the share price goes up."

The loss of public confidence in the integrity of the system persists. It is worrying because the proponents of the capital market model are at least right about the importance, both political and economic, of how capital is allocated. The way it is deployed around the world matters greatly for stability and economic prosperity. With the

ageing of the populations of so many countries in the developed
world, it is also vital that people remain confident about the merits
of saving and investing for their retirement. Yet the system is not
working as it should. Nor is this just a reflection of Enron, WorldCom,
the dotcom bubble and the other excesses that occurred at the peak of
the 1990s' bull market. Looked at from a broader perspective, the
globalization of capital flows is incomplete and imperfect. Indeed,
extraordinary though it sounds, the allocation of capital around the
21st century world is in some respects less efficient than in the 19th
century when telecommunications were rudimentary and computers
non-existent. So the vital challenge for a post-Cold War world in
which capitalism faces no competition from a systematic alternative
view is how to make the process work better, in the interests of the
citizens of both rich and poor countries.

Yet the Anglo-American establishment is losing the globalization
argument because it is hopelessly out of touch. Not only has it failed
to engage with the arguments of anti-globalization protesters, it has
failed to recognize that *within its own terms* the liberal capital market
model is not working properly. And its politicians, business leaders
and investment bankers display blatant double standards in peddling a
version of the model abroad that is notably harsher than the one that
they tolerate back at home. Part of the argument of this book is that
the resulting gap between rhetoric and reality has become so wide that
politicians around the world will baulk at the idea of convergence on
the Anglo-American model.

Globalization has enormous potential to improve living standards
in both the developed and the developing worlds. Yet it cannot be
ignored that, while the lifting of constraints on international capital
flows has made global economic growth more stable, national growth
has often been less stable, especially among developing countries.
And in the developed world, the intensification of competition has
obliged people in mature industries to confront continuing painful
adjustments. To put up with the resulting insecurity, they have to
feel that there is inherent legitimacy in the way the system works.

The risk in the great globalization experiment has always been that the liberalizing tide will turn as a result of the hard-headed calculations of developed-world politicians rather than the squeals of protesters. And few appear to grasp how far the developed-world governmental backlash against the free movement of capital across and within national boundaries has already gone. To that extent, the worries of anti-globalization protesters about the waning power of the nation state can be seen to be greatly oversimplified. Governments are busy imposing more curbs, with varying degrees of effectiveness, on global capital in an attempt to tame what they perceive to be wild markets, just as they are doing in a more obvious way with trade barriers. They are also, as we shall see, preparing to use the full powers of the state to ensure that there is no uniform convergence on the Anglo-American model. The story of the first decade of the new millennium will be as much about the limits of global convergence as about the onward march of triumphant Anglo-American capital. The tension is already apparent. The only question is what impact the attempt to prevent further capital market integration will have on economic growth and human welfare.

The American writer and journalist H. L. Mencken once remarked that for every complex problem there is a solution that is neat, plausible and wrong. Proof of the wisdom of his remark can be seen in the main US legislative attempt to restore confidence in the system, the Sarbanes-Oxley act of 2002, which is a mixture of the sensible, the hasty and the ill-conceived. That is a salutary warning to anyone who ponders the challenge of how to restore legitimacy and efficiency to the workings of capital. The suggestions for policy that are scattered through the rest of this book, and more especially in the final chapter, make no claim to be a comprehensive or definitive set of prescriptions. They are simply the best contribution that the author can offer, on the hoof, to a fast-moving debate that will run and run.

2

The Third World ghetto

Whether you believe that capital is being efficiently used around the world rather depends on where you come from. Since 1970 the US and UK have been the world's dominant suppliers and users of private capital, investing huge sums and absorbing huge investments from elsewhere.[1] So it is not entirely surprising that the chief apologists for the status quo in global capital markets come from the Anglo-American camp. If, on the other hand, you stand in the shoes of an African like Sanou M'Baye, it looks very different.

I first met Sanou M'Baye in the early 1990s when he was a senior official at the African Development Bank (ADB) in London. An economist from Senegal, he had been attracted to the bank because he wanted to engage with its mission, which was to promote economic development and alleviate poverty. These aims were in tune with his religious beliefs – he was a devout Muslim. But over the years I realized that he was becoming increasingly disillusioned with the job. It was not difficult to see why. On any reckoning this regional development bank was making precious little mark on the poorer countries of a region where a vast expansion of the population was magnifying the damaging impact of deteriorating economic perform-ance on incomes per head.

---

[1] Source: *World Economic Outlook*, October 2001, p. 151 (International Monetary Fund).

As far as M'Baye was concerned the ADB was little more than a machine for financing Western exports to the region. There was a growing divorce, he felt, between what the bank said and what it did. And he was unimpressed by the frenetic trading activity going on all around him in London's international markets, which seemed largely irrelevant to the needs of the developing world. M'Baye became an increasingly rebellious bureaucrat, questioning policy within the bank and venting his frustrations by writing articles for publications such as *Le Monde Diplomatique* and *Jeune Afrique*. Eventually he decided he had had enough. He retired prematurely to spend more time in Senegal where he immersed himself in Sufism, the Islamic form of mysticism. It was a similar protest, but in a civilized and humane form, to that of the Islamic terrorists who wrecked the twin towers in New York – a profound expression of impotence, marginalization and despair.

A central challenge for Western capital, as for Western foreign policy, after the atrocities of 11 September, 2001, is to engage more constructively with the developing world. Poverty may not be the root cause of terrorism, but it is surely one of many contributory factors. And if Western capital fails to engage, there must be a risk that more poor countries will become a seedbed for instability and international terrorism. So the retreat into religious contemplation by Sanou M'Baye, an exceptionally talented and normally extrovert member of Africa's intellectual elite, highlighted for me the extent to which private capital was not making the right global connections. What has been going wrong?

In answering that question Western policy-makers usually put most of the emphasis on flaws in the developing countries' policies. Yet it is also revealing to look at the behaviour of the suppliers of private capital, not least because the emerging market countries had the misfortune to be caught up in the euphoria of the 1990s' US stock market bubble. For Western portfolio investors in the last decade of the old millennium, emerging markets became an exciting new fad. When the Berlin Wall came down in 1989 many concluded that the capitalist system was finally reverting to its pre-1914 global frontiers.

Not only did the period of increased state control of markets from 1914 to 1989 suddenly strike many economic liberals as a historical aberration, there was also the probability that three billion people in state-managed economies who had been unable to realize their full productive potential would come back into the market system. Emerging markets held out the promise of much higher investment returns than in the mature economies of the developed countries. And they were heavily promoted by Washington's official institutions such as the International Finance Corporation, the private sector lending and investing arm of the World Bank. The World Bank itself encouraged the euphoria with research publications such as *The Asian Miracle*, which puffed the achievements of the Asian tiger economies and, as the title suggests, promoted a controversial view of their industrialization process as something new and different in economic history.[2]

For their part, developing countries were more inclined after 1989 to buy the arguments of the Washington consensus about the advantages of opening up to foreign capital. There appeared to be no alternative. Many dismantled long-standing capital controls that had operated as barriers to foreign inflows. The world thus appeared to many in the financial community to be ready to embark on the most broadly based and productive economic upturn since the dawn of the industrial era. New eras are, of course, the stuff of bubbles. And this was a new era to end all new eras. According to the American sage Francis Fukuyama, it represented the end of history, by which he meant that, in place of the clash of communist and capitalist ideologies, there was now the prospect of progress toward universal adherence to the values of post-Enlightenment Western modernity.

The world to which economic liberals were hoping to return was both remarkably similar and importantly different from the present era of globalization. Its nature is well captured by John Maynard Keynes in a nostalgic (and characteristically elitist) passage in *Economic Consequences of the Peace*, written in 1919:

---

[2] The World Bank/Oxford University Press, 1993.

What an extraordinary episode in the economic progress of man was that age which came to an end in August 1914. The inhabitant of London could order by telephone, sipping his morning tea in bed, the various products of the whole earth, in such quantity as he might see fit, and reasonably expect their early delivery on his doorstep; he could at the same moment and by the same means adventure his wealth in the natural resources and new enterprises of any quarter of the world, and share without exertion or even trouble, in their prospective fruits and advantages; or he could decide to couple the security of his fortunes with the good faith of the townspeople of any substantial municipality in any continent that fancy or information might recommend.

He could secure forthwith, if he wished it, cheap and comfortable means of transit to any country and climate without passport or other formality, could dispatch his servant to the neighbouring office of a bank for such supply of the precious metals as might seem convenient, and could then proceed abroad to foreign quarters, without knowledge of their relation, language, or customs, bearing coined wealth upon his person, and would consider himself greatly aggrieved and much surprised at the least interference. But, most important of all, he regarded this state of affairs as normal, certain and permanent, except in the direction of further improvement, and any deviations from it as aberrant, scandalous and avoidable.[3]

This was a period in which capital markets were highly integrated. Between 1870 and 1913 Britain directed about half its savings overseas, and by the end of the period its foreign assets were worth one and a half times its gross domestic product. Some 45 per cent of UK capital invested abroad went into the US, Canada, Australia and New Zealand, known to economists as the Western Offshoots. The majority of foreign capital was invested in the debt of governments and railways, with smaller shares going into the exploitation of natural resources and utilities. Investors were expecting to benefit from superior returns in these developing economies, which were growing much faster than the more mature economies of Europe.

Their expectations were justified. Between 1870 and 1913 the annual average compound growth rate of those four economies was 3.9 per cent compared with 2.1 per cent in Western Europe and 1.9 per cent in the UK. Other European countries also invested heavily in

---

[3] *The Collected Writings of John Maynard Keynes*, Vol. 2, published for the Royal Economic Society by Macmillan and Cambridge University Press, 1972.

foreign bonds, though not on the scale of the British. It needs to be said that the pre-1914 world was frequently beset by financial crises and investors were fleeced from time to time by unscrupulous entrepreneurs and company promoters. Governments also defaulted on their bonds. But within its own terms the system of global capital flows worked reasonably well, transferring surplus savings from mature economies in Europe to younger countries where the profit opportunities were far greater.[4]

Where the comparison with today's form of globalization starts to break down is in the workings of the labour market. In the 19th century, labour was as mobile as capital. From 1870 to 1913 around 17.5m people left Europe for the Western Offshoots. Now, in contrast, the poor of the developing world have been largely locked out of the rich countries unless they have exceptional advantages such as skills in high technology, which provide an instant passport to places like California. According to the Public Policy Institute of California, Silicon Valley employed about 9,000 Chinese PhDs and 4,500 Indian PhDs at the end of the 1990s, while 24 per cent of high-tech firms in Silicon Valley had chief executive officers who were Chinese or Indian immigrants.[5] Yet this import of privileged human capital is the exception, not the rule. In the main, private capital now has to beat a path to immobilized pools of labour, whether in the developed or the developing countries. Labour cannot move freely to where the private capital is generated. Europe, in particular, is becoming more hostile to immigrants as politicians of the extreme right exert a growing influence. Symptomatic of this trend was the emergence of the leader of France's extreme right National Front, Jean-Marie Le Pen, as the main opposition candidate to Jacques Chirac in the French presidential election of 2002.

---

[4] Figures from Angus Maddison, *Monitoring the World Economy 1820–1992*, OECD, 1995.

[5] Quoted in David D. Hale, *Can America Achieve a Soft Landing after Its Stock Market Boom or Why the Equity Market Boom Is an Experiment in Corporate Resource Reallocation*, Zurich Financial Services, January 2000.

The composition of capital flows has also changed significantly. In the 19th century investors bought bonds – IOUs of governments and companies. This was relatively stable, long-term financing from the point of view of the borrower. Investors could not pull their money out until the bond reached a specified date of maturity. The risk to the borrower was that the flow of new capital would dry up if the debt interest went unpaid (which can still be very painful as Argentina found to its cost in the financial crisis of 2001–2). In the 1970s and 1980s, in contrast, most cross-border financing was conducted by syndicates of banks lending to governments, or sovereign borrowers. After the Latin American lending crisis, which erupted in 1982, sources of capital first dried up for several years, then became more diverse. In the 1990s the biggest flow of private capital to the emerging markets – just over 50 per cent – came in the much more stable form of foreign direct investment carried out by multinational companies.

Unlike most 19th century corporate borrowers of foreign capital, which had a single purpose such as investing in a new railway or infrastructure project, multinational companies now organize their production, marketing and other operations on an international basis. A large proportion of world trade and global capital flows is conducted internally by these corporate investors. And the range of activities over which they deploy capital is much wider than in the 19th century. Cross-border investment now extends into banking, insurance and other service activities, as well as manufacturing. In the last decade of the century portfolio capital also played a renewed part in financing emerging market economies. Around 16 per cent of the capital flows were in the form of equity and 15 per cent in bonds. Bank lending, the most short term of the various kinds of finance, had fallen to only 12 per cent of the total.[6]

These cross-border capital flows were supported by an infrastructure that scarcely existed in the more *laissez-faire* 19th century. In the modern financial world central banks more frequently act as lenders

---

[6] World Bank, *Global Finance Report 2000*.

of last resort when domestic economies are hit by financial crises. International institutions such as the International Monetary Fund (IMF) and the World Bank facilitate and monitor capital flows. And a battery of financial regulations, accountancy requirements and audit arrangements exists to promote orderly and transparent markets. In short, the intensity of capital integration at the start of the new millennium goes far beyond the norms of the era before the First World War.

Then, into this interdependent, modern financial world came the attack on New York's twin towers, which was to have an important impact on the behaviour of global capital.

The end of end-ism

The initial response from a number of commentators was to declare the end of globalization and an end to the end of history. John Gray, a passionate anti-globalizer from the London School of Economics, was among the more pungent. Writing within a fortnight of the terrorist action he said:

> The dozen years between the fall of the Wall and the assault on the Twin Towers will be remembered as an era of delusion. The west greeted the collapse of communism – though it was itself a western utopian ideology – as the triumph of western values. The end of the most catastrophic utopian experiment in history was welcomed as a historic opportunity to launch yet another vast utopian project – a global free market. The world was to be made over in an image of western modernity – an image deformed by a market ideology that was as far removed from any human reality as Marxism had been. Now, after the attacks on New York and Washington, the conventional view of globalisation as an irresistible historical trend has been shattered. We are back on the classical terrain of history, where war is waged not over ideologies, but over religion, ethnicity, territory and the control of natural resources.[7]

Gray was obviously right that the notion of a world moving in short

---

[7] John Gray, *New Statesman*, 24 September 2001. Gray's chief blast against globalization is in *False Dawn – The Delusions of Global Capitalism*, Granta Books, 1998.

order toward some uniform, free market-oriented image of Western
modernity was untenable in the light of the terrorist attacks. Yet,
when looked at from the perspective of capital flows, it is striking
that what Gray calls the Utopian project had advanced far less than
appears at first sight, at least from the perspective of the developing
world. For the wonders of capital market integration were largely
confined, in the late 20th century, to the rich countries. In fact,
more than three-quarters of the record flows of foreign direct investment in 2000 were between developed countries. Moreover, the portfolio capital tide to the Third World started to retreat long before the
assault on the twin towers. The real turning point was the Asian
financial crisis, which began with a run on the Thai currency in
July 1997.

Immediately after the Asian crisis the emerging market economies
accounted for no more than 7 per cent of the value of the world stock
market capitalization as measured by the Morgan Stanley Capital
International index, despite representing 45 per cent of world
output, 70 per cent of the world's land area and 85 per cent of the
world's population.[8] So it is apparent that the advances on the 19th
century in the breadth and depth of financial interdependence were
largely confined to the developed world. The logic and direction of
capital flows at the end of the 20th century was not only entirely
different from a hundred years earlier. It left emerging market economies more vulnerable to sudden outflows.

In the five worst hit economies in Asia, the reversal in capital
flows between 1996 and 1998 came to nearly $150bn. This exodus of
what Anne Simpson, head of the Organization for Economic
Cooperation and Development (OECD)–World Bank-backed
Global Corporate Governance Forum, has rightly dubbed "fast but
foolish capital" was equivalent to around 15 per cent of those
countries' combined gross domestic product before the outbreak of

[8] David Hale, *Can America's Stock Market Bubble Prevent a Global Downturn?*, Zurich
Financial Services, 30 November 1998.

the crisis.[9] While the international banks' role in cross-border capital flows had substantially diminished since the 1980s, it was still enough to create nightmares for the emerging market economies. In fact, three-quarters of that reversal of flows reflected a dramatic change of sentiment among commercial banks, which chose not to renew their loans, while the remaining quarter was a consequence of portfolio outflows. What was most galling for the countries concerned was that they had been pursuing interest rate and budgetary policies that were widely recognized as sustainable. It was chiefly the mismanagement of their exchange rates and private sector borrowing that left them vulnerable to the switch in market psychology from greed to fear. Only foreign direct investment remained fairly stable.[10]

The resulting losses of output and employment were on a horrific scale by the standards of the developed world – a penalty out of all proportion to the policy errors and one which was imposed extraordinarily swiftly. In 1998 the shrinkage in real gross domestic product in Korea was 6.7 per cent, in Thailand 10.4 per cent, in the Philippines 0.5 per cent, in Malaysia 7.5 per cent and in Indonesia 13.2 per cent. Countries that accepted financial help from the IMF and World Bank were also obliged to put up with a raft of humiliating structural conditions that involved substantial erosions of their sovereignty. There were also demands for improved corporate governance to address crony capitalism, the industrial and financial policy arrangements whereby business provides money to politicians, while the politicians provide lucrative monopolies and other forms of patronage to business.

Asian crony capitalism was undoubtedly corrupt. It also operated to a large extent at the expense of foreign and other non-family investors. Even so, the scope of the international clean-up was unprecedented. In the extreme case of Indonesia these conditions were extraordinarily detailed, ranging from reform of restrictive market

---

[9] Speech to the International Corporate Governance Network annual conference, New York, 14 July, 2000, on shareholder activism in emerging markets.
[10] Institute of International Finance, *Capital Flows to Emerging Market Economies*.

agreements for cement and paper to changes in the taxation of charit-able contributions. The supreme irony was that in countries such as China and India, which had resisted Washington's siren call for the liberalization of capital, growth held up quite well and there was little problem with financial contagion.[11]

Damn bankers

It would be wrong to call this a failure of Anglo-American finance capitalism. The financial exodus was chiefly down to Japanese and continental European banks. But equity prices in the region none-theless halved within a year of the onset of the crisis. The IMF, together with flag-bearers for the Washington consensus like Robert Rubin, the former investment banker from Goldman Sachs who was a treasury secretary in the Clinton administration, must share some blame for encouraging capital market liberalization in countries that lacked financial institutions capable of withstanding exceptionally volatile hot-money flows. It was a similar policy mistake to the dis-astrous encouragement of rapid privatization in Russia, which lacked the political integrity, legal infrastructure and strong civil society necessary to make privatization work. The IMF also compounded the errors in Asia initially by imposing unduly tough fiscal tightening on countries like Thailand where public sector budgets were in reasonable shape, thereby reinforcing the slump caused by the capital outflows. It was obsessively concerned with monetary and fiscal reform rather than protecting vital services such as health care and education. These and other shortcomings in the IMF's approach to its mission have been the subject of a devastating attack by the former Chief Economist of the World Bank Joseph Stiglitz in his controversial book *Globalization and its Discontents*.[12]

Whether Stiglitz's prescriptions for managing the Asian crisis would

---

[11] Figures from *World Economic Outlook* (International Monetary Fund).

[12] W.W. Norton, 2002.

have been better than those of the US Treasury and the IMF is a moot point. But his critique is hard to fault. And it remains extraordinary that, despite the extensive financial infrastructure in modern markets, financial crises today actually produce more dramatic falls in output than before 1914, while in modern currency crises the subsequent recovery is slower. In the absence of the fixed exchange rates of a gold standard, foreign banks and investors are reluctant to pour capital back into a crisis-torn country for fear that the collapse of the currency will lead to high rates of inflation.[13] The gold standard admittedly had the disadvantage that it helped transmit the shock waves of financial crises around the world. Yet today's mixture of free and managed exchange rates is just as prone to contagion, while lacking the stabilizing capacity of the gold standard.

It also seems plausible that the growth of trading in derivative instruments such as currency forwards, futures, swaps and options has contributed to the increased severity of crises. One reason why two-thirds of the $1.5 trillion a day turnover in the currency markets is conducted through these derivatives is that they reduce the cost of betting against fixed exchange rates. This is because they permit a small amount of capital to purchase very large exposure to the risk of currency fluctuations – the phenomenon known as leverage. The IMF itself has suggested that high levels of such leverage in derivatives trading may have caused financial systems to become more likely to make costly mistakes during periods of euphoria. Leverage also magnifies the adverse consequences of negative shocks to the financial system.[14]

---

[13] See Michael D. Bordo, Barry Eichengreen and Douglas A. Irwin, National Bureau of Economic Research Working Paper 7195, *Is Globalization Today Really Different than Globalization a Hundred Years Ago*. They conclude that the more damaging impact of modern crises is an "unprecedented and disturbing" aspect of the current age of globalization, while remaining surprised that the damage is not even worse, given the higher degree of integration than a hundred years ago.

[14] IMF, *International Capital Markets*, 1999.

Reformist zeal

International monetary and financial policies played an unusually large role on the agenda of the US administration under President Clinton. And, partly because of that, the scale of the international policy response to the Asian debacle has been colossal. New bodies have been established to encourage financial stability and improve what is rather grandly called the financial architecture of developing countries. A plethora of international standards and codes has been introduced to encourage better economic policy, better financial regulation and supervision, increased transparency, and better bankruptcy procedures. The World Bank and the OECD are trying to facilitate capital flows to emerging markets through initiatives such as the Global Corporate Governance Forum, which seeks to explain the corporate governance concerns of investors and lenders. Some of this reformist energy has even gone into improving transparency and efficiency in the workings of the IMF. Most important of all, the US after the Asian crisis was willing to act as an importer of last resort for the world. The US Federal Reserve put policy into expansionary mode and the current account of the US balance of payments was allowed to sink further into deficit in the interests of maintaining economic growth.

The positive outcome was that IMF loans and World Bank programmes did, in the end, help pave the way for an export-led economic recovery in which US demand played a vital part. By 1999 it looked as though Indonesia alone would be a continuing victim of the crisis and that victims would not suffer the prolonged misery that affected Latin America after its financial crisis in the 1980s. Yet it should be noted in passing that countries like Malaysia that spurned IMF and World Bank help also recovered, which suggests that the contribution of the Washington financial institutions was probably modest. And the US recession in 2001 hit Asia particularly hard, since Asian industry had prospered on the back of the US high-tech investment boom. Many of those like Taiwan and Singapore that had escaped the worst of the earlier financial crisis slumped. And as far as capital flows were concerned, most of the policy effort on financial architecture went for nothing. The sad reality is that total net private capital flows to the emerging market economies collapsed from $120bn in 1997, the first year of the Asian crisis, to $33bn in 2000. Apologists in the international financial community argue that the dramatic decline in capital flows to Asia is not quite as bad as it looks because international banks have bought up local banks and made consequent reductions in cross-border lending. Reform of financial systems has also encouraged local borrowers to take out domestic instead of foreign loans. Yet it is hard to escape the conclusion that, in capital markets, globalization is simply not working as it should. And much less of it is going on than the volume of protest from anti-globalizers would lead us to believe.

Some economists argue that this may not matter. The theoretical case for liberalizing capital flows has always been much weaker than the case for free trade.[15] Importing capital has not been a uniform feature of economic take-off in the developing world, and many Asian countries have successfully financed rapid economic development from domestic savings. Yet there are such obvious and visible benefits from inward investment in several emerging market countries that it seems more sensible to conclude that in capital markets globalization should be made to work better, especially in the light of the Asian debacle.

Leaders and laggards

There is an obvious and worrying parallel in the drying up of capital flows to emerging markets with Western foreign policy's failure to engage more constructively with the world's more troubled regions. Global inequality is, after all, at a level unprecedented in history. In 1998 the income gap between the world's richest countries, the

---

[15] See, for example, Jagdish Bhagwati, "The Capital Myth", Foreign Affairs, May–June 1998.

Western Offshoots, and the world's poorest region, Africa, was 19 to 1.[16] Such statistics admittedly need to be treated with caution. Over the past 20 years the number of people in absolute poverty has fallen. The inequalities between countries and regions also become less stark when weighted by population. But they remain real for all that, to which adherents to the Washington consensus respond that the laggard countries are usually command economies that deservedly pay a price for failing to open up to international trade and capital.

As for the victims of financial crises, the conventional view is that these emerging market countries have been weak in insulating their finances from domestic political pressures. In the words of the Federal Reserve Chairman Alan Greenspan:

> To close the gap between the financial demands of political constituencies and the limited real resources available to their governments, many countries too often have bridged the difference by borrowing from foreign investors. In effect, the path of least resistance has been external borrowing rather than confronting politically difficult trade-offs. Periodically, as an economy borrows its way to the edge of insolvency with debt denominated in foreign currency, government debt-raising capacity appears to vanish virtually overnight. It is this vanishing capacity that characterises almost all financial crises.[17]

On this view the problems of the emerging market economies are their own fault. To win back foreign capital what they have to do is to provide stable politics, a legal system that strongly underpins property rights, sound fiscal and monetary policies and increased official reserves to provide a buffer for the currency against outflows of foreign capital. Once nations meet what Greenspan calls "the market test" they will no longer need to put up "collateral" in the form of outsized official reserves to certify their financial prudence.

These are powerful arguments. It has to be said that growing inequality is inevitable in a world where some countries industrialize while others do not, because industrialization and trade transform

---

[16] Angus Maddison, *The World Economy: A Millennial Perspective*, OECD, 2001.

[17] Robert P. Maxon Lecture, George Washington University, 3 December 2001.

growth rates. As long as countries continue to opt out of the liberal trading system and remain reluctant to open capital markets, inequality between the leaders and the opted-out laggards can only increase. Nor can private capital be expected to play a significant role where states have failed, or where they close themselves to the outside world by adopting autarky – the policy of economic self-sufficiency. Nor again can it be expected to provide an external financial cushion against emerging market governments' political failures.

Yet the sweeping nature of Greenspan's equation of "almost all financial crises" with excessive foreign currency government debt is revealing, because it is, in fact, such a poor characterization of most of the crises that infected Asia in 1997. And the arguments are un-balanced from a political as well as an economic perspective. For a start, a more far-sighted realpolitik would acknowledge a moral ambiguity in the developed countries' advocacy of a globalization process that does not extend to labour markets. If the West will not accept many of the developing world's immigrants, it has to export more capital to the developing world to help prevent it from becoming a breeding ground for disaffection and, in extremis, terror-ism. That is in its own interest.

Moreover, capital is not rewarding the behaviour that Alan Green-span advocates. Since the Asian crisis Western policy-makers and politicians in many developing countries have made huge efforts to address precisely these points. Why, then, have their efforts had so little impact in securing an improved flow of private capital? When in Spring 2002 I asked this question of James Wolfensohn, President of the World Bank, his response was that it all takes time. In due course, he argued, an improved investment climate in the developing world would attract funds back. And he quoted Costa Rica and Senegal – scarcely significant in the global picture – as examples of countries that had successfully put in place investor-friendly policies.

It has to be said that the World Bank confronts a fundamental difficulty here. It was designed for the immediate post-war world in which most capital flows were between official bodies such as governments and central banks. Much of its lending effort has been directed to governments. Now that private capital is vastly more important – and potentially more productive – than official capital, it is much harder to define a helpful role for the World Bank. It cannot switch the flow of private capital on and off in response to its own policy goals for specific countries. The priority has to be to improve the investment climate in emerging market countries, rather than to advance money to governments.

That said, I believe that James Wolfensohn is right in one respect. There will certainly be an upturn in the flow of capital to the emerging market economies, if only on a cyclical basis. But what is ignored in current policy toward the developing countries is that the flow will be unbalanced because there are substantial distortions in the Western financial architecture that make it very difficult for private capital to reward good behaviour in emerging markets. To put it another way, Western capital's rules of engagement are ill-designed to bring about appropriate flows of capital to the right emerging market economies in the requisite volumes.

Basket case

As far as bank-lending is concerned, regulation heavily distorts the flows. In the emerging market boom of the 1990s the relevant regulations concerned the amount of capital banks were required to use to support their lending activity. These were outlined in the 1988 Basle Capital Accord, an international agreement that provides the basis for bank regulation. Since capital is costly, a rule requiring banks to put up greater or lesser amounts of capital for a given type of lending is a very powerful influence on their behaviour. In the run-up to the Asian crisis the Accord imposed a lesser capital requirement for short-term lending than for long-term lending. The inevitable result was that countries borrowed too much on a short-term basis, leaving them vulnerable to greater volatility of inflows and outflows.

Volatility was further exacerbated by the banks' and the markets' reliance on credit-rating agencies. In the Asian crisis the agencies failed to downgrade countries as their finances deteriorated before the crisis, but then they worsened the crisis by bringing down the ratings as panic spread through the markets. In other words the agencies lag, rather than lead, the market. Or, in the more colourful phrase of veteran US financial commentator Martin Mayer, they shoot the wounded.[18] Proposed reforms to the Basle Accord that have emerged since the Asian crisis seek to correct the bias in favour of short-term lending. But they also call for the credit-rating agencies, which are unregulated, to be given a more formal role in a new accord. In the view of many experts, of which more in Chapter 3, the proposals are likely to exaggerate the swings in the economic cycle and increase the risk of financial crises. By making the returns on international lending more volatile, the flow of capital to the developing world may be less than it would otherwise be. Incredible though it must seem to anyone outside the narrow world of international financial diplomacy, some bankers go so far as to argue that the new Basle regime could make lending to lower income developing countries hopelessly uneconomic.[19] And by giving big banks with the most sophisticated risk management systems a capital advantage, the proposals will impose a competitive disadvantage on banks in the developing world that lack that degree of sophistication.

The market test is also flawed where equity and bond flows are concerned. The rules of engagement here are based partly on a theory, developed mainly by American academics, of how portfolio capital is supposed to flow around the world. It rests on the case for diversification or, in simple terms, the need to put eggs in more than one basket to reduce the risks to the investor. If Western professional investors really took the theory of diversification to heart there would be enormous scope for increased cross-border flows because so many of them have a home country bias. At the start of the new millennium

---

[18] Martin Mayer in *The Fed*, The Free Press/Simon & Schuster, 2001.

[19] This conclusion emerged at a joint seminar on 27 September between the Société Universitaire Européenne des Recherches Financières (SUERF) and the Centre for the Study of Financial Innovation, a London-based think tank with which the author is associated.

US pension funds held assets worth $8.1 trillion. Of this only 10 per cent was invested in international equities and 1 per cent in international bonds. The pension funds do, of course, acquire some exposure to foreign economies through the international activities of US companies in which they invest. But even allowing for that they are, by textbook standards, overexposed to any shocks in the US economy and stock market. Much the same argument could be made for Japan, even though Japanese pension funds' exposure to foreign equities and bonds was higher, at 26 per cent, or for the UK, where the comparable figure was 28 per cent. Why, then, do these pension fund investors fail to diversify further?[20]

One answer is that many professional fund-managers have concluded the theory is flawed. In practice, the more capital flows become global the less effective diversification becomes. In the period of extreme turbulence around the Asian crisis, the Russian default and near-collapse of the Long-Term Capital Management hedge fund in 1998, all the world's equity markets moved in sync as contagion transmitted the shock from one market to another, often regardless of the health of the individual economies concerned. So the whole purpose of overseas portfolio diversification, which is to provide some insulation from shocks, was nullified.

The theory works best when markets are not volatile. But even then the diversification benefit tends to come more from the movement of currencies relative to the home currency than from the performance of the stocks or bonds. So it is not much help to the emerging market economies, especially those whose currencies are pegged to the dollar. And if such economies embrace the prescriptions of Washington's economic liberals, fostering open domestic capital markets and funded pension systems, the consequences might be very unhelpful. Textbook investment theory would require pension fund investors in small open economies in the developing world to export a majority of their money to other countries. The perverse outcome would be that developing countries would end up sending

---

[20] Figures from Phillips & Drew, *Pension Fund Indicators*, 2000.

scarce savings to economies whose need for capital was less. Their own savings would make a lesser contribution to the development of their domestic financial systems. That is not how the Asian tiger economies succeeded in generating the fastest rates of economic growth in history.

For American investors the experience of international diversification has been unrewarding in a more direct sense. The reason so many of them have lost their appetite for emerging market equity is that the returns appeared dismal in the 1990s compared with the return on domestic equities. The explanation is not hard to find. The bubble in US securities continued long after the bubble in emerging market securities collapsed. And much of the money withdrawn by Western fund-managers from Asia in 1997–98 will have gone to inflate the US bubble further. So the Anglo-American financial world has been overtaken by perverse logic. At the turn of the millennium professional investors were comparing depressed emerging market stocks with overvalued US stocks and then buying more of the overvalued variety. This is the economics of the madhouse – the very opposite of efficient capital allocation. Yet many policy-makers and fund-managers are completely oblivious to the wider impact of such thinking on the developing countries.

The difficulty arises partly because professional investors in the US and UK, the two biggest investors in emerging markets, are obsessed with the short term. Understandably so, because the performance of so many of them is appraised by myopic pension fund trustees over as little as three months or a year. As a result they are driven in a herd by worries about their performance relative to their competitors and the potential loss of their pension fund clients. Staying close to the herd takes precedence over the quest for high absolute returns because it minimizes the competitive threat to the professional fund-manager's business. And the fund-managers' experience in the emerging markets has been discomfiting in other respects.

One of the biggest omissions in American textbooks on portfolio diversification is any reference to corporate governance – the system of checks and balances that ensures that management has the right incentives and investors' rights are properly protected. Some textbooks also ignore political risk, including the possibility that companies may be nationalized without compensation or the rights of shareholders arbitrarily altered. Yet an equity stake in the form of ordinary stocks and shares in a company in Taiwan, Korea or even Japan or Germany is very different from an equity in the US or UK.

In the Anglo-American world the law requires that companies be run primarily in the interests of shareholders. Elsewhere company directors may have divided responsibilities that extend to other stakeholders such as employees and the community. In pre-crisis Asia, banking systems in countries such as Korea were used as an instrument of government industrial policy without regard for their profitability. The legal and regulatory structures in such jurisdictions may offer little protection for shareholders who are not part of the inside group of crony capitalists who control the company. In other words, the rewards for shareholders in companies outside the Anglo-American world tend to be at the discretion of the managers or family owners who control the enterprise. In the wilder reaches of the global equity market where corporate governance discipline is minimal, it is common for managers and controlling family owners to milk the company at the expense of outside shareholders.

Burned again

In practice, standards of corporate governance vary enormously across the world's markets. Ira Millstein, the leading US lawyer who helped set up the OECD–World Bank Global Corporate Governance Forum after the Asian crisis, argues that any solution to the interrupted flow of capital to the developing world must take into account an obvious fact about capital – namely, that it is more likely to flow to countries and companies that demonstrate a responsiveness to governance issues. Increasingly, share prices in these markets do reflect the risk of poor regulation, governance and company law infrastructure and reward efforts to improve governance. Yet many professional investors rushed indiscriminately into emerging markets in the 1990s and were burned. And having learned the lesson in the Asian crisis, they promptly forgot it again, when technology stocks in emerging markets started to share in the euphoria of the US high-tech bubble in 1999 and early 2000. Disillusion inevitably followed.

Another kind of disillusion was manifested by Calpers (California Public Employees Retirement System), the giant pension fund, when it announced in 2002 that it was selling all its equities in Thailand, the Philippines, Malaysia and Indonesia on governance grounds. The criteria used by consultants Wilshire Associates in establishing a "permissible country list" for Calpers included labour market standards, democracy and civil liberties, as well as more mundane tests such as the efficiency of the infrastructure for share-dealing. The result of Wilshire's efforts, which included input from two other consultants, Oxford Analytica and Verité, was that Argentina was ranked top, despite being wracked by a financial crisis and civil strife. Then Wilshire discovered it had wrongly classified the Philippines by failing to note the upgrading of stock exchange settlement procedures. This was a curiously marginal basis on which to decide whether a country was to be regarded as a pariah or a favoured candidate. It was also an inauspicious beginning for Calpers' kind of screening.

Whether this approach constitutes responsible investment is anyway a moot point. The trouble with such blanket-screening is that it resembles redlining, the approach whereby home-lenders shun lending to neighbourhoods in which the poor or large ethnic groups are heavily represented. The result is that creditworthy borrowers are penalized along with the less creditworthy. Screening also responds inflexibly to countries that are in the process of making significant improvements in governance. This crude, discriminatory approach to global investment also raises an important question about legitimacy. Calpers, after all, was an investor both in the quoted stock of Enron, the bankrupt energy-trader, and in an unquoted private partnership of Enron. Citizens of any developing country might reasonably ask why they were on a blacklist when Enron was not. There were plenty of examples of poor governance at the company, ranging from non-executives whose independence was impaired because they were awarded consultancy contracts by Enron, to big political donations that reeked of crony capitalism. So here we have a striking example of Western double standards.

Even allowing for the probability of an improved flow of private capital, the emerging markets are unlikely to escape from their marginalized position in the world's capital markets. They are a ghetto, accounting in 2001 for less than 4 per cent of the total worth of global equities. This is not in the Western interest, not least because one of the contributory forces behind terrorism is the sense of frustration experienced by people who have been marginalized while their concerns have been ignored. Failed states presiding over debilitated economies are also relatively defenceless against terrorists who seek a haven against their enemies.

To be shunned by global capital is also a disaster for enterprise in the developing world because a lower share price raises a company's cost of capital. For those aspiring to compete in global markets this is a big competitive handicap. And it can lead to perverse outcomes, whereby the best companies abandon local stock markets and seek a listing on the larger markets of the developed world. South Africa is an obvious case in point. While it contains some of the globe's poorest people it has one of the most sophisticated stock markets in the developing world, together with relatively good standards of corporate governance. It also has companies that are internationally competitive in sectors such as mining, information technology and financial services.

Because they are pigeon-holed as emerging market investments by professional fund-managers around the world, these companies are tarred with the brush of high political risk and poor corporate governance, even where a majority of their revenues arises outside South Africa. The local market is not big enough to provide capital on a scale that would allow South African companies to make a global impact. And because of Western investors' faddish approach to emerging market investment, the volatility of share prices means that windows for raising capital tend to open and close very fast.

These companies therefore have a powerful incentive to shift their domicile and stock exchange listing. Many have done so. In mining, Anglo American and Billiton have moved their main stock exchange listing to the UK, while AngloGold has listed in the US. South African Breweries, the insurer Old Mutual, financial services outfit Investec and the high-tech group Dimension Data have all moved their listing to London. The paper and pulp company Sappi is another to have decamped to the US. The change of listing often results in the markets according a higher value to the company concerned, especially if it is big enough to go into one of the main market indices such as the FTSE 100 in the UK which guarantees the backing of all the funds that track the index. Since index-tracking funds hold more than a fifth of the companies in the FTSE 100, this is a further benefit to the share price. As well as holding out the prospect of reducing the company's cost of capital and improving its access to new equity, the change of home base means that the company's shares will be more acceptable as a currency in future takeovers. And the political risk that South Africa might follow the catastrophically self-destructive path of Robert Mugabe's Zimbabwe is conveniently diluted – though few dare to make the point publicly.

Yet this is not good news for any emerging market economy, since it may threaten the country's tax base. In South Africa's case, it has created political tensions. The Congress of South African Trade Unions (COSATU) regards the exodus as an unpatriotic flight of white capital from the country – an understandable concern given the fraught history of apartheid. So the government has been obliged to introduce a more restrictive set of hurdles for companies seeking to list their shares offshore. At the very least it is a bizarre consequence of globalization that it provides incentives for the best emerging market companies to evacuate when global capital has never been more mobile. And any diminution in the number of companies that are potentially attractive to international investors is singularly un-helpful to the developing world, because it exacerbates the biggest impediment to inflows of Western capital. That is, the sheer imbalance between the size of funds looking for an outlet in global equities and the capacity of emerging markets to absorb external capital.

In the 19th century cross-border investment was carried out mainly by private individuals who were chasing the higher bond returns available in the developing world. In the late 20th century individual savings have been substantially collectivized in pools of money managed by investment banks, mutual funds, self-administered pension funds and insurance companies. These investors have a natural appetite for equity that, at first sight, appears an ideal form of financing for the developing world. It cannot be withdrawn like bank finance because the investor has to find a buyer in order to make an exit. And because dividends, unlike interest, are not fixed and can be changed to reflect the extreme swings of a developing country's economic cycles, there is an inbuilt cushion. The snag is that in the US and UK, the biggest global portfolio investors, this money observes specific legal and regulatory constraints, along with a set of widely accepted investment conventions, which can pose overwhelming obstacles to investment in emerging markets.

Consider the position of the top three investment banks, Merrill Lynch, Morgan Stanley and Goldman Sachs, which together managed $2.7 trillion of other people's money at the end of December 2000.[21] This was more than twice the combined value of the stock markets of Hong Kong, Taiwan, Singapore, Korea, China, Malaysia, Thailand, Indonesia, the Philippines and India. The giant US pension fund Calpers alone managed $155bn in 2001, and targeted 19 per cent of that sum, or $29.5bn, at international markets – a larger tally than the value of any single Latin American market apart from Brazil, Mexico or Chile.

Gulliver in Lilliput

It follows, first, that it is almost impossible for such large funds to do much for their investment performance by investing in emerging

---

[21] Figures compiled by the author from annual reports.

markets. Any investment would simply be too small to make an impact on the overall return. So devoting time and effort to these markets may not appear worth the trouble for the giants of global fund management, except through intermediaries such as smaller specialist mutual funds or hedge funds. Harsh reality dictates that since the collapse of the Asian bubble and the disappearance of the post-Cold War euphoria, emerging markets have ceased to be an important area of attention for big global money.

The other consequence of this imbalance is that it is anyway difficult for Western capital to take an interest in emerging markets without destabilizing them. Relatively small inflows create stock market bubbles, which promptly collapse when the money tries to move out. And the smaller specialist funds tend to see these markets as an opportunity for speculative trading, which condemns them to a high degree of volatility. So there are structural impediments, often overlooked by Western policy-makers, to an increased flow of equity capital to the emerging market economies. Those same impediments apply to some extent to bond finance, with an added disadvantage. Emerging market borrowers faced extraordinarily high interest rates at the start of the new millennium, which were hard to reconcile with the fact that sovereign debt defaults on bonds were running at historically low levels. With interest rates well in excess of rates of economic growth, few could borrow without quickly making their debt burdens unsustainable.[22]

Emerging equity and bond markets have thus been condemned to ghetto status. So the best hope for developing countries to escape from the instability of short-term bank finance or exclusive reliance on domestic saving is to attract increased foreign direct investment by multinationals. For those categorized by the United Nations as least developed countries, with per capita gross domestic product of less than $900, foreign direct investment likewise looks appealing as a

[22] For a discussion of this phenomenon, see the speech by Mervyn King, Deputy Governor of the Bank of England, to the Indian Council for Research on International Economic Relations, *Bank of England Bulletin*, August 2001.

complement to official development assistance, a surprisingly volatile source of finance. Such investment can bring access to technology and know-how as well as to international markets. In other words, the social return is higher than the private return, not least because it can provide a means of upgrading the skills of the workforce and obtaining organizational expertise, two vital components of enhanced productivity, the great engine of economic growth.

Yet there are snags. Foreign direct investment may not be as stable as it looks, because the capital flows it entails may be conducted via multinational companies' inter-company accounts. So foreign subsidiaries in emerging markets may borrow domestically and lend the money to the parent company back in the developed world. Or the parent may recall outstanding debt at the foreign subsidiary at short notice. More fundamentally, and unfortunately for the world's poorer regions, multinationals are driven by concerns very different from those of 19th century investors. The rates of return on foreign direct investment in Africa and the Middle East were respectively 19.4 per cent and 18.9 per cent in 2000, compared with 15.1 per cent for Asia-Pacific, 8.3 per cent for Latin America and 10.9 per cent for Europe. Yet Africa and the Middle East attracted only $1.1bn and $1.9bn, respectively, of direct inflows that year, compared with $21bn for Asia-Pacific, $19.9bn for Latin America and $76.9bn for Europe.[23] A higher reward is clearly required to compensate for the higher risk of investing in these two poor regions. There may also be some element of distortion in the figures that inflates these returns. Even so, for Africa, the pariah of the capital markets, the share of the world's foreign direct investment inflows in 2000 was extraordinarily low at 0.6 per cent. And for developing countries generally, the share declined to 19 per cent compared with a peak of 41 per cent in 1994.[24] For the poor of the earth it is nothing less than a catastrophe.

What this demonstrates, among other things, is that multinationals

---

[23] Figures from US Bureau of Economic Analysis, quoted in HSBC's *World Economic Watch*, 11 October 2001.

[24] United Nations Conference on Trade and Development, *World Investment Report 2001: Promoting Linkages*.

invest on a basis that does not primarily reflect investment returns and risks. The level of inflows is more closely correlated to the size of the country's market, its recent growth rate and the average income of the residents. The result is a high degree of concentration. Five countries – Argentina, Brazil, China (including Hong Kong), Mexico and Korea – received nearly two-thirds of all the flows of foreign direct investment to the emerging market economies in 2000.[25] This mirrors the concentration in portfolio investment, where Hong Kong, Korea, Singapore and Taiwan are the biggest beneficiaries. The striking point, especially in the case of Asian countries that have high domestic savings and current account surpluses on their balance of payments, is that these are often the emerging markets least in need of inflows. And private capital is not showing itself uniformly responsive to good political or corporate governance. China's record on a range of things from human rights to the security of property rights is not one that should allow it to qualify as a member of this magic circle of beneficiaries of large-scale foreign investment.

Against that background the terrorist action in September 2001 has made things worse. Like the oil shock in 1973–74 – another gesture of protest from the developing world over perceived mistreatment and neglect by the West – the impact on psychology in Western boardrooms has been to increase risk aversion. Investment plans are more frequently stress-tested against worst case scenarios, leading to less adventurous business behaviour – "animal spirits" in Keynes's phrase – around the globe. So the likelihood is that these Islamic extremists, having failed to destroy the Western capitalist system, have succeeded in turning more Muslim countries into no-go areas for Western capital. In the aftermath of the New York and Washington attacks the International Institute of Finance, a Washington think tank backed by 300 banks, slashed its estimate for growth in emerging market economies in 2001 by half. It estimated that capital flows to emerging markets would fall by more than a third in 2001 and

---

[25] Bank for International Settlements, 71st Annual Report.

that direct investment would decline from $130bn in 2001 to $108bn in 2002.

For my friend Sanou M'Baye, late of the ADB, this has deepened his pessimism about the future of Africa and the poor of the developing world. Small wonder. The message seems to be that capital will flow to those who need it least, while the Western policy agenda in this area, for all the efforts put in after the Asian crisis, is biased. It has been more concerned to make the world safe for US capital than to make US capital safe for the rest of the world. And policy remains hostage to the endless financial crises in the emerging market economies, with the result that firefighting takes precedence over strategic thinking.

Given that insufficient attention is being paid to the Western capital market flaws that constrain capital flows, as opposed to the weaknesses in the emerging market economies, there is a high probability that many countries will find that adherence to Washington's prescriptions does not deliver. Meantime the baleful outcome of these constant currency and financial crises provides explosive ammunition to anti-globalization protesters. And the attack on New York's twin towers has confirmed many hard-nosed policy-makers and pundits in the West in their conviction that the poor of the developing world are bringing their plight upon themselves. The globalization of capital flows still has enormous potential to alleviate poverty and promote economic growth. But, contrary to the widespread perception, woefully little globalization of capital is actually taking place.

3

Dr Pangloss comes to Wall Street

Economics has been dubbed the dismal science, while economists have been accused of forecasting 43 of the last 6 recessions. Yet the subset of the species that inhabits Wall Street is given to unconquerable bouts of optimism. At the start of the new millennium the in-house economists of the big investment banks were more than usually inclined to believe, like Dr Pangloss in Voltaire's *Candide*, that all was for the best in the best of all possible worlds. The general assumption was that the Federal Reserve had pulled off the trick of delivering stable economic growth and low inflation on a permanent basis. Thanks to innovations in information technology, industrialists appeared to be adjusting their production schedules more rapidly in response to changes in demand. This led, in turn, to suggestions that cyclical fluctuations in investment and in the inventory of products that industrialists kept in their factories had been softened or abolished. And there was some historical evidence to support this optimism. When economists looked back 15 years and made comparisons with the 15-year period before that, they noted that the volatility of US growth and inflation was cut by more than half.[1]

This optimism was shared, if more soberly expressed, by the central bankers at the Fed. Having shown scepticism about the stock market's

---

[1] See Stephen Cecchetti in "Halfway to vanquishing volatility", *Financial Times*, 22 August 2001, for evidence and caveats. Cecchetti is Professor of Economics at Ohio State University and formerly an economist at the New York Federal Reserve.

enthusiasm for the so-called new economy in 1996 in a now famous reference to "irrational exuberance", Fed Chairman Alan Greenspan became increasingly sympathetic in his public statements to the new-era view of the US economy. Even many of those who did not believe in the new economy felt that by setting interest rates chiefly with a view to achieving stability in consumer prices the Fed had steered the economy toward the maximum output and employment it could manage on a continuing basis. In killing off retail price inflation, the central bankers reckoned they had done all they could to achieve sustainable economic growth and minimize the age-old risk of a boom-and-bust business cycle, which is the ultimate goal of monetary policy. Yet these assertions about economic stability sat rather oddly with the financial background, which was more unstable than it had been for years. This was in some respects reminiscent of the *laissez-faire* period of free global capital flows before 1914 when financial crises were endemic. The question at the turn of the new millennium was whether the world was simply reverting to a kind of free market state of nature or whether financial instability was sending a disturbing message about the future path of the world economy that the optimists were overlooking.

There can be no doubt that the financial world has in some respects gone back to an older pattern of behaviour. The economic historian Charles Kindleberger has highlighted the extraordinary fact that financial crises tended to appear at roughly 10-year intervals over a 400-year span.[2] Periods such as the two and a half decades after the Second World War in which financial conditions were relatively tranquil have been the exception, not the rule. The existence of the semi-fixed exchange rate regime put in place at the Bretton Woods conference in the United States at the end of the war in 1944, along with a host of complex regulations introduced after the 1930s' Slump, curbed financial instability and prevented its transmission across national borders.

---

[2] Charles Kindleberger, A *Financial History of Western Europe*, George, Allen & Unwin, 1984, p. 269.

But exchange rate agreements cannot work for long unless the participants commit themselves to pursue compatible policies. And controls in financial markets tend to lead, over time, to a growing misallocation of resources as people find ways of circumventing them. The Bretton Woods system collapsed in the early 1970s largely because the US had been reluctant to levy higher taxes to pay for the Vietnam war. A deficit on the US external account caused unwanted dollars to pile up in European central banks, causing trans-atlantic friction. This was unilaterally resolved when the US decided, under President Nixon, to suspend the dollar's convertibility into gold and devalue the currency. A wave of deregulation ensued in the financial markets of the English-speaking countries.

New-Age finance

That is significant because investment manias, or bubbles, have tended to follow the lifting of legal and regulatory restrictions imposed after earlier financial excesses. In 19th century Britain, for example, the railway mania followed the repeal in 1824 of the Bubble Act that had been introduced at the time of the South Sea Bubble in the early 18th century. New freedoms, together with the loss of any memory of earlier financial disasters and a belief that a new age is dawning, provide the basis for sudden inflations, as in the 1970s. Or they may contribute to the creation of stock market bubbles in which market euphoria – or irrational exuberance in Alan Greenspan's phrase – causes prices of stocks and shares to rise wildly out of line with prospective returns on investment.

Crises also result from the innate instability of commercial banking. Commercial banks borrow on a short-term basis from depositors who can withdraw their deposits on demand. They then lend over longer periods to customers from whom they cannot instantly reclaim their advances. Provided depositors do not try to withdraw their money all at once, the system works. But in a panic, a run can develop on the banks, which are unable to liquidate their assets fast enough to repay all the depositors. So there is an incentive for depositors to beat their fellow savers to the exit in the hope of salvaging more of their money.

As often as not, banking crises are precipitated by bubbles, which afflict stock markets and property markets with surprising regularity. The risk is that when the bubble bursts, the collapse of a bank becomes contagious and spreads to other banks. The whole financial system is then in jeopardy as sound banks suffer a loss of deposits alongside the weak and a severe recession follows, together with the risk of deflation. To counteract this threat governments in the developed world have introduced deposit insurance schemes, while central banks have taken on the role of lender of last resort to the banking system. In crises, they pump money – liquidity in the jargon – into the system. Where a failing bank is so big that it poses a threat to the whole financial system, they bail it out. The snag is that the existence of this safety net encourages imprudent behaviour by the management of banks. Depositors no longer have the same incentive to monitor banks' behaviour. So bankers have to be policed by regulators who set rules, and supervisors who monitor compliance with those rules, to prevent banks running up losses on a scale that might threaten the system.

The trouble with today's markets is that there has been an alarming acceleration in the pace and scale of financial crises and a rise in volatility far beyond anything seen in the 19th century. This points to something more than a mere reversion to the historic norm of free markets.[3] The International Monetary Fund (IMF) has estimated that between 1975 and 1997 there were no less than 82 banking crises and 158 currency crises.[4] And the gaps between the larger crises appear to be becoming shorter. In the mid-1970s the US and UK banking systems were beset with problems in property-lending. A Latin American lending crisis came to a head in 1982 when Mexico declared that it was unable to service its debts. Soon after, the American

---

[3] For data on the increased volatility of international capital flows, see World Economic Outlook, October 2001, pp. 163–4 (International Monetary Fund).

[4] World Economic Outlook, Chapter IV on financial crises, May 1998 (International Monetary Fund).

savings and loans, the US equivalent of British building societies, became a financial disaster zone.

In the early 1990s the American and British banks were overtaken by an astonishing collective memory loss, overextending themselves in property once again. Their experience was replicated this time all across the developed world, with banks in Continental Europe and Japan suffering similar disasters, while the Nordic banking systems had to be bailed out by their governments in a wave of nationalizations. A currency crisis then swept through Europe, starting with Britain's ejection from the European exchange rate mechanism in 1992. Mexico ran into trouble again in 1994. Then came the Asian crisis in 1997–98, followed by the near-collapse of the Long-Term Capital Management (LTCM) hedge fund, to which several big banks had lent imprudently. Since then there have been serious crises in Brazil, Turkey and Argentina. Avinash Persaud, Managing Director and Head of Global Research at State Street Bank and Trust Company, refers to the 1990s as the decade of financial dislocation. He calculates that the financial system was in crisis for 40 of the decade's 120 months.[5]

There are, of course, many more states, currencies and financial systems in existence today than in the 19th century, so the scope for crises is inevitably multiplied. Even so, that tally of financial disaster is awesome, bearing in mind that such crises can lead to devastating losses of output, income and employment in the countries concerned. And the US stock market bubble of the second half of the 1990s was extraordinary by any historical yardstick. Many analysts argue that the bubble was confined to technology, media and telecommunications stocks. And certainly the euphoria was most extreme in those areas. Yet the wider market was also subject to an unprecedented inflation in stock prices. From the start of the bull market in 1982 the value of the US stock market rose from 33 per cent of gross domestic product (GDP) to 181 per cent at the peak in

---

[5] From *Developing Countries and the Global Financial System*, edited by Stephany Griffiths-Jones and Amar Battacharya, Commonwealth Secretariat, 2000.

March 2000. This was more than double the level achieved before the fabled 1929 Wall Street crash, when stock market capitalization amounted to what then seemed the astonishing figure of 81 per cent of GDP. When looked at in terms of how much investors were prepared to pay for the earnings or assets of quoted companies, the market valuation was similarly extreme. Why, you might ask, did America experience a bubble of even greater proportions than in the 1920s, given that so much more money was now in the hands of supposedly canny professional investors rather than private individuals? And why, today, has the wider financial world become so much more volatile compared with earlier periods?

A first and fundamental difference, when compared with the 19th century, is that American military strength, however impressive, does not provide a comparable degree of global political stability to the Pax Britannica. Nor is there a gold standard today to provide an anchor for the monetary and financial system. A shared commitment to convert currencies into gold at a fixed parity puts a constraint on the expansion of credit and is thus a force for stable prices and financial stability. It also reduces currency instability, which largely explains why modern financial crises appear to do more damage than those in the gold standard period before 1914. Without that standard, the world depends on central banks and governments to keep things stable. Over the past 20 years they have indeed succeeded in conquering inflation. In that, the Wall Street economists and the central bankers at the Fed are right. But in the words of Andrew Crockett, General Manager from 1994 to 2003 of the Bank for International Settlements, the central bankers' bank in Basle, lower inflation has not by itself yielded the peace dividend of a more stable financial environment, as central bankers had expected. So instability has risen to the top of the international economic policy agenda and it stubbornly remains there.[6]

---

[6] Andrew Crockett, speech to the Société Universitaire Européenne des Recherches Financières (SUERF), April 2000.

The monkeys take charge

There is a large paradox in this. Financiers have traditionally made their living by matching the needs of people with surplus funds to the requirements of other people who believe they can find a productive outlet for the money. Yet over the past quarter of a century the balance of financial activity has changed, especially in the Anglo-American world. More of this intermediary role has been taken over by markets, as companies have discovered they can bypass the banks and raise money more cheaply by issuing securities and IOUs such as commercial paper. Savers have withdrawn deposits from the banking system and put more money into the securities markets.

Equally important, to cope with increased volatility resulting from the tidal wave of deregulation and the growth of incredibly rapid computerized trading, financial systems have developed new markets to cope with risk. With governments no longer stabilizing markets by way of tight regulation, banks and companies take out private insurance against unexpected changes in interest rates, currencies and security prices through the use of derivative instruments such as swaps, futures and options. In this new American-dominated financial world, exposure to risks can be bought and sold separately from the underlying financial assets. Complex computer systems monitor these risks, which metamorphose on a minute-to-minute basis as banks shuffle their financial assets and liabilities and change the shape of their balance sheets in response to the needs of clients and their own trading positions. These changes were made possible by advances in the mathematical theory of option-pricing, pioneered by American academic economists.

A consequence of this shift in the workings of high finance toward the management of risk is that central banks have lost their grip on a vital part of the system. Without an expensive army of supervisors permanently stationed on every dealing floor, they cannot police the high-octane trading that drives activity in global markets, whether for hedging purposes or speculation. They can only examine banks' risk management systems, impose rules for the amount of capital that must be used to support a given exposure to risk and call for increased transparency. With the biggest banks these capital rules are applied to risk management models of their own devising. The central bankers are dependent on experts in private banks to ensure that the plumbing of the system is capable of handling safely the complex trading strategies initiated by derivatives dealers. This new, but diminished role for the central banks is euphemistically known as "process-oriented regulation". Banking experts insist that it has the great merit of flexibility. But that cannot disguise the fact that banking supervision has been semi-privatized by default, leading to a genuine erosion of the power of the state and of its agents in the central banks. Crudely put, the monkeys are now in charge of the zoo.

The paradox lies in the fact that despite huge resources being poured into the technology of risk assessment, everyone in high finance knows that risk management is fundamentally flawed. In part, this stems from an error of omission. Nobody has been able to find a way of using derivatives to hedge against liquidity risk – the problem banks face when depositors panic. The big error of commission arises because the banks are exceptionally skilled in assessing the *relative* risk between different kinds of financial instruments and financial relationships. But they are flummoxed when it comes to evaluating *absolute* risks arising from such basic things as changes in the economic or financial cycle. Contrary to the protestations of Lawrence Summers in Chapter 1, these worries are not confined to people who know nothing of markets. Andrew Crockett, the central bankers' banker, puts it like this:

> Indicators of risk tend to be at their lowest at or close to the peak of the financial cycle, ie, just at the point where, with hindsight, we can see that risk was greatest. Asset prices are buoyant, credit spreads are narrow and loan loss provisions are low. There is a sense in which risk *accumulates* during upswings, as financial imbalances build up, and *materialises* in recessions. The length of the horizon here is crucial. Yet, so far, the ability to anticipate, and hence prepare for, the rainy day has proved inadequate.[7]

---

[7] Andrew Crockett, SUERF speech.

Worse, the system of capital charges imposed on banks encourages them to over-lend in booms and under-lend in recessions. This is Alice in Wonderland territory – not least because a proposed reform of the regulatory regime for bank capital, prepared under the aegis of the Bank for International Settlements in Basle, threatens to exacerbate existing flaws instead of eliminating them. Some of the world's best monetary economists have concluded that the proposed new system is so perversely designed that it will, in and of itself, produce crashes.[8] As if to compensate for the fact that central banks cannot police high-octane trading more directly, the proposed system is hugely prescriptive to the point where some leading bankers have complained to me that they are not sure how to incorporate it into their existing risk management models. So finance capitalism in the post-communist era appears to suffer from what Marx called internal contradictions. Bizarre though it may seem to anyone outside the financial world, the whole thrust of risk management is directed at the less important threats. The risk-managers' black boxes send hopelessly misleading signals about the big threats that can cause painful losses of output and employment in individual countries while potentially destabilizing the global financial system.

Rational and irrational exuberance

A similar myopia may have been at work in the US stock market bubble. The world economy, with the US providing the main impetus, has in recent years experienced conditions that would

---

[8] Jon Danielsson, Paul Embrechts, Charles Goodhart, Con Keating, Felix Muennich, Olivier Renault and Hyun Song Shin, *An Academic Response to Basle II*, Special Paper No. 130, Financial Markets Group, London School of Economics, 2001. See also Charles Calomiris of Columbia University in the June 2002 issue of *The Financial Regulator*. His pithy verdict on Basle II is: "At the most basic level the focus on book equity capital relative to risk-based assets is simply not workable and should be scrapped. Book equity capital is not measured accurately. Risk-based assets do not accurately measure risk. Furthermore we have no evidence as to whether 8 per cent is the right target capital ratio. The numerator is phoney, the denominator is phoney and the target ratio is phoney! Apart from that, it is a great system."

have been familiar to 19th century Americans. Technological innovation led to an investment boom in the 1990s, which encouraged
investors to raise their expectations about future profits to absurd
levels. The bursting of the bubble was followed by recession in 2001
resulting from surplus capacity, declining profits, rising unemployment
and waning consumer confidence. This was very different from the
typical post-war economic cycle in which recessions were precipitated
by rising interest rates as central banks moved to curb accelerating
inflation. The pattern is more redolent of the inherently volatile
cycles of creative destruction described by the Austrian-born economist Joseph Schumpeter that were experienced in the late 19th
century.

It is clear that professional investors, being human, are no less
prone to euphoria than ordinary private investors. The bubble phenomenon and the psychology of investors in the new Internet age has
been brilliantly explored by Robert J. Shiller in his book *Irrational
Exuberance*.[9] Yet it is often overlooked that there were rational as well
as irrational elements that help explain why this bubble was so much
more extreme than anything seen before – rational at least in the
sense that the motivation of the participants was in their own self-
interest if not that of the wider community. One important and
extraordinary factor here is that many professional fund-managers
are no longer really interested in making money for their clients.
They are preoccupied chiefly with their investment performance
relative to their competitors, because they know that if they underperform by a wide margin they will lose the mandate to manage the
client's money.

This has led fund-managers to rely on complex computer models
that measure the volatility of investment returns against a benchmark
index. In simple language, they are more interested in sticking close to
the pack of their fellow fund-managers than in whether the stock
market goes up or down. By defining risk in this narrow, self-serving
way, many failed to alert clients such as pension fund trustees to the

---

[9] Robert J. Shiller, *Irrational Exuberance*, Princeton University Press, 2000.

fact that stock markets were becoming overvalued and highly dangerous in the 1990s. Those who chose not to follow the herd risked losing
their jobs as clients with short-term horizons melted away. (The
famously bearish Tony Dye of London fund-manager PDFM, who
took a contrarian view during the bubble, was a notable victim of
this syndrome. His departure from PDFM coincided almost exactly
with the peak of the bubble.) Once again, bizarre though it may seem
to ordinary mortals, immensely sophisticated techniques were being
applied to the management of those risks that mattered least for the
efficient working of the market system.

As pension fund trustees have become disillusioned with the medi-
ocre performance that resulted from the professional fund-managers'
obsession with staying close to benchmarks, they have increasingly
put their money into funds that track an index. When large sums are
devoted in this way to replicating the performance of stock market
indices, herd behaviour becomes endemic. It is a strategy that assumes
the level of the market is always "right", even in an extreme bubble.
So fund-managers end up overexposed to expensive stocks while
remaining underexposed to cheap ones. They can also become vulnerable to the grandiose, but ill-judged takeover plans of large companies
where management knows that index-tracking investors will be forced
to increase their exposure to the company as it issues more shares in
exchange for expensive acquisitions. And companies become vulnerable to market distortions wrought by the mechanics of index construction. When in July 2002 Standard & Poor's decided to remove
foreign companies from the S&P 500 index in the US, the Canadian
telecom company Nortel saw its stock price fall 14 per cent in a single
day, while shares in Royal Dutch Shell fell 9 per cent. Since the share
price determines a company's cost of capital, the outcome is that
resources are misallocated. Increasingly, then, fund-managers are
abandoning the task of pursuing *absolute* returns to the hedge funds,
another Anglo-American financial phenomenon.[10]

---

[10] For a thoughtful discussion of these issues, see Barry Riley, *Financial Times*,
5 October 2001.

Hedge funds borrow heavily and invest hyperactively on behalf of both private and institutional investors. They have provided a convenient scapegoat in successive financial crises and have a knack, which is important in the present context, of exposing the weak points in financial supervision as well. Yet they are not quite the villains they are often painted. The readiness of some of them to take a contrary view, unlike so many conventional fund-managers, is healthy for the markets. Their arbitrage operations contribute to the efficient allocation of capital around the globe when they work according to plan. Leading hedge fund-managers are also among the more acute critics of the workings of financial markets. The pre-eminent example is George Soros, chairman of Soros Fund Management, who argues that financial markets, far from being an unalloyed economic boon, have an innate destabilizing capacity. He nonetheless does a fair bit of destabilizing himself while simultaneously urging in the media that the authorities should not leave the markets to their own devices. Much of the profit Soros earns in this curiously ambivalent fashion has been devoted to philanthropic causes, notably in the transition economies of Eastern Europe.

Yet hedge funds come in different forms and many of them are momentum-traders. That is, they try to make money in the very short term by following a market trend, thereby reinforcing it regardless of whether it makes sense in relation to economic fundamentals. This was a factor in the rise and rise of America's high-tech market NASDAQ whose value went from $2.9 trillion in January 1999 to $6 trillion in March 2000. At this level NASDAQ companies were being valued, on average, at 245 times their annual earnings – an astonishing figure that partly reflects the fact that many NASDAQ companies were not earning anything, but piling up losses. While the surge on NASDAQ is often said to be the work of private investors and day-traders, the professionals were in there too. They had to be, because many of the biggest high-tech companies such as Microsoft preferred a listing on NASDAQ to one on the New York Stock Exchange.

Many hedge funds, though by no means all, are heavily leveraged, whether through borrowing or through the use of derivatives that give them large exposure to risk and reward in relation to very small amounts of capital. At its simplest, this means that, instead of buying a security, they place a bet on the movement of a security. So for a small stake, they gain exposure to the same profit or loss as if they had bought the security itself. This, together with the fact that many are based in offshore jurisdictions beyond the reach of effective supervision, means that they can exert a destabilizing influence on markets that is hard for government watchdogs to prevent. The classic instance was that of LTCM, the secretive hedge fund run by the former Salomon Brothers bond-trader John Meriwether, which came close to collapse in September 1998. This was a historic landmark that took central banking into new territory.

Nobel seal of approval

LTCM was neither long term in outlook, nor much good at managing capital. At one point its borrowings had reached more than $100bn on a slender wedge of equity capital of just under $1bn. Despite the presence on the board of two Nobel Prize-winning economists, Robert Merton and Myron Scholes, pioneers of the financial theory that contributed to the development of derivatives, LTCM's risk management systems were far from shock-proof. Their models were based on historical simulations, which were useful enough for managing day-to-day risks in humdrum markets. But in the volatile circumstances that followed Asia's financial crisis and Russia's default on its government bonds in the summer of 1998, LTCM's black box was useless.

Part of the trouble was that too many of the big players in the financial system were using very similar black boxes with risk limits geared to the movements of the markets. If, in such circumstances, markets become unexpectedly volatile, too many financial institutions reach their risk limits at the same time. Everyone then tries to sell in order to restore their position, which causes further market weakness and volatility. More financial institutions then hit their risk limits. Because the world's biggest financial institutions are all moving in a herd-like way, and because their black boxes exclude extreme risks, the outcome is that risk management systems that are assumed to be conducive to more stable markets actually end up destabilizing them.[11]

In the specific case of LTCM the black box had not predicted that the hedge fund would be capable of losing half a billion dollars in a single day. The bankers took fright and demanded more collateral for their loans. When the troubled hedge fund was unable to stump up, the Federal Reserve felt obliged to step in to help broker a rescue.

It was the first time a central bank had ever acted to help a hedge fund in distress and it raises important questions about the workings of the Anglo-American market system. The theology of bailouts, which was developed by the 19th century British economist and political theorist Walter Bagehot, requires support to be extended only to commercial banks and then only where there is a risk to the whole financial system. Bagehot also stipulated that such help should be confined to solvent banks that were temporary victims of the prevailing financial panic. Keeping insolvent banks afloat is a recipe for undermining those that are solvent.

The difficulty with the theology is that it is always hard to assess whether an imminent banking collapse is a real systemic threat. Central banks tend to err on the side of extending a safety net, not least because this helps disguise their earlier failures of regulation and supervision that allowed the banking crisis to develop. In practice, banks that run into trouble are more often than not insolvent. Yet if they are large, they will be deemed "too big to fail". And the taxpayer will end up paying a bill for the rescue.

There is no doubt that if LTCM had been allowed to collapse there would have been substantial disruption to markets on a global basis. The Bank for International Settlements has estimated that LTCM was the world's single most active user of interest rate swaps in

---

[11] See Avinash Persaud's inaugural lecture as visiting professor at London's Gresham College on 3 October 2002 for a cogent and more detailed explanation of this innate flaw in conventional risk management.

1998. At the time of the rescue mission, it had exposure to derivatives with a value of $1 trillion, of which three-quarters consisted of interest rate swaps with about 50 financial institutions around the world. None of those institutions knew the extent of LTCM's overall exposure. When the fund tried to raise cash to meet its obligations that summer, it caused shock waves in some of the world's biggest markets.

Whether this constituted a systemic threat or not, a number of things were clear. One was that the centre of gravity in financial markets had shifted decisively away from conventional banking activity such as deposit-taking and lending. By 1998 the over-the-counter derivatives markets – the ones in which banks sell customized derivatives to individual clients – were dealing in sums comparable with the total cash positions in the whole of the world's old-style banking and securities markets. More than 40 per cent of the sums outstanding in this opaque part of the financial jungle related to hedge funds and other non-bank institutions.[12]

Yet the commercial banks were at risk, because they financed the investment banks that financed the hedge funds. John Reed, the then Chairman of Citigroup, has revealed that he was called while in San Francisco by William McDonough, Head of the New York Federal Reserve, and asked to attend a meeting to sort out LTCM. He declined because Citigroup had no loans to the troubled hedge fund. But while he was on the plane returning to New York it dawned on him that Citigroup was the lead bank to Goldman Sachs, which had overextended itself to LTCM, and to others on Wall Street that would be rocked by LTCM's failure. He joined in the rescue.[13] The Federal Reserve, meantime, cut its interest rates.

Whatever the theology, the politics of the rescue were plain enough. John Meriwether and his failing hedge fund were holding the global financial community to ransom. He was able to do this partly because the New York Fed was seriously rattled about the

---

[12] Bank for International Settlements' Annual Report, 1999.
[13] Quoted in Martin Mayer's, *The Fed*, The Free Press, 2001. For a full account of the LTCM episode, see Roger Lowenstein, *When Genius Failed*, Random House, 2000.

extent to which his investment bank creditors posed a threat to the system. This was, as mentioned earlier, a novelty in central banking. In the previous economic cycle Drexel Burnham, the investment bank that foundered because of the activities of junk bond king Michael Milken, was allowed to go to the wall despite having a sizeable balance sheet and a string of relationships with the world's leading banks. But LTCM's was a larger and more complex collapse. Meriwether and his investment banking friends also enjoyed one advantage that Drexel Burnham and Milken had lacked. The financial establishment was in bed with LTCM.

The usual suspects

David Mullins, a former vice chairman of the Federal Reserve and a friend of Alan Greenspan, was on the board. This was eye-catching in itself because Mullins had been closely involved in the Fed's investigation of a Treasury bond-rigging scandal that resulted in John Meriwether being forced to resign from Salomon Brothers. David Komansky, Chairman and Chief Executive Officer of Merrill Lynch, had a personal investment of $800,000 in the hedge fund, while fellow Merrill executives had more than $20m in the pot. Donald Marron, Chairman of PaineWebber, was another leading Wall Street figure with personal money in the fund as well as a $100m investment on his firm's account. So this was crony capitalism, American-style.

True, market professionals are not immune from euphoria. These people had bought the hedge fund's sophisticated marketing patter. Part of Meriwether's marketing genius was that he had discovered a novel inversion of the 19th century aristocratic guinea pig – the titled director who lent lustre, but not brains to a dubious board and took fees that were traditionally paid in guineas. LTCM's decorative Nobel Prize-winners had more brains than judgement. But their lustrous imprimatur looked wonderfully impressive and unlike their Victorian antecedents they put in work for their money. The big Wall Street professionals were also in bed with LTCM because its frenetic dealing activity constituted a huge source of revenue for the investment banks in their capacity as providers of broking, market-making and settlement services. It was also important for them to know at first hand what such a big player in global markets was doing. Yet with so much at stake, both personally and through their firms, these giants of Wall Street were involved in potential conflicts of interest, not least in deciding whether their shareholders' money should be used to back a costly rescue.

No taxpayers' money went into the bailout, so this was not one of the more egregious examples of crony capitalism. But senior Fed officials freely admit that the Fed's role in securing funds for LTCM did involve a degree of moral hazard – the phenomenon whereby the existence of a safety net tends to encourage imprudent behaviour. Interestingly, John Meriwether was doing the rounds of the financial institutions in a matter of months to raise fresh capital. By November 1999 he had found investors willing to back him with no less than $250m. So here lies an important clue to the acceleration in the incidence of financial crises and the extreme nature of the US stock market bubble. The general perception of the US model of capitalism as a Darwinian struggle in which the weak founder and markets rule is entirely misleading. The reality is that the Federal Reserve under Alan Greenspan, the world's most powerful central banker, has been intensively managing the economic and financial cycle and putting a safety net under the markets.

Consider how much propping and rescuing has taken place on Alan Greenspan's watch. He became Chairman of the Fed in August 1987, just in time for the stock market crash in October that year. There was a serious risk of a breakdown in the settlement of securities transactions and of securities firms going to the wall so the Fed announced that it would support the economic and financial system by standing ready to pump liquidity, or money, into the markets. Interest rates were cut and Fed officials twisted the arms of those banks that were reluctant to support clients that were still creditworthy despite the market collapse. In the event, confidence was restored so quickly that the Fed had no need to buy large quantities of government bonds from banks through open market operations – the practical way of injecting liquidity into markets. The effect of the rescue mission was to extend an economic cycle that would otherwise have come to a painful halt.

By early 1991 Greenspan was back in rescue mode again, this time in response to a crisis in banking. There had been the bubble in the US commercial property market, together with a vast increase in corporate debt levels as a result of leveraged buyouts and takeovers. Consumers were also over-indebted. Banks had become reluctant to lend, and there were rumours that the biggest US commercial bank Citicorp, as it was then known, was in trouble. Greenspan cut interest rates, which reduced the banks' cost of funds. And he tried to encourage bank supervisors to be less zealous about the need to write down the value of bank assets to levels that might threaten the banks' solvency. In due course improved profitability allowed the banks to emerge from intensive care. Then came the Asian crisis in 1998, followed by the LTCM debacle. As we have seen, this prompted similar cuts in interest rates. The Fed also flooded the market with liquidity around the new millennium to deal with the Year 2000 (Y2K) computer problem – a threat that turned out to be vastly overblown. This swept the bubble in technology stocks to its peak. And the Fed repeated the trick in response to the terrorist attacks on New York's twin towers.

A welfare system for capital

In each case there is an obvious justification for extending the safety net. Yet the cumulative effect of such behaviour is to erode capitalism's immune system. Participants in the markets observe that, whenever prices plunge, the safety net comes out. They also observe that nothing is ever done to impose a ceiling when prices rocket. So those that are not under financial pressure see financial crises as a potential buying opportunity. This subverts the purpose that crises serve within the capitalist system, which is to correct excesses and imbalances that build up in the upswing of the economic cycle.

The conventional wisdom among central bankers, which was shared by Alan Greenspan and his colleagues at the Fed during the bubble, is that it is wrong to turn asset prices, whether in the stock market or in property, into targets for policy. They believe that asset prices should be taken into account only in so far as they are likely to contribute to future inflation. And they claim that the practical difficulties of identifying and pricking bubbles are overwhelmingly complex. All of which leads to the conclusion that their job should be confined to stabilizing prices in the market for goods and services. As Greenspan likes to put it, spotting a bubble in advance requires a judgement that hundreds of thousands of informed investors have it all wrong. The task, as he sees it in relation to bubbles, is to mitigate the damage after the bubble bursts. Yet the so-called asymmetry in this approach to monetary policy – providing a safety net, but imposing no ceiling on asset prices that are soaring – is perfectly designed to foster rational exuberance. In other words, just as banks can become too big to be allowed to fail, markets can rise too high to be allowed to fall. If the US stock market bubble in the 1990s was so much more impressive than its predecessors, the explanation is surely here. Alan Greenspan's Fed helped create the bubble.

In one sense this constant resort to the safety net brings the American model of capitalism closer to that of Europe, where governments have tried to soften the rigours of the economic cycle by putting the safety net under the labour market. Yet it creates incentive effects that can be similarly counterproductive. If much of the financial pain is taken out of unemployment, as it is in Europe, people will devote less effort to rejoining the labour market. The generosity of European social security payments is one of the factors behind the much higher rate of unemployment and the lower rate of participation in the labour market in Continental Europe compared with the US.

By putting a safety net under the capital markets, the US runs a different risk. It stabilizes the economic cycle in the short run, but the rise in equity prices creates a wealth effect: around three to five cents of every additional dollar of stock market wealth is eventually reflected in increased consumer purchases.[14] As consumer outlays rise in relation to disposable income, household savings decline because, in the words of the Wall Street commentator James Grant, people conclude that the stock market is doing their saving for them.[15] And since rising equity prices lead to a reduction in industry's cost of capital, companies invest more. In effect, both consumers and companies bring forward spending decisions. Because industry's cost of capital is artificially low, it ends up investing in uneconomic projects. The result is a build-up of private sector debt and a deteriorating balance of payments, as a shortfall of savings against investment has to be made good from overseas. Thanks to these so-called imbalances Joseph Schumpeter's boom-and-bust cycle may, in the long run, be exaggerated rather than mitigated by policy even if the short run effect of policy is benign. So the central bankers who argue that the movement of asset prices is relevant only in helping make judgements about future inflation miss the point. After a bubble collapses, the greater risk is of deflation as falling asset prices shrink the collateral of the banking system and precipitate a credit crunch in which banks stop lending even to creditworthy borrowers. Governments are then forced to consider risky policy options such as running large fiscal deficits and resorting to inflation to extract themselves from this bind.

A related problem is simply that a central banker's safety net can become threadbare from continuing use. So if an overvalued stock market runs into an unexpected shock or dramatic change in sentiment, investors may not respond in the same cheery way when the central bank pulls the interest rate lever in yet another attempt to perpetuate the levitation in stock prices. For when heavily indebted companies and private individuals discover that their earlier assump-

---

[14] See Chapter 2 of *World Economic Outlook*, April 2002 *A Financial History of Western Europe*, George, Allen & Unwin, 1984, p. 273.

[15] James Grant's newsletter *Grant's Interest Rate Observer* bears witness to the absurdity of Alan Greenspan's contention that bubbles cannot be identified before they have burst. Not only did Grant identify the bubble, as it expanded he identified many of the accountancy loopholes that were subsequently to spook investors in such companies as IBM and Tyco International.

tions about asset prices have proved wrong, they may be more anxious to increase savings and reduce debts than to respond to lower interest rates by spending more. This then exacerbates the deflationary pressures in the economy as the laws of financial gravity reassert themselves.

Politics of the rescue culture

Why, given these risks, did the Federal Reserve create a rescue culture for the markets? It has to be said that the central bankers' arguments about the difficulty of adjusting interest rates to prevent bubbles are not just hot air. A decision by the US Federal Reserve to raise interest rates to dampen speculation was, after all, the proximate cause of the disastrous 1929 crash. But the Fed, at that time a new and relatively untested institution, left the decision too late. Toward the end of the century there was far greater understanding and sophistication in economic management. Plenty of independent economists and not over-smart financial journalists managed to diagnose the Japanese bubble of the 1980s and the US bubble of the 1990s. It beggars credibility that Alan Greenspan, one of the world's most astute students of financial markets, could not do the same. His own coinage of the phrase "irrational exuberance" suggests precisely that he did.

The most plausible explanation for the Fed's reluctance to puncture the bubble lies not in the practicalities of targeting asset prices, but in the politics of US monetary policy. For the politics did indeed change in the 1990s thanks to the great increase in the exposure of private individuals to the risk of stock market fluctuations. At the end of the 1990s some 35 million Americans owned equities directly, while nearly 50 million were exposed to the stock market via pension plans invested in mutual funds. In this they differed from the Continental Europeans who relied more heavily on the state for their pensions and on the banks to keep their savings. At much the same period German bank assets were almost five times as large as the value of the German stock market, whereas the assets of the US banking system had shrunk to a mere third of the value of the US stock market. American citizens held only 16 per cent of their financial assets at the bank, compared with 43 per cent in equities and 41 per cent in bonds.[16]

With so many Americans exposed to equities, the stock market was driving the US economy as much as the US economy was driving the stock market as people adjusted their spending in response to changing perceptions about their own wealth. But wealth effects also work in reverse. The rise in the number of individual owners of stocks and shares meant that a market collapse had far greater potential economic and political consequences than in earlier periods of US history.

The problem for central bankers in confronting a stock market bubble is that it may make economic sense to raise interest rates pre-emptively to prick the bubble and cause a mild recession so as to avoid a much bigger recession at a later date. But they may end up being blamed for the recession, while gaining no credit with politicians and public for avoiding a worse recession or depression later. Andrew Smithers and Stephen Wright argue plausibly in their book *Valuing Wall Street* that, if the Fed had raised interest rates in early 1995 when the US equity market first started to became noticeably overvalued, President Clinton might not have reappointed Alan Greenspan as chairman of the Fed. A mild recession, they add, might also have stopped Clinton from being elected.[17]

In such circumstances Wall Street's Panglossian punditry can provide useful cover for a Federal Reserve that is reluctant to prick a bubble. Innocently so, in the case of those economists and investment strategists whose belief in the New Paradigm caused them to flunk the test of diagnosing the greatest bubble of the 20th century. By looking at the economy exclusively through the rear-view mirror, they mistook a very long economic cycle for a non-cycle, failing to

---

[16] Figures from David D. Hale, *Can America Achieve a Soft Landing after Its Stock Market Boom or Why the Equity Market Boom Is an Experiment in Corporate Resource Allocation*, Zurich Financial Services, January 2000.

[17] Andrew Smithers and Stephen Wright, *Valuing Wall Street*, McGraw-Hill, 2001.

recognize that for all its merits new information technology could not remove from industrialists the risk of overestimating the demand for their products. And they also forgot the important lesson of history that much of the benefit of productivity miracles goes to consumers, not shareholders.

For, while productivity growth rose inexorably in the second half of the decade, profits of non-financial corporations in the US peaked in the third quarter of 1997 in relation to both GDP and shareholders' equity. So, extraordinary though it sounds, the climactic years of the bubble were supported by a dwindling stream of profits. Yet there were also less innocent behavioural factors at work because the investment banking pundits were involved in deep conflicts of interest. Most were under pressure from their bosses to justify the overvalued level of the market because investment bankers make more money in rising markets when the volume of financial transactions is high. When everything is going up, the economists, investment strategists and analysts share in the higher bonuses too.

Threadbare safety net

A number of conclusions follow from all this. For a start, the standard continental European view of the US model of capitalism as a Hobbesian war of all against all, in which the values of the market triumph over social values is, at the very least, out of date. The Fed's bailout culture casts the US model in a very different light. In effect, the Hobbesian financial world, complete with full-scale financial crises, collapsing banks and economic slumps, is now largely confined to emerging market countries. At the same time, the belief of the anti-globalizers that the state and its agents in the central banks are no longer able to influence markets and companies is clearly wrong. Policy was partly responsible for the bubble. And while the financial watchdogs have lost some of their power over the markets, regulation nonetheless continues to influence markets profoundly. The problem is that these regulatory powers come shackled to the law of unintended consequences.

Regulation has contributed to financial crises by creating perverse incentives. The rules about how much capital banks need to support a given type of risk, which are contained in the international accord known as the 1988 Basle Capital Adequacy Regime, created a greater incentive in the 1990s for banks to lend to unregulated hedge funds than to the giants of industry and commerce. The rules also imposed low capital charges on over-the-counter derivatives – those traded over phones and screens between banks and their clients – relative to those traded on more transparent exchanges. So derivatives business has unintentionally been driven into a black hole in the markets where central banks are unable to monitor adequately what goes on.

Where the stock market is concerned, some argue that it was better to have had the party than not. Because the euphoria was taking place in the capital markets, there was less of a threat to the perennially vulnerable banking system than there was in the property bubble of the late 1980s or in the Japanese stock market bubble where the banks were hit by the collapse in the value of their shareholdings in client companies. As for the wider economic risks posed by the bubble, it is only fair to give credit to Alan Greenspan for the remarkable way in which the US economy in 2001 survived not only the sharp fall in equity values, but a severe retrenchment in capital-spending and the appalling terrorist acts of 11 September. By encouraging ordinary Americans to borrow and spend while US industry struggled, the Fed's very rapid interest rate cuts in the face of looming recession guaranteed an earlier recovery than during the post-bubble period in Japan.

In effect the economic impact of a falling equity market on people's wealth was offset because the Fed succeeded in inflating the property market, thereby protecting wealth by another route. And Fed Chairman Alan Greenspan felt able to give himself a testimonial in the Spring of 2002 when he opined that "the imbalances that triggered the downturn and that could have prolonged this difficult period did not fester." In his view, information technology, together with financial innovation and deregulation, had made it possible to address and resolve economic imbalances far more rapidly than in the past and thereby reduce cyclical swings in economic activity.[18] The implicit suggestion was that the US had experienced the first stock market binge in history not to have been followed by a hangover, in the shape of a banking crisis or a slump.

The trouble with this rationalization of events is that despite the Fed Chairman's soothing words, the imbalances had not, in 2002, been addressed. Private sector indebtedness was still at its highest level for half a century in relation to GDP, while the size of the current account deficit was unprecedented. In effect, the Fed had risked creating a house price bubble in order to escape from the consequences of the stock market bubble. So if the imbalances had not "festered", as Greenspan put it, they had not gone away either, which meant that the economy remained fragile and vulnerable to any loss of confidence. With the US public sector moving from surplus to deficit under George W. Bush, foreigners who were previously keen to finance private sector investment in a seemingly robust economy were by 2002 being asked to finance public and private sector consumption – a much less attractive proposition than financing a private sector investment boom. There was also the risk that some of those investors, among the largest of whom were central banks such as the People's Bank of China, would be reluctant to continue financing the US if it pursued controversial foreign policy initiatives in Iraq or elsewhere. As the year progressed, foreign investors did indeed start pulling out, contributing to a simultaneous weakening of equities and the dollar.

Compounding the problem was the fact that by 2002 the stock market safety net had indeed become dangerously threadbare. For when investors finally recognized that Enron was just the first of many corporate scandals, they lost confidence in the earnings figures on which high stock market values depended for their support. With the target for the federal funds rate down to a mere

---

[18] Speech to the Institute of International Finance, 22 April 2002.

$1\frac{3}{4}$ per cent, there was far less room than previously to cut interest rates to bolster confidence and a big question as to whether the expedient would work any more. The threat of deflation arising from an over-rapid adjustment of the imbalances in the economy looked increasingly real.

By then there were still some people who were willing to believe that the Fed Chairman was a genius who had subtly honed his central banking skills to deal with the new challenges of the information age. An alternative view, to which I subscribe, is that this exceptional Fed Chairman belongs to a much older banking tradition encapsulated in the remark of the 19th century German financier Bleichroeder on his fellow banker Bethel Henry Strousberg: "The man is very clever, but his manner of undertaking new ventures in order to mend old holes is dangerous, and if he should encounter a sudden obstacle, his whole structure may collapse and under its ruins bury millions of gullible shareholders."[19] And one fact about Greenspan remains damning beyond dispute. In the biggest bubble the world had ever seen he persisted in talking the market up with his enthusiastic new-economy rhetoric when a more prudent central banker would have tried to talk it down. On that, the verdict of history will surely be punitive.

But, whatever the economic outcome, there is no escaping the fact that the American model has not lived up to the claim made for it by the propagandists in Washington and Wall Street that it allocates capital with supreme efficiency. Because capital became too cheap in the bull market, too much of it financed a wasteful investment binge. The result was a savage capital-spending recession. And in the absence of changed policy at the Fed, there is a risk that at some point in the future when the threat of deflation has been forgotten capital will be misallocated again in another bubble. Robert Shiller, the author of *Irrational Exuberance*, explains some of the wider consequences better than I can:

---

[19] Quoted in Kindleberger, A *Financial History of Western Europe*, George, Allen & Unwin, 1984, p. 273.

How we value the stock market now and in the future influences major economic and social policy decisions that affect not only investors but also society at large, even the world. If we exaggerate the present and future value of the stock market, then as a society we may invest too much in business start-ups and expansions, and too little in infrastructure, education, and other forms of human capital. If we think the market is worth more than it really is, we may become complacent in funding our pension plans, in maintaining our savings rate, in legislating an improved Social Security system, and in providing other forms of social insurance. We might also lose the opportunity to use our expanding financial technology to devise new solutions to the genuine risks – to our homes, cities, and livelihoods – that we face.

In short, if capital goes off the rails, it is not a trivial matter. And a greater price may yet have to be paid for the greatest investment binge since the railway mania of the 19th century.

4

Europe pulls up a drawbridge

Continental Europe has as many varieties of capitalism as it has countries. But in so far as there is something distinctively and overwhelmingly different about the Continental European approach to capitalism, it lies in the emphasis that European politicians place on what they call social peace. In a continent that has suffered centuries-long cycles of destruction through war and that was at the geographical front line in the ideological battle between capitalism and communism, this desire for cohesion has an obvious historical *raison d'être*. It also helps explain why many Continental European politicians are profoundly suspicious of "Anglo-Saxon" capitalism, with its hire-and-fire labour markets, volatile capital flows and income inequality.

Nowhere more so than in France, where a right-of-centre French former prime minister Edouard Balladur once remarked: "What is the market? It is the law of the jungle, the law of nature." And what is civilisation? It is the struggle against nature.[1] A left-wing prime minister Lionel Jospin subsequently sang from the same song sheet, when he famously argued that the French would tolerate a market economy, but not a market society. Such sentiments reflect a wider distrust in Europe of the streak of libertarian individualism in US culture and a view that the social costs imposed by unfettered markets are unacceptably high. This has been further fuelled by the

---

[1] *Financial Times*, 31 December 1993.

spate of corporate scandals in the US after the collapse of Enron. And many Continental Europeans harbour a profound suspicion of financial markets. Typical of this attitude is the remark of French intellectual Alain Minc who rails against "the dictatorship of the jittery people in the markets."[2]

Euro-pessimists in the international financial community have an equal and opposite distrust of this commitment to social peace, which they regard as a pious cover for the European habit of buying off interest groups, whether farmers, truck-drivers or rail-workers, at tax-payers' expense. They likewise argue that Europeans are being priced out of work by the high payroll taxes needed to finance welfare benefits, by high minimum wages and by other inflexibilities in the labour market. And it has to be said that there is a fair measure of hypocrisy in the Continental politicians' antipathy toward the Anglo-American model, given that social peace appears to have delivered such a poor dividend to the European workforce over the past decade or so. The level of unemployment in the big Continental European economies has been substantially higher than that in America for years. At the start of 2000 the jobless numbers in Germany, France and Italy stood respectively at 7.9 per cent, 9.5 per cent and 10.5 per cent, compared with a mere 4.0 per cent in the US and 5.5 per cent in the UK.[3]

The US, meantime, has pursued more interventionist labour market policies than most Europeans have noticed. The expansion of the country's earned income tax credit, which raises the pay for the poorest workers by having government pay part of the wage bill, has helped reduce unemployment and made post-tax incomes less unequal. Since labour market conditions tightened in the 1990s, companies across North America started to educate and train inner city youths previously regarded as unemployable. European politicians appear reluctant to give America due credit for this approach to social peace and seem to draw consolation from their vision of US

---

[2] Quoted in Bernard Connolly, *The Rotten Heart of Europe*, Faber & Faber, 1995.
[3] OECD standardized basis, *OECD Economic Outlook No. 69*, June 2001.

cities as an urban hell. Yet the rise of the extreme right in Continental Europe suggests that the politicians have been unduly complacent about the rising tide of violence in their own cities back at home. And while unemployment rose sharply in the US with the onset of recession in 2001, few doubt that the US economy will continue to be better at creating private sector jobs than Continental Europe. The desire for social cohesion has also resulted in Europe denying itself the opportunity to increase the labour force through immigration. And the immigration that does take place is perceived as increasingly threatening. In this there is a sharp contrast with the US, where immigration continues to make a significant contribution to economic growth by swelling the labour force.

That said, the European Union has recently been moving in a more market-friendly direction, not least in relation to capital. Securities markets across the eurozone have been reformed, as have tax systems. The European Union summit in Lisbon in March 2000 – which coincided inauspiciously with the peak of the dotcom bubble in the stock markets – was notable for its recognition of the need to make European markets work better. In announcing the grandiose goal of becoming the "most competitive and dynamic knowledge-based economy in the world", Europe's leaders, with Britain's Tony Blair to the fore, proposed a raft of radical liberalization measures at the so-called dotcom summit.

Despite the rhetorical trench warfare, then, Europe's different models of capitalism are moving closer to the Anglo-American benchmark. And Europe can still teach the US a thing or two about corporate scandals, most notably in Italy where corporate corruption has not only been rife but stretches right up to the office of Prime Minister Silvio Berlusconi, the media magnate turned politician who contrives to make George W. Bush look like a saint. Yet the differences of perception between the US and Europe are no less real for that and have encouraged people in think tanks to talk of a transatlantic "values gap". Indeed, the fear of market instability and of globalization was an important strand in the construction of European monetary union (EMU) and Europe's new currency, the euro. For many European politicians the European Union is, among other things, a vehicle for managing economic interdependence and taming the markets. Monetary union offered a way of raising the regulatory powers of member states to a more effective regional level. At the same time the introduction of the euro eliminated currency instability within Europe and was expected to pose a challenge to the dollar without.

That desire to provide competition for the US currency reflects a powerful streak of economic nationalism among Europe's political elite, tinged with old-world hauteur. It is no coincidence that in the French referendum over the Maastricht Treaty, which paved the way for EMU, the government-orchestrated pro-EMU advertising campaign featured an overweight American cowboy and a Japanese sumo-wrestler bestriding the globe. The message was that the only way for France to escape subjugation by these uncouth forces was to integrate further into the European Union. Yet for all the scratchiness of the transatlantic relationship Europe has embraced a great deal of the Anglo-American capital prospectus.

Frisky Trojan horses

The post-war British foreign secretary and trade union leader Ernest Bevin once remarked of the Council of Europe, in a fine melange of myths, that "if you open up that Pandora's Box you never know what Trojan 'orses will jump out." The same could be said of EMU and the liberalizing measures of Europe's single market programme, if we substitute Anglo-Americans for Trojans. As far as the capital markets are concerned these have provided an entrée for two very significant Trojan incursions. The first stems from the fact that the single currency has facilitated the creation of a unified European bond market in which the IOUs of both governments and companies can be floated and traded. This is really the last nail in the coffin of bank-dominated finance of the kind normally associated with what the French call "Rhenish", or Rhineland, capitalism – a model much admired, until recently, by left-of-centre British and American commentators.

In Germany, companies have traditionally enjoyed a close relation-ship with a single house bank – a "universal" bank that engaged in securities business as well as conventional deposit-taking and lending. In the post-war period the banks enjoyed a monopoly in lending to a given client company in exchange for an implicit agreement to provide support if the borrower ran into trouble. At large companies the bank was also represented on the supervisory board and thus had a role in corporate governance, ensuring that managerial power was subject to proper oversight and discipline.

Bank-dominated systems have usually evolved where capital markets were underdeveloped or disrupted by shocks such as war, so that laws were uncertain or difficult to enforce. Their strengths, as exemplified by post-war Germany, include the mutual long-term com-mitment of both borrower and lender. And the banks' judgements on whether to rescue a troubled company tend to take into account all the value that the company adds to society, including to workers, customers and local communities. In Germany this was part of a wider compromise between capital and labour, which included the unique system of co-determination, or worker participation. The outcome was a degree of long-term security that allowed workers to commit to the company in a way that American or British workers could not.

Within this system, outside shareholders were often disadvantaged. For investors based in the civil code jurisdictions of Continental Europe have enjoyed poor legal protection compared with those in the English-speaking common law countries. Controlling share-holders, whether in bank-led or family-dominated systems, frequently used their political clout in the post-war period to ensure that they enjoyed the greatest possible benefits of private control of their com-panies, sometimes at the expense of the non-controlling shareholders. Yet it also needs to be said that on other occasions they imposed a governance discipline on management from which outside share-holders gained. The problem for outside investors, in the absence of more formal legal and regulatory protection, was that they could not be certain whether they would be fleeced or whether they would enjoy a profitable free ride on the coat-tails of the holders of large controlling stakes. They were, in consequence, more reluctant to put money into the stock markets than people in the English-speaking jurisdictions, so making it harder and more costly for companies to raise capital. For large companies that financed themselves mainly from retained profits, this scarcely mattered. It was young companies that paid the penalty, since it was difficult for them to raise capital to finance new investment.

Until the 1990s Continental Europe's financial systems and corporate governance arrangements were essentially national. Nowhere more so than in Germany, where the bank-dominated approach worked to best effect on the basis of limited mobility of capital and labour. But as capital controls were lifted all across Europe, German companies suddenly found they were no longer locked into their historic accommodation with the workforce. Managers directed more of their investment to countries in Eastern Europe, which were able to offer much cheaper labour and were close enough to permit just-in-time production methods back in Germany. German companies also came to recognize that their house bank was a middleman and that it was just as easy to cut out the middlemen in financial markets as anywhere else. Despite the closeness of their past relationships, German businessmen are in practice no more enamoured of their bankers than anyone else. They were delighted to discover that they could bypass the bank and raise money more cheaply from the markets.

So the banks lost much of their incentive to monitor corporate performance. Nationally negotiated coordination between capital and labour was eroded. The big banks, realizing that their core corporate lending business was threatened by competition from the markets, moved into American-style investment banking. Deutsche Bank, the largest of them, bought itself a significant presence on Wall Street by buying Bankers Trust and shifted much of its corporate business operations to London. Others followed it into the London markets. The development of a pan-European corporate bond market thanks to EMU has put the seal on this process. In 2000, companies raised more than $200bn in the new euro-denominated market in corporate IOUs. As this market evolves, it will reach further down the rungs of Europe's corporate ladder, further eroding traditional banking relationships.

This move in an Anglo-American direction has been reinforced by the arrival of another Trojan horse in Europe, courtesy of privatization. Back in 1900 the capital markets in France and Germany were much closer in character to the modern US market than to the stakeholder models of the second half of the 20th century. But in the 1930s Depression, Europe shifted toward much greater state ownership of industry and commerce, as companies and banks collapsed. In the extreme case of Italy, the government of Mussolini transferred so much of the equity of large companies to a public holding company, the Istituto per la Ricostruzione Industriale (IRI), that public ownership substantially replaced the securities markets. This was in sharp contrast to the US, where the state chose to regulate private markets after the 1929 Crash instead of acting as a substitute for them.

All that changed significantly in Europe in the final decade of the old century. Of the $850bn of state assets across the world that were transferred to the private sector in the 1990s, around 40 per cent were in Europe, including the transition economies of the former Soviet bloc.[4] This move to shift assets into the private sector was less ideologically driven than in the UK, which pioneered privatization in Europe during Margaret Thatcher's term as prime minister. The attraction for continental politicians lay as much in the ability to use privatization proceeds to reduce bloated government deficits as in the potential for improved economic efficiency. It also followed a different pattern to the UK privatization experiment because the state could not rely on the buying power of large private pension funds to absorb state assets.

---

[4] OECD estimates, from Kevin Brown, *Financial Times* survey "Europe Reinvented", 26 January 2001.

The big three Continental economies of Germany, France and Italy handle pension provision primarily through pay-as-you-go state pensions, whereby pension contributions of the working population pay for the pensions of retired people. So there was an ownership vacuum in the private sector that could only be filled thanks to globalization. Capital from America, Britain and elsewhere poured into Continental Europe. The result is that many of the largest companies on the Continent are majority-owned by Anglo-American investors – a very receptive audience for takeover bids as a lever for managerial change and a more efficient use of capital. It was no coincidence that two-thirds of the equity capital of Mannesmann, the giant German conglomerate that succumbed to a path-breaking hostile bid in 2000 from Britain's mobile phone group Vodafone, was owned by foreigners.

Crony euro-capitalism

The existence of these large foreign holdings created a new pressure on European industrialists to increase the return on capital, which was low compared with the US. It also gave London-based investment bankers their chance to promote the takeover habit on the Continent and to break the stranglehold of the old-style European investment bankers such as France's Lazard Frères and Mediobanca in Italy. The skills of these European institutions had been learned in the context of bank- or family-dominated controlling share stakes. They knew how to handle the European form of crony capitalism in which insiders often controlled large business empires via a cat's cradle of friendly cross-shareholdings or capital structures in which the outside shareholders had restricted voting rights. Breaking up these protected concentrations of often inefficient ownership held out the prospect for rapid structural change in the Continental economy.

Privatization was not the only means by which governments were prepared to help in the loosening up process. In Germany the Schroeder government's tax reforms included a relief on capital gains that potentially unlocked long-standing bank shareholdings in German industry and commerce. The swingeing tax penalty on the sale of such shares was removed. Measures were also introduced in Germany and elsewhere to curb the use of restricted voting arrangements, whereby outside shareholders enjoyed fewer voting rights than family owners and employees.

At the same time many family shareholdings established by a post-war generation of European entrepreneurs were coming onto the market as their children and grandchildren chose other career paths, or ownership became more dispersed. For the first time a market in corporate control started to operate in the larger economies, culminating in an outbreak of hostile takeovers. Gucci of Italy was attacked by French luxury goods and drinks group LVMH in what came to be known as the handbag wars. Olivetti made a hostile bid for Telecom Italia, the former state telecoms monopoly. Leading Italian insurance group Ina fell to a hostile bid from its larger rival Generali. In the French energy sector TotalFina made an unfriendly bid for Elf, which had been in talks with Italy's leading energy group Eni. Hostile bids also played an important part in the restructuring of French banking.

And foreign shareholders started to engage in more direct shareholder activism. The most revealing case concerned the French mining group Eramet, where TIAA-CREF, manager of America's biggest pension fund for teachers and university academics, put a hostile shareholder resolution in an attempt to reinforce the company's independence from its majority shareholder, the French government. This was an unprecedented and bold move in a country where the state had traditionally exercised considerable power over the corporate sector. The battle arose following a move by France's centre-right government in the mid-1990s to strip the company of a nickel concession in New Caledonia. It wanted to give this asset to Kanak nationalists before a referendum in which the French overseas territory was voting on whether to separate from France.

This attempt to use the company's assets to promote French foreign policy interests at the shareholders' expense caused outrage among international investors. By the time TIAA-CREF's resolution was put at the company's annual meeting in 1997, Lionel Jospin's socialists had come to power. The new government chose not to do battle with Anglo-American investors at a time when it was considering the privatization of state assets including a minority interest in France Télécom. The outcome perfectly illustrated the new balance of power in the globalized capital markets. To win access to capital on the best terms it was necessary for both governments and companies to observe the Anglo-American rules.

Since then French markets have seen sporadic outbreaks of American-style aggression. US-based arbitrageur Guy Wyser-Pratte led foreign shareholders in a successful putsch to clear out the board of French fashion retailer Groupe André. An activist campaign on behalf of foreign shareholders also succeeded, with the help of a sympathetic French court, in procuring better terms for outside shareholders in the Schneider takeover of Legrand, a company with a two-tier capital structure that incorporated both voting and non-voting shares.

At the lower end of Europe's corporate economy new markets sprang up, such as the Neuer Markt in Germany, the Nouveau Marché in France and the Nuovo Mercato in Italy. These were open to young and more risky companies that lacked a sufficient track record to qualify to raise capital on the main stock markets. This provided a spur to venture capital – the financing of unquoted businesses – since a vital requirement for success in venture capital is to be able to exit from an investment by floating the company on a stock market. Many countries offered new tax breaks for venture capital. And for the first time investors in Germany, France, Italy and many other EU countries acquired a taste for equity investment, as well as putting money into traditional havens such as bank deposits and bonds.

For European companies that were potentially competitive on a global basis, the growing emphasis on shareholder value was often welcome. Many enjoyed the increased flexibility that came from operating in liberalized markets and were at ease with the Anglo-

American business culture. In Germany boards of some of the largest companies adopted English as the boardroom language. Flamboyant French business people such as Jean-Marie Messier revelled in the opportunity to make takeovers abroad. Messier's frenetic wheeling and dealing while at the helm of Vivendi Universal secured him a large media and entertainment empire in the US, along with a string of other interests in Europe. Italian banks and insurers, meantime, seized the chance to reposition themselves both at home and in the wider European financial services market through acquisitions and mergers.

A bas, les Anglo-Saxons

To suggest that any economic disadvantage Europe suffers relative to the US is largely down to capital being poorly allocated is by now questionable. On the American side the speculative excesses of the late 1990s and the excessive amounts of capital directed at fragile telecom and Internet companies have cast some doubt on the argument. Meanwhile much restructuring is taking place among quoted companies in the Continental European economy, underlining the catch-up potential in relation to the US. After a period in which markets had become sclerotic, the region found itself, in the run-up to the introduction of the EMU, in a position not unlike that of Britain in 1979 when Margaret Thatcher came to power. International capital had become very pessimistic in the 1990s about the prospect for the big three economies of Continental Europe, just as it had for Britain after the country's dismal economic performance in the 1970s. Yet, with a brand new currency, substantial liberalizing measures in train and industrialists increasingly keen to restructure mature industries, the region looked ripe for an economic renaissance.

Yet Continental Europe's politicians do not share the Thatcherite appetite for radical policy. And they were particularly rattled by the takeover battles in the capital markets. The backlash started with the German move in 2001 to sabotage Europe's common takeover code, which was intended to encourage pan-European restructuring. The European parliament, egged on by the Schroeder government, rejected central proposals in a takeover directive that had taken 12 years of tortuous negotiation to draft. The Germans then enacted a national statute of their own that, while removing some obstacles to the takeover process, deliberately set out to make hostile takeovers more difficult. At the same time Lionel Jospin's government insisted that the European Union examine the potential for a so-called Tobin tax on currency transactions with a view to attacking speculative capital movements and addressing financial instability. This backlash was as symbolic, in its way, as the gesture in which anti-globalization protester José Bové acquired heroic status in France by destroying the local McDonald's.

The Tobin tax, admittedly, is an absurdity in this context, not least because derivative instruments could easily be used to avoid its impact. It will not happen. In contrast, the consequences of restraining takeover activity are likely to be far-reaching because globalization is now driven by capital flows to a greater extent than by trade, with foreign direct investment playing the central role. And in the developed world cross-border mergers and acquisitions are the main stimulus behind such direct investment. By mid-2002, meantime, in the run-up to the German elections, the Conservative opposition candidate Edmund Stoiber announced that he wanted to re-examine the removal of the capital gains tax on corporate asset sales before the change had been given a chance to free up cross-holdings of equity and improve the allocation of capital. The social democratic government that had introduced the reform immediately came under pressure to reconsider its position. Gerhard Schroeder's subsequent return to power at the head of a Social Democrat–Green coalition in September 2002 did not herald any kind of step toward radical restructuring via the capital markets.

The move to pull up the European drawbridge against global capital flows and to limit the process of convergence on the Anglo-American model coincided with a waning enthusiasm for many of the liberalizing measures adopted with such fanfare at Europe's dotcom summit in Lisbon. The politics of this retreat were clear enough. The Berlin government was reflecting a widespread concern in Germany that those elements of the consensual German model that remained intact needed to be preserved. Many feared that American-led globalization would cause disruption and unemployment on a scale redolent of the 1930s, bringing with it the worrying prospect of a revival of the extreme right. Outside Germany there was a suspicion that the take-over of Mannesmann had provoked nationalist sentiment against foreign takeovers of large domestic companies.

These suspicions were well founded, for the takeover issue had a particular resonance for Gerhard Schroeder when he was standing for re-election in 2002 and was anxious to project himself as the guardian of the interests of both German workers and German companies. Early that year the German chancellor went out of his way to make a special pledge to the workers at Volkswagen. As long as he held office, he promised, the workers had nothing to fear from EU-inspired takeover proposals. The choice of Volkswagen for this high-profile election pledge reflected Schroeder's close historic relationship with the motor manufacturer. When he was Governor of Lower Saxony, which owns a stake of nearly 19 per cent in the company, he sat on the supervisory board. So he was naturally the target of fierce lobbying by management and unions. The intensity of their efforts was no doubt increased by rumours current at the time that Volkswagen was a potential takeover target for Ford Motor of the US. Yet Schroeder's pledge was clearly intended to be heard all across Germany. It amounted to a big and significant volte-face on his earlier more liberal position because Volkswagen perfectly exemplified Continental Europe's relaxed attitude to capital efficiency. The company's target rate of return on investment was set at 9 to 11 per cent – well below the hurdles imposed by comparable companies in the US.

It was not just Europe's politicians who took exception to the accelerating pace of takeovers. Central bankers became nervous too. The Bank of Italy blocked hostile bids by Unicredito for Banca Commerciale and by San Paolo-IMI for Banca di Roma. The Italian central bank's intervention was widely interpreted as reflecting a dirigiste urge to have the restructuring of Italian banking follow its own blueprint rather than that of the market. The deep vein of economic nationalism in the Continent's political and bureaucratic elite had unquestionably been stirred by the Anglo-American invasion.

Designer poison pills

Yet the collapse of the takeover directive did not mean that takeovers were finished in Continental Europe. The European Commission responded to the setback by attempting to revive the directive by other means, inviting a group of experts under the economically liberal Dutch academic lawyer Jaap Winter to make new recommendations. A new draft directive subsequently emerged from the Commission, which fell some way short of advocating a fully open market in corporate control. The implication is that for the foreseeable future Continental European bid battles will be fought on a dirtier basis involving the use of all the poison pills currently sanctioned by national legislation. Poison pills take a variety of forms. A target company may issue shares cheaply to its existing shareholders in order to raise the bidder's cost of acquisition. They may involve variations in voting rights designed to put more votes in the hands of insiders or those friendly to incumbent management.

Another such defence involves the conditional sale of assets by a target company, so that the hostile bidder finds that the target may turn into a less attractive or less valuable animal on takeover.

Poison pills and other dirty tricks have featured particularly heavily in the big takeover battles for Italian companies. In the handbag wars Gucci escaped the clutches of LVMH only thanks to the ploy of diluting the value of the outside shareholders' stake by issuing new shares. Pirelli took control of Telecom Italia without making an offer to outside shareholders at all – a move that would be impossible in the UK where the buyer of a certain percentage of the target company's shares has to buy the rest of the shares on the same terms. The Pirelli chairman Marco Tronchetti Provera ended up controlling the whole Telecom Italia group through a relatively small personal shareholding at the top of a complex pyramid of companies with intertwined shareholdings. Analysts argue that in the absence of a European directive it seems unlikely that Italy will clean up its take-over act because Prime Minister Silvio Berlusconi is a key player, through his media group, in the web of shareholdings that criss-crosses Italian industry and commerce.[5]

So the takeover process in much of Europe will discriminate in favour of insiders against outside shareholders and be less conducive to economic efficiency in those jurisdictions that permit poison pill defences. It was precisely the move to outlaw such defences, unless shareholders agreed, that prompted the European parliament's action against the takeover directive.

It was no coincidence that the chief opposition to the directive came from Berlin because the Germans had more at stake than other members of the EU. Their slow, consensual approach to policy-making in this area reflects the historic priorities of the immediate post-war period when powerful checks, balances and restraints were put in place in a conscious effort to prevent a repeat of the circum-stances that allowed Hitler to come to power. Moreover, under German law, companies have explicit societal obligations and the directors have duties toward stakeholders such as employees.

Most French managers likewise believe that companies should be run in the interests of all stakeholders and that employment should be kept stable even at the cost of cutting dividends to shareholders. In the normal course of events, management has no difficulty in balanc-ing its responsibilities to the various stakeholder constituencies. No company, whether in the US or Europe, can succeed if it consistently neglects the expectations of its stakeholders, whether they be cus-tomers, shareholders, employees, suppliers or the community. Yet the Anglo-American hostile takeover process, as exemplified by the

---

[5] See, for example, "The land of Machiavelli", in *Strategy Ideas*, 6 August 2001 (HSBC).

Vodafone–Mannesmann battle, has an exclusive focus on shareholder requirements and little time for employees or the wider community interest.

Corporate performance is assessed by British and American investors chiefly on narrow financial criteria, despite the fact that conventional accounting is ill-equipped to capture much of the intangible value such as human capital that contributes to competitiveness in the modern company. And the culture of Anglo-American capital markets requires information about impending takeovers to be confined to a handful of top executives. The employees are kept in the dark. Among other things, this deliberate lack of consensualism is designed to inhibit insider-trading by employees on the stock market. So there is a fundamental incompatibility between these two very different cultures of capitalism.

The hostile takeover has the potential to subvert the legal obligation to society and what remains of the long-termism fostered in the old German model because management survival depends on putting the shareholders' requirement for narrowly defined financial performance first. Managers thus have less incentive to keep workers on the payroll if the company is vulnerable to the attention of predators. For their part, employees have less incentive to invest in acquiring skills that are specific to their firm, or to share knowledge with fellow employees, if they believe that a new management will break these implicit contracts after a takeover. The rewards for loyalty disappear. Continental Europeans also fear that more takeover activity will lead to family disruption, higher divorce rates and social dislocation.

There are, then, large costs in abandoning a model that takes into account the interests of stakeholders other than shareholders. Yet there is also some truth in the allegation that managers of many European companies have exploited the shelter from accountability that the stakeholder ethos can sometimes provide. Continental economies, most notably Germany, tend to be over-dependent on manufacturing and under-represented in technology. Information and communications technology in Germany, France and Italy in 1997 accounted respectively for 1.6 per cent, 2.2 per cent and 1.4

per cent of gross domestic product, compared with 5.2 per cent in the US.[6] That points to a need for more active recycling of capital. And for many leaders of European business, the priority in the first decade of the new millennium is rapid change rather than a quiet life. As Michael Rogowski, President of the Federation of German Industries, put it in 2001:

> In view of the hesitant pace of reforms and the inferior quality of policy, it is no surprise that the pace of growth in the EU is slackening. The financial markets have every reason to be sceptical about the EU's ability to act and its capacity for innovation. The reluctance to implement the planned structural reforms is reducing Europe's chances in global competition. The aim of taking over part of the engine of global economic growth from the US seems increasingly fanciful, as part of a distant future.[7]

An economic purist would argue that Rogowski's concern with European competitiveness is wrong-headed, because it adopts a flawed concept of national (or supra-national) competitiveness which implicitly assumes that there is a limited quantum of global prosperity for which nations compete. In reality, competition in trade and investment constitutes a positive sum game from which all the participating countries benefit. And given that the countries of the eurozone were collectively running a current account surplus on the EU balance of payments at this time, the region could not be said to be labouring under the burden of an uncompetitive exchange rate.

That said, Rogowski's diagnosis makes a wider point about the EU role in the world economy that commands attention. This relates to the way the world has long been over-dependent on the stimulus of US demand. The world's second largest economy Japan has been struggling for years to fend off deflation and has been in no position to impart much stimulus to the rest of the world. It appears unlikely to do much better on that score for the foreseeable future. As for Europe,

---

[6] Numbers from OECD, quoted in *European Growth Prospects*, November 2001 (HSBC).

[7] Article for the sixth annual conference of the German–British Forum, October 2001.

despite being free from acute problems of the kind that afflict Japan, it has been similarly over-dependent on external stimulus from the US to keep growing.

While the US sorts out the imbalances in its post-bubble economy, which will involve rebuilding domestic savings and reducing the current account deficit on the balance of payments, the EU ought to be picking up the baton. It would make sense for it to complement US stringency with a more growth-oriented approach, thereby helping to drive the world economy forward. In the short and medium term, that is chiefly a matter for fiscal and monetary policy – and it is not easy to be optimistic about the outcome on either count given the parochial remit of the European Central Bank and the poorly conceived rules governing EU member states' fiscal policies, of which more in Chapter 11. But over the longer run, it is the structural reform agenda that matters. And there is no likelihood that the EU will match the potential growth rate of the US without a much more vigorous attempt to tackle its structural problems.

Of course European restructuring has not come to a complete halt as a result of the collapse of the takeover directive. The consequence of the politicians' second thoughts on takeovers will simply be that there are fewer mergers and acquisitions, and those that do happen will encourage less creative destruction than would otherwise take place. This underlines a fundamental point about the Anglo-American model. Takeovers do not work in isolation. Their efficacy and their contribution to economic growth depends on their interaction with other markets and on the incentives that influence the behaviour of all those involved in the process, from shareholders, to managers, to employees. It is a point that applies with as much force to the English-speaking countries, as we shall see in Chapter 5, as to others. But in the case of Continental Europe, the inflexibility of labour, housing and other markets can only subvert a healthy takeover process.

In many Continental countries tight labour market regulations make it so difficult and costly to fire employees that the standard cost-cutting takeover that contributes to the restructuring of mature

American or British industries is simply not feasible. And the politicians often believe that they can have their cake and eat it by adopting a pick-and-mix approach to capitalism. Goeran Persson, the Swedish Prime Minister, argued eloquently before the Barcelona summit of EU leaders in 2002 that Europe urgently needed common rules on takeovers to promote dynamic restructuring. Yet he also wanted employees to have a say in the process. If that say were of any value, employees concerned for their own job security would be most unlikely to support cost-cutting takeovers. Turkeys do not vote for Christmas.[8]

This labour market inflexibility is, incidentally, particularly important in the high-tech area because most of the rate of return from newer technologies comes from cost reduction – especially the reduction in labour costs. It follows that if European firms are constrained by law and regulation from implementing such cost cuts, the prospective rate of return on newer technologies will be lower. That in turn means that the incentive to introduce them will be less. Europe may then find itself at a greater potential productivity disadvantage to the US.

It also means that in practice many of the mergers that have taken place across Europe have had more to do with baronial reconfigurations of industrial and financial power than genuine rationalization. Much acquisition activity has been about ego-tripping conglomeration rather than carefully focused strategy. This was undoubtedly so at Vivendi, where Jean-Marie Messier's acquisition spree in the US and elsewhere ended up costing shareholders a fortune. Messier's cavalier attitude to shareholder value emerged all too clearly when he declared that the multi-billion losses on his acquisitions were of no great importance because they had been paid for in the paper currency of Vivendi shares.

Other Continental European takeovers have been inspired by a political desire to build national champions. Under Lionel Jospin the French government in the late 1990s saw the state-owned

---

[8] See his article, "Europe's missed deadlines", *Financial Times*, 14 January 2002.

France Télécom as a suitable vehicle for its aspiration to promote a global player in a key high-tech industry. Yet because the government wished to maintain a big ownership stake in the business, France Télécom had to finance its strategic acquisitions with debt rather than equity. As with earlier putative national champions such as Crédit Lyonnais in global financial services, the outcome was disastrous. France Télécom's acquisitions were ill-judged and, at the government's behest, badly financed. The resulting damage to the company's balance sheet left it hopelessly behind in the global telecommunications race. It also left the French government with a financial and industrial headache.

It is possible, too, that the combination of an active capital market and a rigid labour market could leave Europe with the worst of both worlds – a higher level of transaction costs in the economy, as companies pay their fees to the investment bankers and other professional advisers, and little enhancement of productivity. Against that background, merger and acquisition activity will remain an awkward foreign implant. Meantime, the thrust of the European Union's proposed pension directive, a crucial measure for the future shape of Europe's capital markets, seems to be at odds with the liberalizing tendency of the Lisbon summit. It will do less than originally expected to remove national portfolio restrictions on pension fund investment in equities and on venture capital investment in fledgling companies, which is hardly the way to make European capital markets less sclerotic.

Transatlantic love–hate

None of this is lost on the international financial fraternity. Indeed, an interesting consequence of the introduction of Europe's new single currency is that it gives global capital an opportunity to pass a transparent verdict on the whole region on a minute-by-minute basis. The weakness of the euro against the dollar in the period after the launch of economic and monetary union may owe something to a technical portfolio adjustment. Since European investors could no longer obtain international diversification by investing in other European countries, they were probably switching funds out of Europe into the UK and US, which would have weakened the euro against the dollar and sterling. But when looked at over a longer period, weakness in the euro and its predecessor currencies could also partly be interpreted as a huge vote of no confidence by capital in the management of the Continental European economy.

As so often, when economies are not performing well, it was the flight of domestic capital that did most to weaken the exchange rate. The capital exodus to the United States involved an annual average outflow of $200bn from Europe between 1995 and 2000.[9] Between 1997 when the statistics started and 2000 there was only one three-month period in which the eurozone foreign inflows of direct investment exceeded outflows – and that was in the first quarter of 2000 when Vodafone bought control of Mannesmann in the biggest cross-border takeover deal Europe had ever seen. Given that Europe was a net recipient of funds in its bond markets, the outflow of equity and direct investment was proportionately greater.

The conclusion must be that Europe's investors and industrialists rated the economic strength and profit potential of the US much more highly during that period than the potential of their home economies, regardless of the European Union's reformist aspirations. So much for the grandiose claims made at the Lisbon summit. Political rhetoric and serious money were at odds with each other here, reflecting a tension that is apparent in many other aspects of Europe's anti-Americanism. Think only of how the French political elite excoriates McDonald's while the French consumer eats sufficient Big Macs to justify 800 or so busy burger outlets around the country. It is hard to escape the conclusion, then, that the capital exodus reflected a pan-European loss of self-confidence, with a growing inferiority complex finding expression in cross-border capital flows.

---

[9] Deutsche Bank, *Emu Watch*, 29 October 2001.

Nothing could have been more convenient for the Americans, who at the turn of the millennium were running a deficit on the current account of their balance of payments at an annual rate of $435bn.[10] European capital made the biggest contribution to plugging the gap. The irony is that Europe's investment has been singularly unrewarding because so many investors and companies jumped in at the peak just before the collapse of American telecom and Internet stocks, the wider fall in the equity and corporate bond markets, and the onset of the US recession. They bought into the American model just when its claim to allocate capital with supreme efficiency was about to look laughably over-hyped.

This saga nonetheless raises a question. Is capital too impatient in its judgement about Europe's prospects? After all, Margaret Thatcher's reforms took time to gather impetus, and there were numerous setbacks on the way. Her governments never offered the electorate anything that looked like a crash programme. Yet once the thrust of her policies became clear, there was never much doubt about the British Prime Minister's ultimate goal or her readiness, as in the crushing of the 1984–5 miners' strike, to take extreme measures to reach it. And in terms of attracting outside capital, the openness of the British economy, together with the liberalizing thrust of policy, offered a clear and increasingly attractive alternative to the US, which appeared to be performing poorly relative to Japan at that time, and to the rest of Europe.

In contrast, the politicians of Continental Europe have a less clearly defined vision. Globalization has deprived their old models of capitalism of their potency. Yet the attempt to articulate a new Third Way has amounted to little more than a critique of the Anglo-American model. To the extent that a Continental Third Way exists, it is a haphazardly constructed halfway house built on political expediency and the principle of taking two steps forward and one step back along the path to a more Anglo-American market model.

---

[10] OECD standardized basis, *OECD Economic Outlook No. 69*, June 2001.

The US economist Mancur Olson argued that stable, socially cohesive societies suffer an important economic disadvantage. They tend to accumulate collusive organizations and interest groups over time, which impairs their capacity to adapt. This leads to economic sclerosis and lower growth. The description fits much of Continental Europe very well, when compared with the melting-pot population and poor social security safety net in the US. And globalization heightens the importance of Olson's perception. Since the Thatcher experiment in Britain the respective time horizons of politics and of global capital in the currency markets have become more remote from each other to the disadvantage of the politicians.

At its simplest, globalization and rapid technological change have put a premium on the speed of response in policy-making and corporate decision-making. So when global capital looks at Europe's poorly articulated Third Way, its weak tradition of entrepreneurship and its combination of inflexible markets and tame capital, the comparison with the US is unfavourable. So, too, with monetary policy, where the European Central Bank's response to recession in 2001 and 2002 looked leaden-footed when compared with the US Federal Reserve.

Currency weakness is admittedly not overly damaging for a vast Continental economy like that of Europe. And fickle currencies overshoot for long periods, understating or exaggerating the real strength of the underlying economies. Dollar strength is not a given of the modern world. By mid-2002 it looked as though the long period of dollar strength might be at an end. Yet in the longer run there are clear risks in Europe opting for the politically expedient, but economically incoherent halfway house. With many of the old disciplines on management such as the house bank system in Germany going by the board, there is a potential corporate governance vacuum. Many companies will continue to be run by insiders enjoying greater protection from proper accountability. The cronyism implicit in the Continental models of capitalism will be reinforced, in the absence of any new discipline such as an effective hostile takeover mechanism.

Because this weakened corporate governance will continue to disadvantage outside shareholders, professionally managed international capital may not be prepared to pay as highly for the shares of European companies as for those in the US or UK. Research conducted by consultants McKinsey into the behaviour of global institutional investors demonstrates a clear sensitivity to corporate governance issues.[11] The risk is that Continental stock markets may be valued on a lower rating than they would otherwise enjoy, with the likelihood that good companies will suffer a higher cost of capital and enjoy poorer access to global equity markets.

In the short run Continental Europe has enjoyed a reprieve on this score. Thanks to Enron and all the other corporate governance and accounting scandals in the US, the more investor-friendly regime in the US has lost some of its lustre. Hence, in part, the strengthening of the euro against the dollar in the first half of 2002. It is possible, too, to exaggerate the importance of the corporate governance deficiencies of Continental Europe for its economic performance, given that much of the strength of Continental Europe's corporate sector lies in its unquoted businesses. Since these are family controlled, they do not suffer from the principal-agent problem that is a central focus for Anglo-American corporate governance in the quoted company sector. And it is anyway moot whether takeovers are as effective a tool for creative destruction as US and UK policy-makers believe, a point that will be explored in Chapter 5.

Yet the European retreat from a hostile takeover discipline remains symbolic, because the rejection of the Anglo-American capital market approach in favour of a quieter economic life is just one of many indicators that Continental Europe is consciously opting for lower growth. Not that it is unreasonable for Europeans to make such a choice. Indeed, the chief reason their per capita incomes are now lower than those in the US is simply that they work far less. Labour productivity in France and Germany, for example, is little

---

[11] Paul Coombes and Mark Watson, "Three surveys on corporate governance", *The McKinsey Quarterly*, No. 4, 2000.

different from that in the US, but German and French employees work up to 40 per cent fewer hours per capita than their American counterparts.[12] (British employees, though less productive, are more workaholic, if not to the same degree as Americans.)

Yet in emphasizing the validity of this European choice it is important to be clear about the consequences. Small differences in relative economic growth rates lead to big differences in living standards over time. And a combination of weaker demography, which will be discussed in Chapter 8, and slower growth in per capita incomes vis-à-vis the US will make it even less likely that the European Union will be able to project power and influence in the world in a way that will command the respect of the world's only superpower. To that extent, the ambitious competitive rhetoric at successive EU summits about matching American economic perform-ance has been pure posturing.

Admittedly, the gap between summit rhetoric and reality is more a reflection of European politicians' capacity for self-deception than a disingenuous attempt to deceive the voters of Europe. No European summit communiqué could anyway be expected to trumpet the EU's de facto motto, which is two steps forward, one step back. But the motto really is the message. And its lack of visionary quality is scarcely designed to win over footloose global capital, which likes nothing better than a simple, unequivocal story.

---

[12] See Mary O'Mahoney, *Britain's Productivity Performance 1950–96: An International Perspective*, National Institute of Economic and Social Research, 1999.

Part 2

Double Standards

5

Uncreative destruction

Henry "Hank" Paulson, Chairman and Chief Executive of the world's pre-eminent investment bank Goldman Sachs, is a tireless promoter of the gospel of free global capital flows. In November 2001 he wrote in the *Financial Times* of the critical need for reform in Europe, which was "a vital battlefield in the struggle over globalisation." Among the reforms he demanded were the further integration of capital and labour markets within Europe, more accountable corporate governance and less intrusive government regulation. Mergers, he complained, were under assault across the European Union and the failure of the European Takeover Directive squandered 12 years of effort. "We must do a better job of making the case for further liberal-isation across the world. And the most powerful way of doing so," Paulson concluded, "is to run our companies for our shareholders."

A European would be entitled to say that this was pretty rich coming from Goldman Sachs because the giant investment bank's governance arrangements had more in common with the cosy "insider" systems of Continental European governance than the shareholder-value-based model in its conventional description. For a start, the bank has been more or less immune from hostile takeover since its stock market flotation in 2000 thanks to the large proportion of its capital that is owned by directors and employees, along with some devastatingly potent poison pills. The board can issue a form of security aptly known as "blank cheque" preferred stock, which dilutes outside shareholders' voting rights and can shrink their share

of Goldman's earnings and assets at the whim of incumbent management. The common stock includes non-voting as well as voting stock.
And the rights of outside shareholders are heavily restricted. Under
Goldman's charter and bye-laws an impossibly high 80 per cent of the
outstanding votes have to be cast in favour before the directors can be
ousted – a so-called supermajority provision. Shareholders are denied
the right to call a special meeting, which can only be done by a
majority of the board of directors. Any attempt to throw out the
poison pill provisions in the charter also runs up against another 80
per cent voting threshold.

The excuse for highly discriminatory corporate constitutions and
voting structures of this kind is that they promote continuity of
existing management and protect human capital. Without them
shareholders would be vulnerable to expensive greenmail, whereby
corporate raiders accumulate a big stake in a target company and
then invite the management to buy them off to avoid a hostile takeover. Such excuses would be instantly recognizable to any Rhineland
capitalist. And the Goldman charter has other echoes of the German
stakeholder ethos. It gives the directors discretion to consider the
impact of their actions on employees and the community as well as
shareholders. The discretion includes actions involving a change in
ownership of the investment bank.

This example of double standards is a private sector version of the
exceptionalism the US so often displays in foreign policy – as, for
example, when Washington tries to prevent poor countries buying
cheap generic drugs to combat HIV/Aids-related disease, while
forcing drugs companies to sell it antibiotics on the cheap in response
to the anthrax scare in 2001. It should be emphasized that double
standards are not, in the capital markets, confined to Goldman, of
which more later. Unlike many other American corporations the big
investment bank can also argue that its immunity from hostile takeover does not fatally undermine accountability because there remains
a strong ownership discipline, with directors and employees holding so
much Goldman stock. That argument cannot be used by the largest
groups that combine commercial and investment banking, since they

have been exempt from takeover discipline for a different reason. During the stock market bubble Citigroup and J. P. Morgan Chase were simply too big for any predator to swallow. It follows that share-holder discipline and accountability in these giants at the very heart of the US capital market system has been less rigorous than it might have been.

Nor is this the only way in which the investment banks appear to be exempt from the normal disciplines of capitalism. When it comes to raising fresh equity capital for companies, the fees charged by investment banks in the US appear to defy the pull of market gravity. Initial public offerings on Wall Street, where companies join the stock market and raise capital from investors, cost the cor-porate client more than twice as much in underwriting commission as they do in Europe and Asia. In addition, the hidden charge whereby shares are issued at a discount to the level at which they are expected to trade in the market has widened enormously over the past 20 years – a period in which deregulation has imposed a tight squeeze on margins in most other areas of financial business.[1] Competitors of the big investment banks have long suspected the existence of an informal cartel. Yet the giants of Wall Street appear to be immune from the normal rigours of competition policy in a country where price-fixing can land you in jail.

---

[1] In a paper to a London School of Economics Financial Markets Group seminar in September 2001, Philip Augar quotes recent evidence as follows: "In the US the gross spreads received by underwriters have long been established at 7 per cent. This is about double the level that prevails in Europe and Asia. Jay Ritter at the University of Florida and others have shown that in recent years over 90 per cent of deals raising between $20–80m have spreads of exactly 7 per cent, three times the proportion of a decade earlier. A similar trend to increased pricing is evident in the second element of charging. Over the last twenty years the discount to the issue price has been steadily widening from 8 per cent over the period 1978–1991, then up to 12 per cent from 1991–1994. In 1995 the initial gain on IPOs exceeded 20 per cent, averaged around 15 per cent in 1996–8 and then soared to 69 per cent in 1999 and 56 per cent in 2000." Augar cites in support Hsuan-Chi Chen and Jay R. Ritter, "The seven per cent solution", *Journal of Finance*, Vol. 5, June 2000; Robert S. Hansen, "Do investment banks compete in IPOs?" *Journal of Financial Economics*, Vol. 59, 2001; and Jay Ritter, University of Florida, bear.cba.ufl.edu/ritter.

Management on top

Maybe this simply reflects the peculiar nature of the capital-raising business. Or maybe it says something about the formidable political clout of the investment banking fraternity, in which top bankers often enjoy the benefit of a smoothly functioning escalator from Wall Street to Washington. Over the course of my journalistic career there have been many examples. Bill Simon, the US Treasury Secretary who played a big part in the International Monetary Fund's bail-out of the United Kingdom in the mid-1970s, was a former bond-trader from Salomon Brothers. In the 1980s Donald Regan, the pugnacious Irish-American boss of Merrill Lynch, left to become US Treasury Secretary in the Reagan administration and subsequently White House Chief of Staff. The Treasury Secretary in the administration of George Bush senior was Nicholas Brady from the establishment Wall Street investment bank Dillon, Read. And Robert Rubin, Treasury Secretary under Bill Clinton, was a former boss at Goldman, where there is a long tradition of close relations with the Washington establishment going back to Sidney Weinberg. Weinberg, the man who reinvented Goldman Sachs after it came close to collapse in 1929, was an informal adviser to Franklin D. Roosevelt and joined his administration as Vice Chairman of the War Production Board in the Second World War.

If this smacks of crony capitalism, it is not necessarily corrupt in the Asian style. But it can look conspicuously cosy. Many commentators noted the convenient consequences for Wall Street of the bail-out of Mexico in 1995, which substantially reduced the losses incurred by American investors at some cost to the US taxpayer. The rescue, masterminded by the former Goldman partner Rubin, escaped Congressional scrutiny because it was financed via the Exchange Stabilization Fund, the only pot of taxpayers' money over which the President enjoyed discretion.

Not only is the corporate governance playing field uneven in the US as between different kinds of company. The problem shareholders face in asserting their rights runs wider, because American company law is very friendly to management at the expense of shareholders. A majority of jurisdictions in the US, including that of Delaware in which more US companies are incorporated than anywhere else, have enacted "stakeholder" statutes that allow managers to frustrate takeover bids at will. The deterrent vehicle, as with Goldman Sachs, is the right to issue poison pill securities that make hostile takeovers prohibitively expensive. Explicit consent is not usually required from shareholders for the issue of these value-destroying securities. Nor is this the only way in which most states choose to tilt the legal balance heavily in favour of management at the expense of shareholders. To take another equally egregious example, it is common for company directors to be permitted to indemnify themselves under their constitutions for liability for any breach of their own duties.

Such excessive powers and protections for management are a consequence of competition within a federal system. States fight to attract companies to incorporate in their own jurisdictions as a form of service industry inward investment, which encourages a regulatory race to the bottom. And they make their pitch to management, not shareholders, because it is the managers who choose the company domicile, or charter. In Delaware, corporate formation and related legal services have become such a big industry that they have a vital impact on the local economy. A fifth of the state's total tax revenues are rumoured to come from this source. And, of course, states share an interest with incumbent management when a local company is threatened by a hostile takeover. Local employment and tax revenues may disappear if companies are taken over by predators with headquarters in another state. Once again the rationale for US stakeholder statutes would be immediately comprehensible to politicians in Germany's federal system.

That is not to say that the US in general and Delaware in particular are impossible places in which to conduct takeovers. There is a high volume of such activity. And despite the tendency of US companies to reincorporate in more manager-friendly jurisdictions as they grow bigger, academics have failed to establish that the resulting damage to shareholders is reflected in stock market valuations. Yet big investment institutions have been fighting a rearguard battle against the toxic takeover deterrents. Peter Clapman, Senior Vice President and Chief Counsel, Investments, at TIAA-CREF, which manages the biggest US pension fund and handled more than $275bn in assets in 2001, has campaigned vigorously to persuade companies to remove their protective pills. Others have followed in his wake. But success to date has been modest.

Coke, burgers and bids

It is, of course, no coincidence that US investment banks rank with the executives of Hollywood, Coca-Cola and McDonald's as the shock troops of globalization. For them, the potential for extending the Anglo-American model of capitalism to the rest of the world represents one of the greatest business opportunities of all time, especially if it can be exported in a more red-blooded form than the US itself is prepared to tolerate. Hostile takeovers, in particular, offer enormous fees to corporate advisers in banking and the professions because managers spend company money with little or no inhibition if their jobs are at stake or they are engaged in the thrill of the chase. It is the shareholders of the bidding company who pay the bills, which is part of the overpayment phenomenon known as the winner's curse. And if industrialists can be persuaded that the answer to their strategic problems lies in acquisitions and divestments, recurring fees will flow into the banks' coffers. Yet regardless of the investment banks' own motivation, there are good theoretical arguments in favour of an active takeover market.

In the first half of the 20th century, corporate ownership was increasingly divorced from control. Shares, which in the 19th century had largely been concentrated in the hands of owner-managers, became more widely dispersed as companies floated on stock markets and became larger. This phenomenon, which was described by Adolph Berle and Gardiner Means in their seminal book *The Modern Corporation and Private Property* in 1932, resulted in managers becoming less accountable.[2] In the absence of significant blocks of shares commanding large numbers of votes, no-one was in a position to fire the managers if they underperformed. In conventional economic literature this conflict of interest between shareholders and management is referred to as the principal-agent problem. The conflict arises because agents usually cannot be relied on to manage other people's affairs or money as well as they would manage their own.

As long as ownership was fragmented the discipline in the Anglo-American system came from four main sources. One was the competition that corporate managers faced in the markets for goods and services. Another was the transparency of capital markets, which ensured that management was subject to constant scrutiny. Then there was the pressure that institutional shareholders could bring to bear for managerial change if a financially stretched company tried to raise more capital. The final discipline was bankruptcy, which arose when a failure to compete effectively in the markets for its goods or services led to declining profitability and the withdrawal of credit by the banks. The genius of the hostile takeover lies in its claim to provide a more timely discipline on management before the money runs out.

In the UK, hostile bids were pioneered in the immediate post-war period by corporate raiders such as Charles Clore, who set his sights on companies with underused or undervalued assets in the balance sheet. The first wave of aggressive takeovers in the US took place much later, starting in the 1970s with the assault by the Canadian mining group International Nickel, known as INCO, on Electric Storage Battery, the world's biggest battery company.

In a climate of hitherto weak management accountability, the effect was similar to a shift in a political system from absolute monarchy to democracy. The existence of a bid suddenly empowered shareholders by giving them the opportunity to choose between different teams of managers competing for the stewardship of the company. And the mere knowledge that the threat of an aggressive

---

[2] Commerce Clearing House, 1932.

bid was always there in the background ensured that managements
had a powerful incentive to use economic resources more efficiently in
order to keep corporate predators at bay.

For the few big institutional investors who were prepared to take
advantage of this new power, there was also potential to influence
underperforming management or even in the UK to clear useless
directors out of the boardroom. In the UK 10 per cent of shareholders
can call an extraordinary general meeting and 50 per cent of those
attending can replace any or all the directors – a power that stock-
holders in the US do not have. In most states of the Union it is
impossible both to call an extraordinary meeting and vote out
directors, unless there is evidence of criminal behaviour in their performance of the job.[3] But, for the great majority of shareholders,
whether personal or professional, the market in corporate control
conforms to the dictum of the philosopher Jean-Jacques Rousseau,
who remarked that people were only free in a democracy during
elections. Substitute takeovers for elections and the same stricture
applies to empowerment in the capital markets.

The hostile takeover can nonetheless be a powerful tool for recycling capital from the less efficient to the more efficient. And the role of
takeovers assumes a new significance in the context of developments
in information and communications technology. These technologies
are net destroyers of jobs. The economic benefits they bring derive in
part from the way they free people to work in other parts of the
economy. That is why, in recent years, the traffic in the job market
has been mainly from large companies to smaller and newer ones.
Downsizing is driven in part by shareholder pressure. But it also
reflects changes in perceptions about the nature of technological
innovation. Bradford DeLong, an economist at Berkeley and one-
time member of the Clinton administration, puts it like this:

---

[3] I am indebted to Robert G. Monks for this comparison. Monks argues that the UK is
unique in the world in the powers that it gives to shareholders on this score and that
it amounts to an important competitive advantage.

Because of changing technology there has been an important shift in the efficient location of new technological development. The extraordinary economic success of the venture start-up system of Silicon Valley is not just a side effect of a stock market bubble, but is the result of a technology-driven decline in the relative competence of very large firms at tasks of developing (but not marketing) new technologies and new products.[4]

Since DeLong wrote that in April 2000 the venture capital market has come through a nervous breakdown. Yet the assertion about the decline of the advantage of very large firms in fostering innovation remains part of the conventional wisdom in the Anglo-American financial community.

Yet, despite the compelling nature of the arguments for mergers and acquisitions as a means of creative destruction, the practice of takeovers is less convincing than the theory. There is a great deal of academic research suggesting that the investment bankers are, in this area, frequently peddling a dud product and that the most consistent winners from takeover activity are not those who initiate the bids, but the shareholders in the target company. Hostile bids do not appear to be consistently directed at inefficient companies. And there is evidence that friendly takeovers and mergers, which are used increasingly as a means of repositioning businesses, destroy more value than hostile ones.[5] As for cross-border takeovers, they appear to be unusually hazardous, as will become clear later in this chapter.

No research on this subject will ever be definitive since many impacts of an active takeover culture cannot be measured. On the positive side, the existence of the threat of hostile takeover keeps managers on their toes and encourages them to use capital efficiently. A more negative aspect is that business people and academics tend to

---

[4] J. Bradford DeLong, *The Coming End of American Triumphalism*, April 2000, on delong@econ.berkeley.edu.

[5] See, for example, Loughran and Vihj, "Do long term shareholders benefit from corporate acquisitions?" *Journal of Finance*, Vol. 52, No. 5, 1997. On the outcome of hostile as against friendly takeovers, see Sudi Sudarsanam, "Friend or foe: Securing shareholder value in mergers and acquisitions", in *Management Focus*, Summer 2001, Issue 16 (Cranfield University School of Management).

measure the outcome of takeovers by reference to narrow financial criteria. They fail to capture the significant losses of human and social capital that can result from hostile or mismanaged takeovers. And nobody can say what would have happened if the takeovers had not taken place.

The tale of two companies

Yet the most powerful case that mergers and acquisitions are not working as intended emerges from practical observation of events in the UK market in corporate control, which is much more open than the US. Thanks to the absence of US-style poison pills and the existence of a very flexible, practitioner-based regulatory regime administered by London's Takeover Panel, the UK system is the most takeover-friendly in the world. It was here that the two greatest names in British manufacturing demonstrated in the late 1990s how large-scale attempts that reposition businesses through friendly acquisitions and divestments could swiftly turn corporate giants into over-indebted pygmies.

Imperial Chemical Industries (ICI), Britain's leading industrial company for much of the 20th century, used to be a research-based giant with a global reach, in which a respected professional management focused its efforts primarily on developing the operating businesses. Then in the late 1980s Hanson, an acquisitive conglomerate, started buying shares in ICI. Hanson's move was widely interpreted as a prelude to a takeover bid for a group that had hitherto been regarded as invulnerable. It was not welcomed by the ICI management under Chairman Sir Denys Henderson, who headed a highly effective public relations campaign that cast doubt on Hanson's credentials as a potential owner of ICI. Lord Hanson and Lord White, the twin potentates who headed the acquisitive conglomerate, were seen off the field.

Yet this run-in with a corporate predator had a profound effect on the psychology of the pre-eminent member of Britain's industrial establishment. ICI's management decided, having prevaricated in the 1980s, that there was no future for it in basic chemicals, a mature business subject to violent cyclical fluctuations. It also decided it wanted shareholders to see more direct benefit from the company's highly successful pharmaceutical business. ICI consisted, in effect, of two very separate groups of technologies. Its bioscience-related activities such as drugs and agrochemicals were in one distinct technological camp, while the traditional bulk chemicals business, making such things as polythene, soda ash and chlorine, was in another. There was little synergy between the two groups. Many in the company also felt that the head office had allocated excessive resources to research and new plant in the mature chemicals businesses and too little to the more promising life sciences area. So in 1992 Sir Denys Henderson announced that the company would split itself in two.

With advice from, among others, a clever and abrasive young corporate financier John Mayo from investment bankers S.G. Warburg, ICI embarked on a big exercise in de-conglomeration. The life sciences became part of a new quoted company Zeneca under Chief Executive David Barnes, with the aim of developing new products, strengthening the worldwide sales organization and improving the productivity of the research and development efforts. Ronnie Hampel, the Chief Executive of the older businesses in a revamped ICI, sought to reduce overheads, raise manufacturing efficiency and achieve global market leadership in the more capital intensive areas where ICI had a technological advantage.[6]

Then, in a break with precedent, the revamped ICI groomed an outsider to take over from Ronnie Hampel when he moved up from Chief Executive to Chairman. Charles Miller Smith, who had spent his career at Unilever, but had been passed over for the Chief Executive job, joined ICI and became Chief Executive in 1995. There followed a dramatic upheaval. In 1997 ICI bought Unilever's speciality chemicals division, which included food, flavour and fragrance

[6] For a full account of ICI's strategic thinking, see the article by Geoffrey Owen and Trevor Harrison in the March–April issue of the *Harvard Business Review*, 1995.

ingredients, for £4.8bn. Miller Smith had run the business while at Unilever. And ICI proceeded, over the next three years, to sell more than 50 businesses including most of its bulk chemicals operations for over £6bn. Of its original portfolio, only the paints operations, which included the Dulux brand, remained in the group. ICI had sold more than half its businesses and reinvented itself as an entirely new group. The Hampel–Miller Smith team believed that the new business, with its National Starch and Quest subsidiaries at the heart of the strategy, would attain higher growth, stabler margins and more robust demand for their products in any downturn in the economic cycle. And the ICI board was reassured in the notion that these acquisitions were resistant to cyclical downturns by high-powered consultants from McKinsey and persuasive investment bankers from Goldman Sachs.

Professional fund-managers and investment analysts were initially impressed by the transition in ICI's modus operandi from managing businesses to buying and selling them. This was similar to restructuring efforts being carried out by other leading players in the chemical industry across Europe. In the first year after the deal with Unilever, speciality chemicals companies were valued in the stock market on higher ratings than pharmaceutical companies like Zeneca. But, with the Asian crisis, demand for the products of speciality companies started to falter. And by the time the world went into recession in 2001 the investment analysts were worrying that the company had escaped from the vicious bulk chemicals cycle only to plunge into a tricky consumer one. Despite the reassurances from ICI's advisers and despite the strong market positions of the acquired companies, flavours and fragrances turned out to be a cyclical business after all. More seriously, ICI had borrowed very heavily to buy the Unilever interests. Despite the influx of cash from the sale of bulk chemicals, the company was unable to reduce its borrowings. An already weak cash flow from operations was being further drained by, among other things, redundancy costs, exceptional payments to bolster a weak pension fund, environmental clean-up costs, imprudently high dividends and high transaction costs for all the acquisitions and disposals.

In 1996 before the buying spree ICI was a business with a turnover of £10.5bn, net profits of £275m, shareholders' funds, or net worth, of £3.6bn and borrowings of £1.3bn. By 2000 it was a business with a turnover of £7.7bn making a net loss of £228m. More important, the once great ICI was technically insolvent, for although it continued to trade, its liabilities exceeded its assets by £216m, while its debts had reached a towering £2.8bn. ICI's auditors KPMG bought the management's story that they would make good the deficiency of assets against liabilities from future profits and tapping the market for fresh equity. So the financial accounts in 2000 carried an unqualified audit report that implied that the company was still a going concern. Yet at the start of the global recession ICI was more vulnerable than it had ever been as a cyclical bulk chemicals business.

The outcome of what Charles Miller Smith called "a journey of change and transformation" was a corporate catastrophe that left this once great company debilitated and at risk of bankruptcy. Fortunately for ICI, it was able early in 2002 to launch a rights issue, calling for £800m of fresh capital to give it breathing space. Yet the result of ICI's frenetic dealings in the market in corporate control had been that it bought into speciality chemicals at the top, sold out of bulk chemicals at the bottom, incurred enormous transaction costs and wrecked its balance sheet in the process.[7]

The only mitigating circumstance, if things were looked at in the round, was that Zeneca, which subsequently merged with the Swedish group Astra, continued to be a world-class drugs business.

Corporate sclerosis

An extraordinarily similar tale of woe took place with the transformation of the old General Electric Company into Marconi. GEC, which is no relation of the US company of the same name, was on a par in the mid-1990s, in terms of profitability, with AstraZeneca. It had enjoyed a reputation second only to that of the unsplit ICI in size

---

[7] All figures from ICI annual reports.

and prestige in UK manufacturing. But it was not a world-class player in any of its main activities. In the period of more than three decades in which Arnold (later Lord) Weinstock was Chief Executive it came to own large chunks of the UK power generation, telecommunications and electronics businesses, which had been relatively protected from international competition. In power and telecoms GEC's interests had been placed in joint ventures with, respectively, Alcatel of France and the German group Siemens, while its Hotpoint white goods subsidiary was jointly owned with General Electric of the US. These ventures were, in effect, poison pills, which were initiated in response to a hostile takeover threat in the late 1980s that failed to materialize.

Weinstock was, in fact, one of the original British pioneers of the cost-cutting takeover. His great achievement was to amalgamate and rationalize the giants of British electrical engineering, GEC, English Electric and AEI. He also steered an important part of Britain's industrial heritage through the high-inflation period of the 1970s, which was an exceptionally tough environment for such capital-intensive businesses. Weinstock's managerial approach was highly centralized, with tight financial controls. After his initial bold moves to rationalize electrical engineering he became exceptionally risk-averse. And, despite an outspoken public commitment to free markets, he was keen to operate in areas such as public sector contracting where profits depended on bilateral bargaining with government over cost-plus contracts rather than the discipline of the market place.

Like many over-dominant chief executives, Weinstock was reluctant to be parted from the company he had shaped. He did not retire from the GEC board until he was 72, by which time City analysts and institutional investors were claiming that he was a dead hand on the company. GEC in the 1990s spent less on research and development and filed fewer patents than its international competitors. Because of its highly centralized managerial and reporting disciplines there was little cooperative exploitation of the company's science and technology base, or constructive dialogue between different parts of the group. So Weinstock appeared out of step with the knowledge economy. The company was over-dependent on contracts with the Ministry of Defence and former nationalized corporations such as British Telecommunications. And, as it continued to accumulate a cash mountain that at times topped £1bn, GEC appeared to miss out on opportunities in newer industries such as mobile phones. Its earnings record in the first half of the 1990s was stagnant and in the 15 years to 1996 when Weinstock finally took his leave, the shares underperformed against the stock market.

Everything changed with the arrival of George (later Lord) Simpson, a Scottish accountant by training, as Weinstock's successor. Simpson had cut his teeth in the car industry, becoming Chairman and Chief Executive of Rover Group. He then became Deputy Chief Executive of British Aerospace when it acquired Rover and later Chief Executive of Lucas Industries, the components manufacturer. GEC seduced him away from Lucas with a "golden hello" payment of £500,000 and a controversial pay package that included £600,000 annual basic pay together with incentives and "phantom" share options that were subject to notably undemanding performance yardsticks. Soon after, Sir Roger Hurn, one of British industry's big establishment figures, was appointed Chairman. Hurn was a former Chairman of Smiths Industries, the aerospace and defence engineering group. He subsequently became Chairman of Prudential, Joint Deputy Chairman of Glaxo SmithKline and a non-executive director of Britain's leading independent stockbroker Cazenove. John Mayo, the investment banker from S.G. Warburg who had helped plan the ICI corporate split, joined GEC from Zeneca as Finance Director. Interestingly, both Simpson and Hurn had been non-executive directors of ICI when it embarked on its corporate buying and selling spree.

Most of George Simpson's career had been spent in the troubled British motor industry, which might not have seemed an ideal background to manage a complex industrial conglomerate that faced big challenges in markets that were being deregulated and where the biggest customers had recently been privatized. But he could at least claim some knowledge of electrical engineering and aerospace, areas where Sir Roger Hurn was well qualified, too. This was no doubt helpful in understanding GEC's core businesses. But Simpson was under considerable pressure to tidy up GEC's poison pill joint ventures, refocus the business in higher growth areas and invest the cash pile. A man of great natural charm, the new GEC Chief Executive quickly had fund-managers, investment analysts and financial journalists eating out of his hand. His declared strategy was to move GEC away from being a heavy industrial conglomerate to a high-tech telecoms equipment provider. As the Internet frenzy gathered impetus the company declared that its strategy for the new gold rush was to make "picks, shovels and maps to harness the power of bandwidth and information." Its three main areas were optical-networking, broadband-switching and access products. As a result of this new focus it had a relatively narrow group of customers who were mainly telecom service providers such as Bell South and British Telecommunications.

This message was music to the ears of the many (and mainly young) City analysts who regarded the old GEC as so much industrial archaeology. And those of them who worked in the large investment banks were, of course, involved in conflicts of interest. The prospect of the hitherto staid GEC doing corporate deals meant larger bonuses for the analysts, since they stood to benefit from any profits their banks earned for advising on mergers and acquistions. So it was only to be expected that most analysts would welcome a series of acquisitions and divestments.[8] GEC floated its 50 per cent joint venture stake in power-engineering on the stock market in 1998 under the new name of Alstom. The defence business was transferred to BAE Systems, the former British Aerospace, in exchange for which GEC's shareholders received shares and IOUs in BAE Systems worth around £6.5bn. GEC also bought out Siemens from its joint venture in telecoms, which was then merged with an Italian-based subsidiary Marconi. After that

---

[8] There were honourable exceptions among smaller brokers, most notably at Collins Stewart where research was consistently sceptical about the acquisition-driven strategies of companies such as GEC-Marconi and Vodafone.

GEC changed its name to Marconi and started buying into the tele-coms industry in the US. In the same year it spent £1.3bn on Reltec, a network and access specialist based in Cleveland, Ohio and £2.9bn for Pittsburgh-based Fore Systems, which was in broadband-switching. Other smaller acquisitions followed. They were all operating in one of the world's most competitive high-tech markets. But they were not in the same league as the likes of Cisco, Lucent or Nortel, although Marconi aspired to play alongside such North American giants, boldly declaring that it intended to be the world's leading communications company. In the high-tech bubble, which accelerated after these purchases, Marconi's share price soared. The outcome of this trans-formation was nonetheless dire.

In the summer of 2001 North American telecoms companies started spewing out profit warnings as the investment boom in information and communications technology went into reverse. Marconi surprised the City with its failure to follow suit. Then it found itself in a tangle over the London Stock Exchange rules when it had to announce the sale of its medical equipment subsidiary at the same time that it was due to report its results. Because the Chairman was reluctant to change the timing of the board meeting to approve the figures, Marconi was obliged to suspend its shares for a whole day – a draconian measure that usually happens only when something is dramatically wrong. Not only did this enrage institu-tional shareholders, the publication of poor figures also left them with the impression that GEC's management had little understanding of the new businesses or the extent of their deterioration. Mayo, by now the Deputy Chief Executive, was forced to resign. The shares quickly halved in value. The scale of the subsequent disaster was, if anything, even worse than at ICI.

In the six months to 30 September 2001 Marconi's net worth went from a positive £4.5bn to a negative – a deficit of assets against liabilities – of £805m, leaving the company technically insolvent. This was largely the result of writing down the value of the businesses such as Reltec and Fore Systems acquired at bubble prices in 1999. Thanks to an astonishing 25 per cent decline in the sales of Marconi's core businesses in the six-month period, the operating loss in the first half of the financial year was an impressive £222m, while the leakage of cash from the group was more than double that amount at £470m. After a string of write-offs including £3.4bn for worthless goodwill relating to its acquisitions, the pre-tax loss came out at a mind-numbing £5.1bn. Thanks to the mismanagement of working capital and an accumulation of excessive inventories, the £2.1bn of debts incurred in the acquisitions of Reltec and Fore had spiralled to £4.3bn, casting an immense shadow over the group's future.[9]

By this time Hurn and Simpson, who would have been admirably qualified to run GEC's old businesses, but were clearly out of their depth with the new, had gone. And shareholders in what had been one of the most stable and financially conservative of British industrial companies had seen their shares lose more than 90 per cent of their value in a matter of months. As at ICI after the Zeneca split, shareholders who had been with GEC before the sale of the defence business to BAE Systems could console themselves with the thought that they had not lost out on their stake in the demerged business. But for investors who had bought into either company late in the day, the losses were devastating. When Marconi renegotiated its finances with the banks in the summer of 2002, the banks swapped much of their debt for equity in the company, leaving the original shareholders with just half a per cent of the total equity capital.

Unhappy hunting

The disasters at ICI and Marconi will be seen as landmarks in business history, if only because of the scale of the two catastrophes. Yet they were not isolated events. All across British industry companies with problems in their core businesses had looked in the 1990s to the market in corporate control as a means of buying and selling their

---

[9] All figures from Marconi annual reports and the interim report for the six months to 30 September 2001.

way out of strategic dilemmas and repositioning themselves in higher growth industries. Usually they looked to acquisitions in the United States. Apart from being a happy hunting ground for high-tech opportunities, it was a much easier market in which to make friendly acquisitions than Continental Europe or Asia. And many companies came unstuck because they bought at the peak of the cycle in industries such as telecoms, which suffered a particularly violent downturn in capital investment and a tough inventory adjustment as the recession set in.

This was not, of course, an exclusively British problem. American companies were facing similar challenges and looking to the market in corporate control for solutions. In areas such as the media sector, they were under enormous pressure because of the threat the Internet posed to their core businesses. Time Warner was the highest profile case in point. At the turn of the millennium the venerable entertainment, television and publishing outfit decided to throw in its lot with a new-media distribution business in the shape of AOL. This was by no means illogical, given that AOL had 34 million subscribers who were potential users of Time Warner's old-media content. There were economies of scale and potential synergies to be reaped.

The snag was that AOL and its assets were wildly overvalued at the time of the merger in January 2000 and its managers were not as good as the people at Time Warner had believed. When the AOL Time Warner stock price collapsed and billions were written off the value of the assets, the old-media managers quickly reasserted control. But, unlike ICI and Marconi, Time Warner did not make the mistake of borrowing to acquire AOL. Despite being sold a pup, it remained solvent after its metamorphosis when the bubble burst. With acquisitive American telecoms operators such as WorldCom the financial strains were admittedly greater. The US nonetheless managed during the bubble to escape a takeover-induced disaster to rank with Marconi in the UK.

Much of this merger and acquisition activity was taking place on the basis of severely distorted stock market prices, especially in the high-tech area. And indeed one of the most revealing things to emerge from the Marconi disaster was the apologia that John Mayo offered for the whole saga. According to Mayo the board held a strategy day in February 2000, just before the high-tech bubble burst. Mayo claims that he told the Marconi directors that they were in the midst of a bubble like the Dutch tulip mania of the 17th century or the South Sea Bubble. He argued that none of the company's plans would be able to sustain a share price in the medium term capable of matching the then level. The size difference between Marconi and the top three companies in its industry was also so great that the British group could not hope to grow its way into the top tier organically, even over a 10-year period. Because the stock market would ultimately cool down and share ratings would fall, he argued, it would be sensible to secure a stronger market position before the growth slowed. So he recommended selling out to a merger partner either for cash, or for a combination of cash and IOUs.

This was rejected by the board, which Mayo regards as the biggest of all the mistakes the company made. Mayo also argues that one of his own biggest mistakes was a failure to secure from the board an agreement for an onward sale of Reltec and Fore Systems. The board rejected this, so Marconi became what Mayo calls a "forced owner" of these companies. If a company puts itself in this position, he argues, the timing of the purchase in the course of the business cycle becomes as important as all the other considerations to do with the strength of the underlying businesses.

These arguments betray an attitude that companies are for buying and selling and that the future shape of a group like Marconi should be dictated by short-term share price movements. Instead of looking askance at the manic valuations placed on information technology and communications companies by the stock market Mayo clearly believed that such share values should be taken seriously as a basis for corporate strategy. That strategy boiled down to a belief in the greater fool theory – the idea that there would always be another sucker in the market place who was prepared to take Marconi off the hook. Yet it is highly questionable whether anyone else would have wanted to buy such a company for cash, when it was performing poorly in the telecoms race and, as Mayo himself admitted, had singularly unexciting prospects. The same stricture would have applied to any sale of the two big US subsidiaries.

This is characteristic of the Anglo-American investment banker's mindset, which equates strategy with mergers and acquisitions. Yet in the real world competitive advantage comes from generating organic growth in the operating businesses of the company by dint of selling goods and services that customers want, not from coming out ahead after making a series of deals. Interestingly, a growing band of economists is retreating from the notion that capital markets are efficient in pricing stocks and shares. The experience of the stock market bubble has given impetus to the theory of behavioural finance, which places greater emphasis on human motivation and market inefficiency. Yet investment bankers and business people appear to put ever greater faith in the verdict of the stock market when making judgements that can have a big impact on output and employment.

High-speed wreckage

Another lesson here is that the development of an active market in corporate control makes it possible for managers to wreck even the very largest companies more quickly than ever before. ICI was, in effect, hobbled by a single deal in 1997, which set it on a course that ended in technical insolvency. In Marconi's case the sale of its defence business and the debt-financed purchases of Reltec and Fore Systems all took place within a matter of months in 1999. An economic liberal would argue that corporate accidents are part and parcel of the capitalist process and that this contretemps in the market place for corporate control was healthy, since it resulted in a swifter transfer of assets to more efficient ownership. Yet it remains questionable whether that is what was really happening in these two cases.

The best complexion that can be put on the ICI experience is that the decision by managers at the old ICI to hive off Zeneca stands up to examination in hindsight. It is also worth noting that the decision to split a company in two, however large it may be, does not require particularly demanding new skills of an incumbent management. Once the decision is made, there is a large technical exercise that calls for substantial inputs from investment bankers, accountants, lawyers, tax and pension experts and so forth. Establishing a new modus operandi for the separate companies is a managerial challenge. But in the end it is not that easy to wreck a business by splitting it in two.

Trying to achieve the wholesale transformation of a company by buying and selling large numbers of subsidiaries is another matter. For a start, the skills involved in buying and selling companies are very different from those in managing operating businesses. They tend to exist in predatory outfits like Hanson, or in large companies like General Electric of the US, which routinely makes more than 100 acquisitions a year, rather than in more pedestrian companies like the ICI of the early 1990s. And part of the reason the revamped ICI's financial problems became acute was that the sales of the underlying businesses were not uniformly clean. Huntsman, a private US company that bought a big chunk of ICI's bulk chemical assets, became too financially stretched to pay for its purchase on time. A further problem was that potential buyers of ICI's businesses knew that the company was in hock to the banks and thus under pressure to sell. In a sane world, managers would behave like home-owners who deem it prudent to sell before they buy. Yet the self-discipline required to shrink an empire before expanding it again, combined with pressure from shareholders to transform the business, makes prudence an elusive quality.

That is not to say that it was foolish for ICI to wish to escape from bulk chemicals, any more than it was foolish for Time Warner to worry about the threat posed by the Internet. The UK chemicals giant was not alone in Europe in believing that mature, cyclical businesses of this kind were unattractive to big professional investors and best left to private companies to run. With hindsight, it is also clear that a more efficient way of recycling capital might have been for ICI to hand back the cash from disposals to its shareholders. It would have been hard for them to do worse with the money than the ICI managers. A former ICI board member told me that while there was some discussion of returning the money to shareholders in the 1990s, it was pretty cursory. ICI's managers would, of course, have been doing themselves out of a job if they had opted to hand back the cash and refrain from acquisitions. In those circumstances shareholder value invariably goes out of the window. This is a central weakness of managerial capitalism.

Yet the Anglo-American view of recycling also relies on a questionable set of assumptions about the efficacy of capital markets relative to companies in fostering innovation. One aspect of this was highlighted in a widely reported speech to the Confederation of British Industry in the mid-1990s by the economist John Kay, who pointed out that ICI's sense of mission had been importantly changed after the predatory intervention of Hanson. Back in the 1988 ICI annual report, the company's declared aim was to be "the world's leading chemical company, serving customers internationally through the innovative and responsible application of chemistry and related sciences ... through the achievement of our aim, we will enhance the wealth and wellbeing of our shareholders, our employees, our customers and the communities which we serve in."

After the battle to keep Hanson at bay, the formula in the revamped ICI changed to "our objective is to maximise value for our shareholders by focusing on businesses where we have market leadership, a technological edge and a world competitive cost base." As Kay pointed out, if that had been the mission in the years before the 1990s, 20 years-worth of loss-making innovation that went into Zeneca's most successful drugs would not have taken place. Of course, it is impossible to say whether that investment might otherwise have been undertaken in smaller bio-tech companies financed by venture capitalists; or whether such investment in their hands might have been less protracted and more productive. But given the short time horizon of most venture capitalists it seems inherently fanciful.

This suggests that the notion of a technologically driven decline in the relative competence of large firms in developing new technologies and products needs some qualification. It seems plausible enough in information technology, where the rate of change is breathtaking. But in bio-technology, where there is a much longer gap between innovation and marketing of the product, it looks less credible. It would be easier to argue, in the light of John Kay's point on ICI, that any decline in the competence of large pharmaceutical companies has been driven more by the impatience of capital and a narrow concept of shareholder value than technological change.

It is noteworthy, too, that the experience in Europe suggests that large companies can still find different ways of rejuvenating themselves and of skinning the high-tech cat. Indeed, the most spectacular European successes often result from internal rather than external corporate transformations. Nokia, the Finnish group that dominates the global market for mobile phones, is the outstanding case in point. It was originally founded as a paper manufacturer in 1865. In the second half of the 20th century it expanded into rubber and electrical cables, then into mobile radio systems and television. But when mobile phones took off in the 1990s Nokia sold all its other interests. Despite this focus on a product that did not exist in the 1980s, most of the top executives were with the company before the mobile phone market began its spectacular rise. Jorma Ollila, the Chairman and Chief Executive who masterminded the development of Nokia's mobile phones in the early 1990s, joined the company in 1985. Thanks to Nokia, and to a helpful European regulatory regime in telecoms, Europe established a strong lead over the US in mobile telephony.

Equally striking is how often in Europe corporate transformation into high-tech industries takes place under the shelter of ownership that is protected from the pressure of impatient capital. In the 1970s, for example, the greatest European success story in information technology was Reuters, a private news-gathering organization jointly owned by a collection of newspapers. Though completely insulated from the capital markets Reuters transformed itself into one of the world's most competitive producers of high-tech dealing systems for currency and financial markets. When the newspaper proprietors decided to float the company, they gave it a constitution that provided protection from hostile takeover. Yet Reuters continued to grow rapidly for two decades, enjoying a high stock market rating and considerable respect in its industry, before it came badly unstuck after the collapse of the stock market bubble in 2000. The Wellcome Trust, one of Europe's supremely successful pharmaceutical groups before its takeover by Glaxo, was similarly protected from capital market discipline. It experienced its most spectacular growth under the ownership of a medical charity, the Wellcome Foundation.

The view of takeovers and mergers as the ultimate tool of creative destruction also needs careful qualification in the light of the haphazard results over the past decade or so. For companies in mature industries such activity is manifestly hazardous. In the light of AOL Time Warner, Marconi, ICI and the rest, it seems clear that Anglo-American managers have yet to learn to use to good effect one of the defining mechanisms of the Anglo-American capital market model. Whatever was going wrong in the internal capital market operated by these companies before they went off the rails, it was nothing like as bad as what happened once the managers decided to plunge into the external market for corporate control. And, despite the enormous increase in the number of takeovers, the task of integrating the businesses merged and taken over does not seem to be becoming any easier if the verdict of most academics and consultants is to be believed.

The takeover market also sits uneasily with newer industries in which the key to competitive advantage lies in human and social capital. The threat of hostile takeover may, for example, foster a defensive culture in which employees become reluctant to share knowledge within the company. They may also be reluctant, if they fear being fired, to invest in training or working practices that are specific to the company and have no value outside. It is striking, too, that in areas such as pharmaceuticals, takeover-driven consolidation has often had a stultifying effect on innovation because highly skilled knowledge workers have been demoralized by the culling of fellow employees.

It is hard, too, in such industries for managers to extract value from takeovers except by cutting costs. Cisco Systems was a notable example of an American information technology pioneer that grew so large that it faced difficulties in maintaining the pace of technological development. Its solution was to buy into technological innovation by resorting to takeovers of fledgling companies in Silicon Valley and elsewhere. Cisco fell from stock market grace in 2001 as investors worried about the number of acquisitions that went wrong. Part of the problem was that many of the entrepreneurs who sold their companies to Cisco simply departed after the takeover.

This highlights an important difficulty in the use of takeovers in the more advanced sectors of the economy. The mobility of human capital is the equivalent of a poison pill whose effect is wholly unpredictable. Walt Wriston, the former Chairman and Chief Executive of Citicorp, explained it pithily when General Electric under Jack Welch prepared to bid for the investment bank Kidder Peabody. Wriston, who was on the board of GE, advised Welch against the acquisition on the ground that Kidder Peabody's assets "went up and down in the elevator". Welch went ahead regardless, only to see Kidder Peabody brought to its knees by a rogue-trader – a particularly toxic variety of negative human capital.

To return to ICI and Marconi, their biggest failures were, in the end, ones of corporate governance – that is, shareholders, non-executive directors and the wider analytical community, including the press, failing to act as an effective check and balance on managements that were under pressure to address exceptionally difficult strategic problems. The restraining task is admittedly a difficult one where directors want to rush into the newest areas of technological innovation – though a company that embarks on a high-tech acquisition strategy ought to have people on the board capable of assessing the business case for such investment. Yet the biggest mistake made by ICI and Marconi lay not so much in the choice of acquisitions as in borrowing and overpaying so heavily that the viability of the business was placed in jeopardy. Borrowing heavily in a disinflationary period is dangerous because inflation makes no contribution to the erosion of the burden of debt. Debt has to be paid down out of hard-won profits, or from the sale of assets or from the issue of new capital. The snag is that businesses are not always saleable, because the markets in corporate control and in private equity sometimes dry up. Even when they are saleable they may not fetch the requisite price. Investors may also be reluctant to put up new equity for a company that is technically insolvent. In Marconi's case the plunge into debt was paradoxical, in that it would have made sense for the company to pay for its acquisitions in equity that its Finance Director believed to be seriously overvalued. Yet it was unable to issue its own paper in the US, according to John Mayo, because it was not compliant with the US Foreign Corrupt Practices Act, which applies criminal sanctions where, for example, companies make payments to intermediaries to facilitate international contracts.

The irony, in ICI's case, was that Sir Ronnie Hampel was the author of the report on corporate governance that provided the basis for the British combined code – the document that lays down governance rules for quoted companies. He made it clear, when preparing his report, that he felt there was too much corporate governance about. Yet the real problem is not that the Anglo-American system imposes too much governance, but that the pressures on management are of the wrong kind. The incentives and penalties under which they operate are tailor-made to encourage them to behave imprudently and without adequate checks and balances. That, as we shall see in Chapter 6, helps explain what the corporate catastrophes at ICI and Marconi were really about. It also highlights the real beneficiaries of the market in corporate control.

At ICI the investment bankers Goldman Sachs and UBS Warburg took handsome fees on both acquisitions and divestments as the ageing industrial giant tried to buy and sell its way out of its strategic dilemma. Then when the company was technically insolvent they took fees on the issue of fresh equity as the company tried to salvage its balance sheet. As I remarked in the *Financial Times* when ICI announced its rights issue, the investment bankers are in a wonderful line of business. They take fees for putting Humpty on the wall, fees for pushing him off and fees for putting him back together again. That, in the modern business argot, is the ultimate win–win situation. As for Charles Miller Smith, the main architect of the disaster, he succeeded in defying one of the iron laws of British public life, which is that failure must never go unrewarded. He became a very rare thing – a former chairman of ICI without a knighthood. But there was a consolation prize to hand from the investment bankers who had profited so mightily from his buying and selling. Miller Smith became an international adviser to Goldman Sachs in 2002.

When all is said and done, it is hard to escape the conclusion after the greatest corporate buying and selling spree in history that the investment bankers' claims for the efficacy of acquisitions and mergers in restructuring an economy are greatly overstated. Despite the supposed aim of enhancing shareholder value, too many takeovers have manifestly been value destroyers. That leaves the intriguing question of why, given the high accident rate from takeovers, corporate moguls are so happy to go along with the blandishments of the investment bankers. The answer will emerge more clearly in Chapter 6.

6

The just-in-time CEO

Regardless of nationality, chief executives usually share certain common characteristics. One is that they enjoy the exercise of power. Another is that they like to have the maximum degree of autonomy in making use of that power. Corporate governance is about trying to give such people enough freedom to drive the business forward while ensuring that there is sufficient independent oversight and discipline to prevent them empire-building at shareholders' expense and otherwise going off the rails.

In the Anglo-American model the shareholders play a pivotal role in governance. Company law gives them responsibility for appointing the directors, including the chief executive officer, or CEO. The non-executive directors then have a dual function. They help in the development of the business, while monitoring the performance of the executive directors. The shareholders are also, in law, responsible for the appointment of independent auditors who give their opinion on compliance with generally accepted accounting principles in the US or, in the case of the UK, on the truth and fairness of company accounts. Shareholders are then supposed to act as productivity chasers, using the voting power attached to their shares as a lever to bring pressure for boardroom change when things go wrong. And if this exercise of the shareholders' control rights still fails to ensure good corporate performance, a predator can be expected to launch a hostile takeover bid in order to remove the underperforming executives.

In the real world the system sometimes comes closer to benign or malign dictatorship by the chief executive. As the American shareholder activist Robert Monks argues:

> While the law provides that the shareholders elect the directors, it is plainly recognized that no one accedes to a board except at the direction or concurrence of the CEO; while directors generally are thought to be responsible for succession planning, the preponderant pattern is for CEOs to pick their successors; emerging notions of good practice recite that CEO pay is fixed by "independent" directors, serving as an "independent" compensation committee, using the service of independent pay consultants. The reality is that all serve at the CEO's pleasure. Nothing proves more clearly the reality of CEO rule as the expansion of top pay from every previously normative ratio to limits unimagined in other times or places. Today's CEO can receive, for a few months of mediocre work, sums larger than the entire annual budget for the government of a country.[1]

This serves as an accurate description for all the larger English-speaking countries, except that CEO pay in the US is in a stratospheric league of its own. Even if the appointment process for directors is farmed out to consultants by a nomination committee of the board, as in the UK, most CEOs try to impose very restrictive criteria for the selection of non-executives. For a start, they like to limit the potential candidates to other experienced CEOs. This tends to perpetuate the dominance on boards of people who are white, male and highly sympathetic to the concerns of a fellow CEO, including his requirement for generous pay. To ask such people to act in the capacity of both player and referee in the corporate governance game is to ensure an unsatisfactory outcome. The independence of non-executives may also be compromised financially. At Enron, the Houston energy-trader that collapsed amid accounting scandals late in 2001, non-executive directors on the audit committee were also paid consultants to the company. They failed to blow the whistle on Enron's habit of concealing losses and debts in murky special-purpose entities that managed to escape proper disclosure in the company's own accounts.

---

[1] Robert A. G.Monks, *The New Global Investors*, Capstone Publishing, 2001.

Uncounted beans

Enron, which became the biggest bankruptcy in US history, also exposed the lack of objectivity in the role of the auditor. Andersen, one of the big five accountancy firms, earned more from consultancy work for this aggressively expansionist company than it took in lower margin audit fees. This tended to confirm the suspicions of critics who claimed that professional firms were using the audit as a loss-leader for more lucrative consultancy business, of which more in Chapter 7. And many of Enron's financial officers were former Andersen partners and employees, which inevitably made for a cosy relationship between the company and its external auditor.

At WorldCom, where Andersen was also the auditor, non-audit fees totted up to nearly four times the bill for the annual audit. While Enron and WorldCom were extreme cases, there can be no doubt that the ethos of the accountancy profession has changed. Indeed, until Enron's collapse, one of the least noticed, but most important shifts in the workings of capitalism over the past quarter century was the bean-counters' metamorphosis from straight-laced professionals to aggressive business people. The big five accountancy firms turned themselves into advisory conglomerates, offering assistance on everything from accounting, legal and actuarial services to human resource consulting and outsourcing. Although the big five have largely hived off their consulting arms in recent years, their non-audit business continues to grow much faster than audit work. At the UK's top-100 quoted companies, for example, non-audit fees in 2001 amounted on average to 2.8 times the audit fees. This was up from 1.6 times in 1998.[2] A similar trend has been apparent in the US. From 1993 to 1999, according to the SEC, the average annual growth of fee income from management advisory and similar services was 26 per cent compared with only 9 per cent for audit services. And the independent Investor Responsibility Research Center found on the basis of analysing proxy statements of

---

[2] Pensions & Investment Research Consultants, Corporate Governance Annual Review, 2001.

1,245 US-quoted companies in 2002 that 72 per cent of the total fees paid to auditors were for non-audit services, equivalent to a multiple of 1.9 times.

Some of the non-audit fees are for tasks such as verifying figures for corporate clients involved in takeover bids. There the incumbent auditor is better equipped to deliver a fast and efficient service than an outside auditor starting from scratch. Even so, the exponential growth of non-audit fee income raises an inescapable question about the independence of a low-margin audit function that delivers a shrinking share of revenue to a rapidly growing conglomerate service industry. Given the role of auditors as guarantors of the integrity of the capitalist system, this is a big fissure in the structure. But there is a more fundamental problem. The appointment and remuneration of the auditor is, in law, the prerogative of shareholders. Yet in reality it is the management that hires, pays and fires the auditor. This fatally undermines independence. To see what that can do to the integrity of auditors, you need look no further than the UK Department of Trade inspectors' report on the fraudulent business empire of Robert Maxwell, published in 2001. In an internal memo a senior partner in Coopers & Lybrand Deloitte (now part of PricewaterhouseCoopers in the UK) described the firm's strategy toward the audit in these terms:

> The first requirement is to continue to be at the beck and call of RM, his sons and his staff, appear when wanted and provide whatever is requested.

The watchdog had clearly turned into a poodle. And there were other important ways in which the professional ethos had been corrupted, notably in relation to the growth of big firms' international practices.

While the big four, PwC, KPMG, Ernst & Young and Deloitte & Touche, use a common name across different jurisdictions, their networks are no more than loose confederations. They are unregulated and unlicensed, with no common ownership, management or control. The right to carry out a statutory audit in most countries is usually only granted to locally controlled firms, so there is a big question about the ability of the networks to enforce consistent audit standards across the world.

The World Bank's assessments of the quality of audits performed by local member firms of the big accountancy networks in developing countries suggest that the quality of audits is very uneven both across and within countries. Yet the use of a common name gives rise to the expectation of "one name, one standard", which multinational companies find reassuring, especially in jurisdictions where the local regulatory regime for auditors is weak. It also makes membership of a big network an attractive business proposition for a local accountancy firm.[3]

Compliance by member firms with the networks' standards of audit performance is nonetheless voluntary. And there is no transparency about the networks' sanctions for failing to match their standards. There is thus a big enforcement problem. In effect, the accountancy firms have franchised their brand names across the world just as McDonald's does with burger outlets. But, unlike McDonald's, they have failed to ensure that the franchisees maintain the quality of the product. As a business strategy it has been a brilliant success for them. Yet these global brand names are dangerously close to being a sham, another indication of how the professional ethos in auditing has been eroded. The fragility of such brands was devastatingly exposed by the extraordinarily rapid disintegration of Andersen after the Enron debacle. From the moment the American part of the organization was in trouble, individual members of the Andersen collective felt no loyalty to the wider organization. It was *sauve qui peut* as each national partnership sought to hook up as advantageously as possible with other members of the remaining Big-Four global confederations.

---

[3] For an exploration of how the networks operate and underperform, see John Hegarty and Claude Trolliet, *Regulatory Reform and Trade Liberalisation in Services: The Benefits and Limitations of Strengthening GATS Rules – Accountancy Services*, OECD–World Bank, March 2002.

Greybeards and money bags

To understand why the chief executives appear to have usurped much of the legal role of the shareholders, it is important to understand how those shareholders behave. In the 21st century relatively few of them are private individuals. They are mainly institutional investors such as mutual funds, insurance companies, pension funds and hedge funds. In the UK, which exemplifies the most extreme form of institutionaliza-tion, individual share ownership went from more than 80 per cent of the equity market in 1939 to just under 17 per cent in 1998. British institutional investors owned around 53 per cent of UK equities in 1998, while overseas investors, mainly institutions, owned 28 per cent.[4] The trend to institutional ownership is common among the English-speaking countries. In 1998, life insurers, pension funds and mutual funds controlled investments worth, as a percentage of gross domestic product, 197 per cent in the UK, 176 per cent in the US and 105 per cent in Canada, compared with 90 per cent in France and just 35 per cent in Germany.

Most of the money controlled by these anonymous collective investors goes toward financing retirement. It comes in the form of pension contributions, which are then invested in equities, bonds and other assets around the globe. Where the biggest companies in the US and UK are concerned, the greater part of the pension money is still in defined benefit pension schemes where the pension is calculated by reference to the employee's pay level and length of service. In other words, the employee has no direct stake in the investments of the pension fund. In a scheme of this kind the employees' property right is nebulous, consisting of no more than a promise. If the pension fund

---

[4] The estimate of pre-war individual share ownership is my own, based on data in the 1959 Radcliffe Committee Report on the monetary system. The later figures are estimates by Phillips & Drew in *Pension Fund Indicators*, May 2000. The figures probably overstate the degree of institutionalization because many private individuals' shareholding are held in nominee accounts that are recorded as institutional holdings. But there is no doubt that institutionalization has gone further in the UK than the US. For an exploration of the growth of pension fund investment in the UK, see my earlier book – *That's the Way the Money Goes*, André Deutsch, 1982.

accumulates a surplus, most of it flows back into the company's profit-and-loss account by way of reduced company contributions. Any additional benefits for the employees are usually at the discretion of the trustees. So the purpose of the fund is not to deliver superior returns to pension scheme members or savers. It is to provide a guarantee to back the pensions promise. And since the company usually has an obligation to top up the fund if it runs into deficit, the directors have an understandable desire to ensure that the trustee, or the majority of a board of trustees, is beholden to management. So employees and pensioners, the so-called beneficiaries, have no substantive claim in this kind of scheme on the fund's assets, except where the company goes bankrupt. And they have little effective say in how the investments are managed.

This is changing, as more companies switch to defined contribution pension schemes where pension levels depend on investment performance and employees shoulder the investment risk themselves. But it is still the case that all those who are professionally involved in managing this pension fund nest egg are enmeshed in potential conflicts of interest. To the extent that pension fund trustees represent management interests, they are unlikely to oppose the grant of generous boardroom pay awards, including stock options. So, too, with fund-managers, who also have an eye on their own stock options. They often argue, disingenuously, that the size of any talented CEO's pay package is trivial in relation to the shareholder value he can create, so pay is not a matter of any great interest to them. It follows that few in the system have much interest in stopping the gravy train.

Exits and entrances

Yet this leads on to a curious paradox. Despite the apparent power of the CEO, the tenure of CEOs has been dramatically foreshortened in recent years. Executive recruitment firms estimate that the rate of CEO turnover in both the US and UK is now down to an average of as little as four years. Some are being offered no more than a year or two to transform the corporation. Yet Jack Welch, who spent over 20 successful years at the helm of General Electric, argues that it takes a minimum of 10 years for a new CEO to make his mark.[5] How can this bizarre contrast between apparent CEO power and absurdly short tenure be explained?

The answer is that a great deal has changed since the 1950s and 1960s when the CEO really did enjoy the status of a philosopher king. In those days institutional investors usually felt that the best response to poor managerial performance was the Wall Street Walk: in a phrase, to sell the shares. They saw themselves as punters rather than owners, with little or no responsibility for acting as productivity chasers. But as more and more money was transferred from individuals to collective savings vehicles such as mutual funds and pension funds, walking away became difficult. For the giants of the savings industry it was impossible to sell shares in all but the biggest quoted companies without the share price moving against them. The big institutions were thus locked in. And the fashion for index-tracking funds, where the investor is by definition precluded from selling shares, further manacled institutional investors to the companies into which they ploughed other people's money.

Yet professional fund-managers remained extremely reluctant to engage with CEOs who were performing badly, preferring to rely on the haphazard hostile takeover mechanism as the remedy of first and last resort. This reflected the conflict of interest in the institutions' own business position. Pension scheme trustees who are directors of the company or who owe their position to management have historically been reluctant to engage in activism. For if activism is given free rein it might one day be directed at them. Most executive directors of quoted companies tend to feel that institutional investors are quite active enough as it is. Much the same goes for professional fund-managers, who are in a highly competitive business. If they are seen to adopt an active interventionist stance at companies in which they invest, they may alienate corporate clients whose pension funds they

---

[5] Anthony Bianco and Louis Lavelle, "The CEO trap", *Business Week*, 11 December 2000.

manage. They may also alienate potential clients. And if they are part of an investment bank, activism may be a deterrent to companies that use the corporate finance services of the bank. In the case of mutual funds, the most pressing conflict arises from the fact that they want to sell companies personal pensions for the employees, known as Section 401k plans.

Industrialists do not hesitate to threaten to withdraw their business if their financial advisers do things that upset them. Moreover, if the fund-managers' bonuses and stock options have performance criteria that relate to the financial results of the whole bank rather than being confined to the fund management arm, the conflict of interest is further entrenched. Their own pay will be affected if their fund management activity alienates the bank's corporate finance clients. Where the fund-manager is owned by an insurance company, the insurer may find that poorly performing companies in the portfolio are also insurance clients who would direct their insurance premiums to a more compliant insurer in response to activism.[6]

There is, in addition, a problem with the economics of institutional intervention. Even if an individual investment institution wants to do something about an underperforming management it will gain only a small part of the reward from its actions, while bearing all the costs and risks. In contrast, passive institutions that avoid intervening gain large benefits from the activism of others while incurring no cost at all. So, as Robert Monks and British businessman Allen Sykes have argued, passivity pays. It is a no-win situation for conscientious institutions trying to look after their beneficiaries' interests and a no-lose situation for passive ones.[7] This is a classic example of the collective action dilemma first identified by the economist Mancur

---

[6] This tension between the investing and ownership roles was explored in my earlier books – That's the Way the Money Goes (see Footnote 4) and A Stake in the Future, Nicholas Brealey, 1997. For a thoughtful business perspective on the conflicts of interest in the position of institutional investors, see Allen Sykes, Capitalism for Tomorrow: Reuniting Ownership and Control, Capstone, 2000.

[7] Capitalism without owners will fail: A policy maker's guide to reform, Centre for the Study of Financial Innovation, October 2002.

Olsen. Market forces have no answer to the free-rider problem, which in this case inhibits the commitment of resources by any individual investor to monitoring management and holding it to account.[8]

Throughout the 1970s and 1980s, then, the corporate sector of the English-speaking countries worked on the principles of a 19th century rotten borough. The institutions were increasingly locked into their investments, but declined to make good use of the voting power that came from equity ownership. So boards were self-perpetuating. A handful of UK institutions, with the Prudential usually to the fore, was prepared to act in particularly egregious cases of bad management. But they tended to summon up their courage late in the day after a great deal of damage had been done. Whenever the public policy aspects of institutional ownership were publicly discussed, fund-managers assured politicians and the press that they were engaged in an active dialogue with management behind the scenes. Yet, in the absence of daylight, this claim was inherently unverifiable.

The Capitalist Manifesto

Anglo-American capitalism finally broke out of this drowsy dialogue thanks to the corporate governance movement and the shareholder value revolution. In the 1980s new US legislation required pension fund investors to regard the voting rights attached to their stocks as an asset of the fund, which should be properly used in the interests of the beneficiaries where it was economic to do so. Big investment institutions such as TIAA-CREF, which manages the pensions of university academics and teachers, and Calpers, the California state retirement fund, started applying pressure in the 1980s to company boards and engaging in proxy battles on issues of governance. Outfits like Institutional Shareholder Services (ISS), founded by Robert Monks, were set up to advise the institutions on how to exercise their voting rights. A more open dialogue was established between American institutional

---

[8] *The Logic of Collective Action*, Harvard University Press, 1965.

investors and the companies they invested in. So in corporate governance the US leapfrogged the UK.

But then Sir Adrian Cadbury's committee on the financial aspects of corporate governance was set up in the UK in response to a series of financial scandals at the end of the 1980s. It established a pioneering code defining best practice on the composition of boards and other governance issues. The code, which was initially attached to the London Stock Exchange's listing agreement and is now supervised by the Financial Services Authority, worked on a "comply or explain" basis. Its impact was reinforced in the 1990s by the growth of consultancies such as Pensions & Investment Research Consultants (PIRC), which, like ISS in the US, advised institutional investors on corporate governance aspects of voting and was prepared to put hostile resolutions on their behalf. (As a former Chairman of PIRC, I have to declare an interest.)

So while boardrooms remain cosy up to a point, Robert Monks's description of CEO power is no longer the whole picture, as he himself acknowledges. There is a growing recognition across the English-speaking countries of the important monitoring function that can be played by independent non-executive directors. The dialogue between investors and company management has become more intense, to the point where an investor relations industry has been spawned to manage it. Big strategic corporate decisions may now be heavily influenced by pressure from institutional investors.[9] There is even some explicit institutional activism. Hermes, which manages the pension funds of the companies that used to comprise British Telecom and the Post Office, has established, with the help of Robert Monks, a focus fund that aims to outperform the market by targeting underperforming managements in the UK and Continental Europe for action. It was following the model of Monks's Lens fund in the US. And managers are barraged with comment from the financial

---

[9] Philip Augar describes how the institutions applied pressure to both Barclays and National Westminster to sell their investment banking operations in his book *The Death of Gentlemanly Capitalism*, Penguin Books, 2001. He has mixed feelings as to whether the institutions' role was constructive.

paparazzi – the extended community of analysts, journalists and non-governmental organizations that monitor the day-to-day behaviour of companies.

All this coincided with the shareholder value revolution. Economists, business people and analysts became obsessed in the 1990s with the question of whether companies were earning a surplus over and above the cost of the capital they used. The analysts' language changed. They talked increasingly about bad management in terms of "value destruction". And the growth of hostile takeovers meant that the former philosopher kings of the Anglo-American corporate world could no longer afford to ignore the concerns of their shareholders. By the late 1990s CEOs were subject to greater pressure than at any time in history, being hostage to the gyrations of the share price and subject to attack for any shortfall of performance against the analysts' expectations. In effect, corporate governance and shareholder value had been turned into a stylized, even ritualistic, game in which all quoted companies were required to show faultless and perpetual growth in earnings, reported in the US on a quarterly basis and in the UK mainly on a half-yearly basis. Any shortfall of earnings against analysts' expectations was and is ruthlessly punished by a savage fall in the share price.[10]

The game of ambush

The most intense manifestation of the game is arguably to be found in the UK because, as indicated in Chapter 5, shareholders have the legal power to fire the directors and a more aggressive hostile takeover discipline than in the US. The very high degree of institutionalization has also brought a growing concentration of shareholdings below the level of the top 100 companies, with the result that the divorce between ownership and control observed by Berle and Means in the

---

[10] This relationship between fund-managers, analysts and company management has been explored with zest and insight in Tony Golding's *The City: Inside the Great Expectations Machine*, Financial Times-Prentice Hall, 2001.

1930s is becoming less absolute. In the UK it is not uncommon for quoted companies to have nearly half their shares in the hands of four or five big institutions, the most frequently recurring names being Merrill Lynch Asset Management, Prudential, Schroders, Hermes, Gartmore and PDFM. What this means is that if anything goes dramatically wrong for which the blame can be laid at any executive director's door, the non-executives feel under immense pressure to eject that director from the board. Usually it is the CEO who is ambushed.

There are a number of curious features about the game of ambush. One is that many institutional investors are still not fully engaged in corporate governance and remain reluctant to make full use of their control rights. In the UK where, unlike the US, there is no compulsory requirement on pension funds to cast their votes at company meetings, the voting turnout at the top 350 companies in 2001 was only 49 per cent. At the immensely fraught Marconi meeting that year the proxy voting turnout was a mere 40 per cent despite the profit warnings, a boardroom resignation and a controversy over the board's attempt to re-price share options in directors' and employees' incentive schemes. At the same time many value-destroying companies seem to slip through the net, with long-serving chairmen and CEOs remaining in charge when their natural shelf life has clearly expired. At any given moment there are usually half a dozen companies or more in the FTSE 100 index of Britain's top companies where there is the widely held view among fund-managers that the CEOs have outlived their usefulness.

Part of the explanation is that the ambush game is not well designed to cope with genteel decline. It works best when there is a manifest crisis, especially if a company is going to need a cash injection from outside investors to address its problems. WorldCom, the telecoms company run by over-acquisitive entrepreneur Bernie Ebbers, was notorious for the uncritical support of the board for its flamboyant CEO. Despite pressure from shareholders, the directors stood by him as the stock market value of the company collapsed from nearly $200bn to just over $7bn. But, when it became clear in

April 2002 that WorldCom faced a difficult challenge in refinancing
its huge debts, these boardroom pussies finally turned into tigers and
hoofed Ebbers out. The stock jumped for joy on the news, confirming
the rightness of their move.[11]

Removing managers also requires courage and solidarity from the
institutional investors. With a wily incumbent like Weinstock, who
had an unrivalled grasp of GEC's very complex business, but only a
modest percentage of the company's equity capital, fund-managers
found it difficult to stiffen their sinews for the battle. Yet perhaps
the oddest thing of all about this power game is that the managers
rarely complain about its evident brutality. Nor do they object to the
short-term horizon it imposes on them in the way they used to do a
decade or so ago.

The only plausible explanation for this acquiescence is that the
corporate governance and shareholder value movements have coincided with a complete change in the structure of incentives in the
boardroom thanks to the growing use of stock options. The theory
behind paying executive directors partly in the form of equity is that it
aligns their interests with those of shareholders. Where options are
concerned, this is hokum because they constitute a one-way bet. If the
share price goes up, the executives make their fortune. If it goes down,
outside shareholders lose money, but the executives do not. Moreover,
this powerful incentive does not motivate executives in the way the
pay and benefit consultants would have everyone believe.

Chief executives know that they have as little as three years before
they become vulnerable to ambush. In most companies they also
know that they cannot transform the operating businesses of the
company in such a short space of time. They are therefore tempted
to look for a transforming takeover deal, preferably with scope for
dramatic cost cuts that will impress institutional investors. Investment
bankers have an exact appreciation of the incoming CEO's problem.

---

[11] It is worth noting that Weinstock originally took the helm at GEC thanks to the
intervention of the Prudential. Because GEC was badly in need of fresh loan capital,
the Pru used this financial lever to eject the then chairman Sir Leslie Gamage, who
complained that he had been pushed around by a "bloody moneylender".

So they deluge the CEO with smart deal-making solutions – for the CEO, that is, not the company. In days gone by, investment bankers used to worry about peddling bad mergers and acquisitions to their clients for fear of damaging their reputation. But in the course of a long bull market in the 1990s they shed their scruples.

Investment bankers make their money by taking small percentages of very large sums. And at the peak of the bull market in 2000 those sums were astounding. The value of all the transactions in the global market for corporate control that year reached $3.5 trillion. The investment banks' incentive structures incorporated even shorter term horizons than those of company executives. Their bonuses simply rewarded them for doing the deal. So there was no pressure on investment bankers to do deals that were successful for the client company – something that can only be measured over a period of years. As with auditors, the professional ethos gave way to short-termism and greed. The bonuses were so large that the recipients felt tomorrow would take care of itself.

At the same time the analysts in the investment banks, who are little more than marketing executives for the mergers and acquisitions people, egg on the CEOs by demanding "corporate activity" from the company to spice up its profile. Corporate activity does not, of course, mean corporate activity in the meaningful sense of running the business. It is a euphemism for any activity that swells the profits of investment banks. For its part the financial press tends mindlessly to follow the predilections of the analysts. But why, it might be asked, would CEOs heed the investment bankers' siren call when they know that so many takeovers turn out badly?

Rewards for fun and failure

One answer is that it is exceptionally difficult to transform large companies and the results of incremental change programmes have been very disappointing. So takeovers offer an alternative to a slow process of change that may disappoint. Another is that stock option incentives are lopsided. Since boardroom pay is partly related to the size of the company, a transforming deal gives CEOs an excuse to demand a fatter pay package. So when, for example, BP made its takeover bid for Amoco in 1999, the pay consultants were through the doors and re-engineering the top pay packages within days of the transaction being completed. If the transforming deal then transforms for the better, the CEOs make a fortune. But if it fails they are still offered a safety net. And many such safety nets were offered when the stock market bubble collapsed. Perhaps the most eye-catching was that of outgoing WorldCom boss Bernie Ebbers. His severance pay included annual payments for life of $1.5m along with the use of the corporate jet. He was also given a long and leisurely repayment plan for his controversial $400m of personal loans from the company at interest rates that looked ridiculously uncommercial – not a bad pay-off for causing nearly $200bn of corporate value to vanish into the ether.

Such egregiously generous rewards for failure irritate some institutional investors, especially in the UK. But many take a more benign view. Andrew Clearfield, Senior Vice President and Chief Counsel of TIAA-CREF, even argues that rewarding failure makes sense, because it is one of the easiest ways of persuading a poorly performing management to leave. For that reason TIAA-CREF has never been opposed in principle to "golden parachutes" – the generous financial payouts that take the sting out of the ambush.

Another explanation for the CEOs' enthusiasm for takeovers is behavioural. Peter Drucker, the doyen of management thinkers, catches the essence of it precisely:

> I will tell you a secret: dealmaking beats working. Dealmaking is exciting and fun, and working is grubby. Running anything is primarily an enormous amount of grubby detail work ... dealmaking is romantic, sexy. That's why you have deals that make no sense.[12]

---

[12] Quoted in Warren Buffett's letter to shareholders in Berkshire Hathaway's annual report for 1995.

There are snags to this combination of excitement and high rewards. Executives may find that their personal assets are dangerously undiversified. To escape from having too many eggs in one basket they may be tempted to make conglomerate acquisitions to achieve diversification via corporate deal-making. Or they may hedge their exposure through the derivatives markets, where the company's investment bank can provide convenient advice. Either approach makes a nonsense of the idea that options align executives' interests with those of shareholders. An alternative and exciting way of addressing the same problem is simply to seek an early exit from the game. This can be lucrative. For if the CEO can procure a buyer for the whole company, the requirement on directors to hold stock options for a given period usually lapses, so ensuring that they can cash in on a bid premium immediately, regardless of whether the takeover makes business sense.

Nor is this the only way in which managers can influence the share price to enhance the value of their options. In the 1990s US dividends were taxed more heavily than capital gains. So American managers substantially reduced the proportion of corporate earnings that they paid out in dividends and at the same time repurchased more of their shares. Since paying a dividend reduces the share price, as value is transferred from the company to shareholders, not paying a dividend is a tax-efficient way of keeping the share price up, which keeps value within the company. This helps support the price of the directors' stock options. And, of course, managers who are rewarded in the form of options have an incentive to shrink the supply of shares on the market by whatever means. In the US they have done so on a massive scale. There is a widespread misconception that the US bull market was driven in the 1990s by ordinary Americans pumping money into mutual funds either directly or via Section 401k pension plans. Yet for much of the decade US households were net sellers of stock, while the corporate sector was the main buyer through takeovers and stock buybacks. This tilted the balance of supply and demand very helpfully from the point of the directors. In the UK, meantime, where the award of options is more often dependent on performance criteria such as growth in earnings per share, buy-backs had the helpful effect for directors of enhancing earnings even when there was no improvement in business performance. The earnings were being divided by a smaller number of shares, so in per-share terms earnings automatically rose.

Yet the outcome of the Anglo-American capital market game has been thoroughly destructive. Many stock buy-backs were a deceptive device, in that they actually destroyed value. This was the case where US companies financed the purchases of their own stock with borrowings at a time when debt finance was more expensive than equity finance. As Andrew Smithers and Stephen Wright point out in their book *Valuing Wall Street*, this was indeed what companies were doing in the late 1990s.[13] The result was a debt-financed transfer of wealth from shareholders to management and employees, which had the overall effect of weakening the balance sheet of the US corporate sector. And the lobbying skills of the Business Round Table, a club for the CEOs of big US companies, pressured the Financial Accounting Standards Board into retreating from a proposal to show the cost of stock options as a charge against profits. This was a case of pulling the wool over everyone's eyes, while reinventing the free lunch. It produced a remarkably forthright response from investor Warren Buffet:

It seems to me that the realities of stock options can be summarized quite simply: if options aren't a form of compensation, what are they? If compensation isn't an expense, what is it? And if expenses shouldn't go into the calculation of earnings, where in the world should they go? ... Managers thinking about accounting issues should never forget one of Abraham Lincoln's favourite riddles, "How many legs does a dog have if you call his tail a leg?" The answer: "Four, because calling a tail a leg does not make it a leg." It behoves managers to remember that Abe's right even if an auditor is willing to certify the tail is a leg.[14]

---

[13] Andrew Smithers and Stephen Wright, *Valuing Wall Street – Protecting Wealth in Turbulent Markets*, McGraw-Hill, 2000.
[14] Letter to Senator Chris Dodd, quoted in Robert Monks's *The New Global Investors*, Capstone Publishing, 2001.

This would all be less worrying if the incentive impact of the directors' options had vastly improved corporate performance for the benefit of shareholders. But as Andrew Smithers and Stephen Wright point out, improvements in corporate efficiency in the 1990s did not go to shareholders. At the peak of the bubble in early 2000 the return on the equity capital of US corporations was 30 per cent above its average since 1948, which sounds very impressive. Yet there was no rise at all over the same period in the return on total assets, as reflected in profits before depreciation, interest and tax. This second yardstick is a better measure of managerial achievement since it excludes things that are completely outside management's control such as falling interest rates and declining taxation. And the comparison between the two yardsticks tells a story that makes sense in relation to the wider economic picture: a larger proportion of corporate revenue had been flowing through to shareholders thanks to a period of disinflation, declining interest rates and reduced corporate taxation. But the benefits of productivity improvements over the period went into increased wages and more competitive prices for consumers instead of higher profits.[15]

Slash, burn, exit

Meantime the extraordinary pressure imposed by the capital markets on managers produced some very strange behaviour at some of America's biggest companies. The *locus classicus* has been Procter & Gamble (P&G) where in mid-1999 Durk Jager took over as CEO with a mandate to carry out a six-year restructuring programme to cut 15,000 jobs and make $1.2bn of savings a year. Feeling himself under considerable pressure from the capital markets, Jager tried to make a bid for Warner-Lambert that failed. He also missed P&G's earnings targets in three successive quarters. As a result, he was

---

[15] Andrew Smithers, *US Profits: Today's Delusions and Tomorrow's Disappointments,* Smithers & Co. Report No. 146, June 2000.

ambushed in less than 18 months and followed by Alan Lafley, who declared that P&G had taken on too much change too fast. Soon after his appointment the same Alan Lafley announced that restructuring had not gone far enough and that a further 9,600 jobs had to go. Meantime *Business Week* had noted, in an article in December 2000, that the combined tenures of Maytag's Lloyd Ward, Campbell Soup's Dale Morrison, P&G's Durk Jager, Xerox's Richard Thoman, Lucent Technology's Richard McGinn and Gillette's Michael Hawley add up to 10 years and 11 months. Equally striking is the speed with which top executives slashed employee numbers in response to the recession of 2001 – the Anglo-American world's just-in-time CEOs firing its just-in-time workers.

To say that this revolving door discipline is in the interests of the shareholders is absurdly simplistic. The shareholders have no means of knowing the cost of the takeover process in terms of human capital destroyed, nor the future cost of training new employees when profits recover. The accounting profession has been slow to find ways of expressing the value of such intangibles. In their world human beings are still a cost, not an asset, so no outsider can be sure whether a cost-cutting CEO is trying to save his skin at the share-holders' expense or engaging in genuine restructuring.

Arguments about the Anglo-American equity culture being particularly favourable to the development of information and com-munications technologies are thus cast in a very strange light. Taking the stock market as a yardstick for boardroom rewards assumes that the market is efficient and will respond rationally to economic events. This is a monumental assumption. It is also fraught with irony because the explosive growth in the use of stock options coincided with the greatest explosion of market exuberance the world has ever seen in the shape of the 1990s stock market bubble. So the stock market provided a hopelessly unreliable verdict on performance during this period. Small wonder that there was so little apparent relationship between performance and reward. And in arriving at that verdict the market had to penetrate a numerical fog in which the only clues the accountants could provide to the intangible values that contribute so importantly to competitive advantage in high-tech business were wholly misleading.

What we do know for sure is that the CEO's short time horizon and the development of the ambush culture mean that many potential liabilities will be left for the CEO's successor to deal with. Among them are likely to be externalities such as the environment and issues like health and safety. Foreshortened time horizons are an invitation to sweep anything difficult, however important, under the carpet. In short, there is a worrying lack of alignment between the interests of the CEO and the interests of society.

Why, it might be asked, do professional investors participate in this short-term game when they are investing to match extremely long-term pension liabilities? The answer is that they, too, are in a very competitive business and their performance is assessed by consultants and trustees on the basis of short-term deviations from their competitors. And while their approach to investment is now very theoretical, with growing reliance being placed on mathematical models, their ability to monitor company management is relatively unsophisticated by comparison. And since monitoring is costly, fewer resources are devoted to the task than it deserves from a wider economic and social perspective.

Demented accountability

In practice this means that fund-managers use an oversimplified model of how companies work. It is a model in which they look to the CEO as a hero, capable of delivering the mirage of unfailing growth. This is, of course, a tall order. Companies in the aggregate will, by definition, deliver only average performance. And while a handful of top managers are genuinely endowed with heroic leadership qualities, most companies perform well on the basis of teamwork rather than individual heroics. This is particularly true of the newer areas of the economy, where authority cannot be exercised from the top downward in the traditional pyramid structure. Human and social capital is more readily fostered in networks of relationships, some of which extend outside the corporation. Such networks require looser and more flexible forms of management organization. Despite this, patient pension capital is transformed into impatient capital in pursuit of an outdated and oversimplified leadership model. It is all part of a demented system of accountability that generates a very different outcome than the one envisaged by the economist Joseph Schumpeter when he talked of creative destruction.

The outcome, in the bowels of the economy, is very similar to what has been happening higher up the scale in monetary policy and the management of interest rates. Rewarding managerial failure has eroded capitalism's immune system. The cultures of the older US and UK industrial giants have more in common with the civil service than anything that resembles entrepreneurship. Top management has been used to allocating capital across industries and around the world in a cautious, incremental process. Yet the growth in use of stock options to compensate directors has resulted in bureaucratic performance enjoying entrepreneurial rewards, without the bureaucrats having to live with capitalism's ultimate discipline, the threat of personal bankruptcy. And the development of the market in corporate control has given these bureaucrats the opportunity to bet the company. The risk, as the economists say, is asymmetric. Most of it is shouldered by the shareholders, very little by the managers. The economic consequences of such distorted incentives are manifestly very damaging.

The game of premature ambush could be quickly stopped. All that is required is to insist that any equity compensation in the boardroom should be in the form of shares, which go down as well as up, not options, which are a one-way bet. Directors should also be locked into the shares for a suitably long period, with no relaxation of the enforced holding period if the directors leave the company. The investment institutions should act to prevent rewards for failure, which subvert the capitalist process of creative destruction. There has been, admittedly, a modest institutional backlash against poorly designed and overgenerous compensation packages in the boardroom. But as British businessman and corporate governance expert Allen

Sykes has argued, it will be difficult to persuade the institutions to hold management to account more vigorously than this without some state intervention.[16] The conflicts of interest inherent in the position of the investment institutions and the inhibitions they feel about collective action militate against a solution. And it remains to be seen whether the political and regulatory response to scandals such as Enron will lead to radical change in the structure of incentives in the boardroom.

---

[16] Sykes was the doyen of finance directors in the UK, having been a pioneer of discounted cash flow techniques for investment appraisal. While at the mining group Rio Tinto Zinc he developed the project financing methods that were ultimately used in financing oil extraction from Britain's North Sea. See Allen Sykes, *Capitalism for Tomorrow: Reuniting Ownership and Control*, Capstone, 2000.

7

Enron, alas

At one moment Enron, the now notorious Houston energy-trader, appeared to stand for everything that was innovative and exciting in the US economy. At the next, like Oscar Wilde's picture of Dorian Gray, it seemed to mirror all that was rotten and hypocritical in what had previously been seen as a remarkably sleek model of American capitalism – a gigantic reproach to the mores of the great bull market of the previous two decades. The profound shock to public confidence derived from the astonishingly comprehensive exposure of systemic flaws that emerged after the bankruptcy of one of America's most admired companies. There was also a powerful element of crony capitalism in the story, given Enron's political donations and the closeness of some of its directors to George W. Bush's administration. Yet the cause of the company's downfall, and of the greatest business scandal for half a century or more, was simply that the people at Enron were doing what everyone else in corporate America was doing, only more so.

There was nothing unique about the company's political donations. It contributed, as did countless other companies, to the presidential campaigns of both Bill Clinton and George W. Bush. Nor was there any secret about the fact that Wendy Gramm, wife of Texas senator Phil Gramm and former Chairwoman of the Commodity Futures Trading Commission, had joined the Enron board in 1993 shortly after standing down from the watchdog that had exempted trading in energy derivatives from supervision. The company was well known for its vigorous lobbying for deregulation, as it transformed itself from a boring pipeline operator into, first, a global energy conglomerate, then an online trader in derivatives.

That ability to avoid supervision was significant because it meant that Enron did not have to meet costly capital requirements, transparency rules and other regulatory restraints. It operated in a regulatory vacuum. Proposals by the Commodity Futures Trading Commission in the late 1990s to regulate over-the-counter derivatives, which are traded outside formal exchanges and were crucial to Enron, were rejected by Congress in the Commodity Futures Modernization Act of 2000. It was another victory for a company whose lobbying skills and route map of the political system were unrivalled. By the end of 2000 Enron was running a derivatives book comparable in size to all but the largest derivatives dealers on Wall Street with a notional value of $758bn.[1] Yet, when confidence evaporated, the lack of a proper capital cushion against adversity contributed to Enron's collapse.

It should be noted in passing that the cronyism surrounding Enron did not work consistently to the company's benefit. Robert Rubin, the former Treasury Secretary who moved to Citigroup, a big lender to Enron, phoned the new bosses at his old department to raise the possibility of government financial support for the ailing energy-trader late in 2001 when confidence was evaporating. He pointed out the similarities with the Long-Term Capital Management hedge fund and the potential threat of a collapse to the financial system. Treasury Secretary Paul O'Neill and Under Secretary Peter Fisher, who was involved in coordinating the LTCM rescue when he was an official at the New York Federal Reserve, decided against a comparable rescue for the energy company. The decision was well judged on purely economic grounds since the Enron bankruptcy did not bring down a major bank. But it was also a political imperative. Given the Bush administration's close links with Enron, a rescue would have provoked outraged allegations of cronyism.

---

[1] Estimate from the Washington-based Derivatives Study Center.

Ramp the price, dump the stock

Yet this was possibly the only check and balance in the system that proved secure. And if ever a management needed to be checked and balanced it was the management at Enron, for the company's chief *raison d'être* and categorical imperative was to raise the stock price and maximize the value of the managers' stock options at any cost. Kenneth Lay, the architect of the company's rise, made a reported $300m from the exercise of options in the 10 years before the company's market capitalization plunged from around $70bn to next to nothing. Where Enron differed from other companies fixated on shareholder value was merely in the means its managers used to pursue their goal. When performance deteriorated they resorted to fiddling the figures through so-called related party transactions. Anything nasty was shovelled out of the accounts into opaque special purpose entities (SPEs) controlled by Enron, but with participation by outside investors, which were used to disguise the true financial position. Partnerships that invested in these vehicles were also indemnified against loss by Enron.

Losses on unsuccessful investments in technology stocks were hidden in this way, as were debts run up to finance unprofitable new businesses. Enron also managed to inflate the value of ailing businesses including its ventures in trading bandwidth, which allowed companies to use the capacity of a fibre optic cable for a given time span. It took profits on these non-arm's length transactions, which were supported by valuations provided or influenced by the Enron management, into its own published accounts. A report commissioned by the Enron board after the debacle from William Powers, Dean at the Texas University School of Law, found that in the first three quarters of 2001 the company's earnings were inflated by almost $1bn through these devices.[2] In short, the scam consisted of ramping up the share price and cashing in the stock options before the

[2] William C. Powers, Raymond S. Troubh and Herbert S. Winokur, *Report of Investigation by the Special Investigative Committee of the Board of Directors of Enron Corp.*, 1 February 2002.

true financial position emerged – "pump and dump" in the Wall Street argot. Outside shareholders and hapless employees whose pension plan money was locked into Enron stock were left high and dry. In contrast, many of those who invested in the SPEs, ranging from Calpers, the giant Californian state pension fund, to leading investment banks and their top executives on Wall Street, made money.

A further element of the scam lay in the participation of Enron employees, including the Chief Financial Officer Andrew Fastow, in the SPEs. They received tens of millions of dollars at Enron shareholders' expense from partnerships that invested in the SPEs. In doing so they incurred virtually no risk. The Enron board chose to waive its ethical code in approving the arrangements whereby the Chief Financial Officer was allowed to serve in the partnerships. According to the Powers report the audit and compliance committee of the board made no meaningful examination of the nature and terms of these transactions.

At the same time a particularly savage peer review process under a performance review committee created a cut-throat culture within the company. To be in the bottom 15 per cent of employees meant an automatic goodbye. In the resulting climate of fear it was difficult for employees to challenge any lack of integrity in the creation of SPEs. And employees worried that if they negotiated too hard with Andrew Fastow's SPEs on behalf of Enron they would be torn to pieces in the peer review, since the reviewers were the people in charge of the off-balance sheet partnerships. At the same time employees who broke the rules were rewarded rather than dismissed if their misdemeanours contributed to swell the company's profits. Penalties and rewards such as these were well designed to drain the corporate culture of all ethical content.

Any lack of diligence on the part of the non-executive directors was understandable. Enron routinely provided its non-executives with lucrative consultancy contracts. Their objectivity was thus impaired. And since they were also awarded stock options, they too stood to benefit from the helpful impact of creative accounting on the stock price. So the checks and balances in the Enron boardroom were fundamentally flawed.

Shred and be damned

Meantime Andersen, the auditors, were providing consultancy advice on the establishment of the SPEs and their accounting arrangements. They then reported on these arrangements in a different capacity as auditors to Enron. Their impartiality was thus compromised by a potential conflict of interest. A majority of their fees came not from the audit, but from higher margin consultancy. It is striking, too, that Andersen and the other big accounting firms were enthusiastic contributors to political campaign funds. Andersen was the third largest contributor to George W. Bush's presidential campaign in 2000 and the biggest campaign donor among the large accountancy firms.

There is little doubt, too, that the accountancy profession's political contributions helped secure Congressional support to block efforts by the Securities and Exchange Commission's then Chairman Arthur Levitt in the late 1990s to force auditors to hive off their consultancy activities. So the audit failure at Enron was symptomatic of a wider problem. The independence of auditors has been fundamentally compromised as they have come to regard corporate clients as the geese that lay golden eggs for their consultancy business. Audit standards have been allowed to drop in order to keep the management happy. Andersen, meantime, will go down in history as the auditor that shredded documents when the balloon went up and was destroyed by the US Justice Department's decision to bring a criminal action against the firm.

As for the analysts, 16 out of 17 in the leading investment banks were still rating Enron a "strong buy" or "buy" before its collapse. Had they been diligent, they would have noted the extraordinarily detailed information about related-party transactions in Enron's published accounts and observed that significant profits appeared to come from these non-arm's length transactions. For, despite the widespread assumption that Enron's misdeeds were carefully concealed, the accounts were liberally scattered with revealing clues as to what was going on. The relevant note to the last published accounts for the year 2000 showed that Enron claimed to have earned revenues from off-balance sheet affiliates of $510m in 2000, $674m in 1999 and $563m in 1998. It also showed that these affiliates had huge liabilities of more than $20bn.

The information was admittedly incomplete and somewhat obscure. But related party transactions are more often than not a warning signal. They studded the accounts of companies run by the British fraudster Robert Maxwell and they provide the means whereby many family-controlled businesses in emerging market economies steal from outside shareholders. At Enron the long list of incestuous dealings referred to in the published accounts should have provided an opportunity to probe. The analysts failed to exploit it because of a fundamental conflict of interest. The company generated a reported $323m in underwriting fees for Wall Street between 1986 and its collapse in 2001, more than half of which went to Goldman Sachs, Salomon Smith Barney and Credit Suisse First Boston (CSFB) alone. Any bank whose analysts criticized this hyperactive wheeler-dealer and alienated its powerful boss Kenneth Lay would not have lasted long at the bank in question.

Proof of this proposition emerged at UBS Paine Webber, to which Enron channelled much of the securities business relating to its employees' 401k pension plans. When Chung Wu, an investment adviser at the Wall Street firm, advised clients by email that Enron's financial situation was deteriorating and urged them to sell, he was instantly fired. The firm reiterated its "strong buy" recommendation and claimed that it was firing its adviser because his emails had not been authorized in line with in-house rules. It has to be said, incidentally, that we in the media performed poorly, too, on Enron, and without the excuse that journalists would have lost their jobs if they had blown the whistle.[3]

In this instance what happened at Enron was no more extreme than events elsewhere. At the height of the high-tech bubble in the 18 months to the end of March in 2000, the investment banks earned

$10bn in fees by raising $245bn for 1,300 companies.[4] Many of these companies were loss-making and subsequently went bust. Analysts in the leading banks were part of the marketing effort to sell the initial public offerings to the investing public and their bonuses reflected their contribution to this corporate finance activity. The intensity of the conflict of interest in the analysts' position emerged in lurid detail when New York Attorney General Eliot Spitzer publicly re-vealed the content of internal emails at Merrill Lynch. The star high-tech analyst Henry Blodget and his team were shown to have described corporate clients as "crap" or "junk" when in public they were referring to the same companies in glowing terms in their effort to promote the stock.

Meantime, on Wall Street and in London, analysts at the house banks of telecoms companies such as WorldCom and Vodafone con-tinued to rate them as "strong buys" when their stock was plummet-ing. Jack Grubman, the analyst at Salomon Smith Barney who helped Salomon raise more money for telecoms companies than any other investment bank, became another focus of Eliot Spitzer's investigations. The suspicion was that his stock recommendations had been compromised by the fees that Salomon had received from telecoms companies. It also emerged that Salomon and others had

---

[3] In October 2002 Marjorie Scardino, Chief Executive of Pearson, owner of the *Financial Times*, publicly declared that journalists had not been up to scratch in reading company balance sheets during the boom. The upset her words caused among FT journalists prompted a quick apology. She was probably wrong to make the statement, because it is always a bad principle for chief executives to rubbish their own goods. The FT journalists also felt the criticism was unfair, since they believed that the paper lacked the resources in the US to carry out investigative journalism on the scale they would have liked. But, in point of fact, she was right. As I look back at the bubble, it seems to me that the FT's editorial writers did well in identifying the bubble – our mailbags were filled with endless complaints from investors who asked why we did not "keep the faith" with the bull market. But, along with the world's other leading newspapers, we failed to demonstrate in our rapportage a sufficiently acute nose for what was going on at companies like Enron.

[4] Figures from Thomson Financial/First Call, quoted in "How corrupt is Wall Street?" *Business Week*, Special Report, 13 May 2002.

been giving clients like Ebbers privileged personal access to stock in initial public offerings during the high-tech bubble.

The accepted view of the Enron scandal is that it demonstrated flaws at almost every point in the workings of American capitalism. That is undeniable. Everyone in the story was involved in potential conflicts of interest. And everyone including the watchdogs had been bought by Enron one way or another. It was a monumental failure of corporate governance. But, while this interpretation is true, it overlooks a more fundamental lesson of Enron, which is that the American model of capitalism has metamorphosed into something very different from its textbook description.

Insiders on the take

The many different kinds of capitalism that exist around the world fall into two distinct groups: the insider, bank-financed models like those of Asia and some countries in Continental Europe, and the capital market models of the English-speaking countries where accountability runs from management to outside shareholders. A key point about Enron is that the Anglo-American system has moved from being an outside system toward a novel form of insider system controlled by managers who have ever-increasing ownership rights thanks to stock options.

In the US the issue of stock options to directors was not automatically subject to a vote by shareholders when Enron was flying high. So the people who ran corporate America took advantage of their inside position to issue stock options to themselves on a lavish scale. In many cases this exceeded the amount of the company's stock that they mopped up through buy-backs. And because big business bludgeoned the Financial Accounting Standards Board into backing down from its proposal to treat this element of the cost of directors' and employees' pay as a charge in the profit-and-loss account, profits were materially overstated in the stock market boom. Their argument was that charging this element of employee costs against profits would be bad for stock prices. And they questioned whether it was possible to value options, given that their ultimate cost depended on the price of the stock at the time the option was exercised.

Yet for anyone who believes in the shareholder value model of capitalism the cost of employee stock options is real and ought thus to be reflected in the stock market's judgement of corporate profitability. Nor is it impossible to value options. Innovative economists have developed standard techniques of valuation, which underpin the workings of the derivatives markets. These values may be approximate, but so are the values of many other assets in corporate balance sheets such as depreciation, which hinges on large assumptions about the longevity of the company's assets. As Joseph Stiglitz, a winner of the Nobel Prize for Economics, has argued, the accounting conventions that prevailed in 2002 put the cost of employee options at zero, which is clearly a vast underestimate. The pretence that these costs do not exist means that resources are inevitably misallocated.[5]

All of which demonstrates that America's managers are powerful insiders who have been exploiting the private benefits of control just like dominant founding families in Korean conglomerates or quoted Chinese businesses. The process whereby the amount of option-related rewards was arrived at was not a market process, but a matter of managerial discretion. And most of the managers treated the options as no more than part of their annual pay and sold the related stock in the market as soon as they were able to do so. Then when markets fell and options became valueless, they were frequently re-priced downward. So not only did they enjoy rewards that were not commensurate with the risks they undertook, they also profited at the expense of outside shareholders, whose ownership interests were diluted as a result of the re-pricing of the options. In fact the outsiders suffered a double penalty because the value of their stock was anyway going down in a falling market.

At Enron there was a particularly vicious twist, in that Chairman Kenneth Lay told employees in an online conference call in September 2000 that Enron stock was a bargain while he was quietly selling

---

[5] Joseph E. Stiglitz, "Accounting for options", *Wall Street Journal*, 6 May 2002.

$16.3m-worth in the market. This was not the only case where managers' actions appeared to betray a cynical disregard for shareholders' and employees' interests. Gary Winnick, boss of Global Crossing, managed to cash in $700m of the telecom company's stock before it went into bankruptcy. Some, like Bernie Ebbers of WorldCom, admittedly hung on to their stock in the company at any cost. Ebbers even persuaded his fellow directors to have the company lend him money to finance his stake in the company when his bankers asked him to put up more collateral as the stock price collapsed. Much the same happened at troubled cable television group Adelphia, where $4.6bn of off-balance sheet loans were advanced to the founding Rigas family. But such behaviour was the exception to the rule that most directors regard stock options as part of the pay package and sell the underlying stock just as soon as they are free to do so.

Worse than the Japanese

There are similarities here with the Japanese model of capitalism before the collapse of the Japanese bubble. In Japan in the 1980s, as in the US more recently, large companies in *keiretsu* groups – loose knit families of companies – paid only paltry dividends. If outside shareholders were not to be short-changed, share prices had to rise indefinitely so that they could be rewarded from capital gains. Much the same was true of America in the 1990s. As long as the stock market went up, outside shareholders did not worry about the dilution of their ownership interest in the US corporate sector as managers grabbed more and more stock options.

Where the systems differ is in the response to the bursting of the bubble. In Japan the outside shareholders were burned. But at least the employees were not taken for a ride. Their stake in the company came from lifetime employment, not from share ownership. And the exposure of the average Japanese worker to the stock market is less than in the US. Because so many big Japanese companies in the 1990s were reluctant to abandon the lifetime employment system, the employees enjoyed some protection from economic stagnation. In contrast, the mild post-bubble US recession of 2001 was accompanied by a sharp increase in unemployment as well as the devaluation of employees' ownership rights because of the decline in the stock market. So the employees were hit twice over, or in Enron's case, three times, because the employees were locked into the stock whereas the top people were not. Outside shareholders, meantime, were milked. In most cases this did not involve egregious related-party transactions, but the dilution of their interests via the issues of stock options in the way described earlier. But the milking was no less real for that.

Enron was emblematic in another important sense. It was a hybrid between the old economy and the new. One part of the business was concerned with generating and transmitting energy. The other was aggressively trading derivatives. Yet the aspiration of the chief executive Jeffrey Skilling was for the whole of Enron to become what he called "asset light". He wanted to shift from managing physical assets such as electricity generating plant to a business in which everything was tradeable and capable of being removed in short order from the Enron balance sheet. He was more interested in financial engineering than energy.

This mirrors the shift in the wider economy to a more transactional culture. Looked at from a historical perspective, it is a trend that goes back to the Glass-Steagall Act of 1933, which aimed to protect investors after the 1929 Crash by insisting that deposit-taking and lending should be completely divorced from investment banking. The legislation put an end to relationship banking on Wall Street, in which a single bank could look after all the financial needs of a given corporate client. It simultaneously put a wedge between the US and European approaches to finance. Glass-Steagall laid the foundations for the modern US capital market model. Refined by the deregulation of Wall Street in the mid-1970s, it culminated in Wall Street's integrated form of investment banking in which all capital market activities ranging from raising money for corporate customers to managing pension fund investments were part of the same operation.

It was an approach to finance uniquely suited to the turbulent market environment that emerged in the 1970s and a good example of how institutional structures – in this case the law and regulatory change – can contribute to a country's comparative advantage. Thanks to this history the US investment banks acquired management and trading skills that enabled them to achieve a dominant position in the City of London after the deregulatory Big Bang on the London Stock Exchange. They had scale and they had trading skills, which stood them in good stead when other European countries followed the British in deregulating their financial systems. And one of the most striking features of the model in the 21st century is precisely that everything has become tradeable.

When a US bank lends money to a home-owner, the chances are that it will sell the loan to an institutional investor. When a vehicle manufacturer provides credit to finance the sale of a car to a con- sumer, the credit will usually disappear from the company's balance sheet into an SPE and be sold to investors. Even bets on the level of interest rates or the stock market are actively traded. The investment banks themselves, meantime, have come to look more and more like hedge funds. The big ones derive a large proportion of their profits from trading in both derivatives and more conventional paper on their own account. And since the recent repeal of the Glass-Steagall Act it is once again possible for banks to engage fully in both capital market activity and deposit-taking and lending. Financial giants such as Citigroup and J.P. Morgan Chase have reverted to the conglomer- ate model familiar before the 1930s.

Integrated conflict

The integrated approach to investment banking involves pressing conflicts of interest. The banks have inside knowledge of their cor- porate clients' trading positions and can exploit that knowledge for their own gain in their trading activities. They make no secret of the fact that the same people manage both own-account transactions and transactions for clients.[6] The transactional culture also means that banking has become semi-detached from industry and commerce. A huge superstructure of financial trading has been built on top of the basic provision of goods and services in the economy. And the corporate client is often little more than a residual consideration in the banks' risk management and trading strategies. For modern invest-ment bankers, companies are for buying and selling, or for generating fees and trading opportunities.

This culture is also prevalent in London, thanks to the dominant influence of the American investment banks. Philip Augar, a former top City broker, has explained the change of ethos from the 1980s to the 1990s like this:

> Bonds used to exist between firms as well as within firms but these have not survived. Screen-based dealing has replaced personal contact and it is dog eat dog in the global market place. Formerly the unwritten code was as powerful, perhaps even more powerful, than the Stock Exchange rulebook. It was very hard to cheat on someone you saw every day. Now people play strictly by the written rules with anonymous counterparties in cyberspace and it is the letter rather than the spirit of the law that matters.[7]

A good example of how relationships are affected by this culture shift can be seen in the credit derivatives market, which by early 2002 was worth $1-1\frac{1}{2}$ trillion, where banks can insure against their loans to corporate clients going sour. Because their exposure is parcelled out to other traders all across the banking and insurance sectors, the collapse of large companies like Enron, Global Crossing, Railtrack or Swissair did not shake the banking system to its foundations. That is a very positive outcome of financial innovation, although it remains to be seen how well the new market stands up to further financial shocks. But, by the same token, banks feel less obligation to help keep an ailing company afloat if they have offloaded most of their exposure in

---

[6] See, for example, Morgan Stanley Dean Witter's accounts for 1999, where Note 9 states: "the Company's trading strategies rely on the integrated management of its client-driven and proprietary transactions, along with the hedging and financing of these positions."

[7] Philip Augar, *The Death of Gentlemanly Capitalism*, Penguin Books, 2000.

an opaque derivatives market in which no-one knows where the risk has ended up. In this system, providing a service to the customer often comes second to profitable trading. All the focus is on the means, not the end. The question is whether a financial system so heavily geared to trading opportunities is really helpful in building sustainable businesses.

Enron typified this kind of financial engineering. Its culture put high emphasis on risk-taking and entrepreneurship. Individualism took precedence over teamwork. For all its faults, the company was impressive in pushing out the boundaries of innovation, dealing in such novelties as telecoms bandwidth or weather derivatives. This may sound bizarre, but it is a legitimate form of financial activity that can undoubtedly be helpful to industry and commerce. By allowing, say, a company that produces cans for soft drinks to hedge against the risk of falling demand when drinks consumption goes down in a cold spell, it permits more efficient management of production and inventories.

Yet the striking thing about Enron was that it was inept in its management of real businesses. Its move from the world of physical assets to financial engineering was driven in part by the recognition that operating conventional energy businesses profitably was difficult. In the end the company used derivatives to fabricate profits in its off-balance sheet partnerships to hide the extent of its indebtedness and to smooth profits from quarter to quarter. And part of the profit it did earn from energy came as a result of exploiting a powerful market position and ramping prices, as it did in the Californian energy crisis. A bizarre feature of the story that emerged after the collapse was how many Enron executives had asked how on earth the rest of the company could be making money if it was managed as badly as their part was managed. Most important of all, the company owed its demise not to fraud or off-balance sheet manipulation, but to unbelievably poor treasury management. There was, in effect, a doomsday lever in the way Enron was financed, in the shape of clauses that said that its bonds would become immediately repayable if the company's credit fell below a certain level. In Enron's desperate circumstances in late 2001 there was no time to refinance. So a simple flaw in treasury management proved fatal.[8]

Techno-libertarians at play

It is important to state that most of the banks and corporations that trade in derivatives markets are not resorting to the flagrant dishonesty that characterized Enron. Yet it could be argued that the whole culture of Anglo-American finance has become Enron-ized in the sense that it is increasingly subversive of regulation, taxation and democratic values, even where it remains within the law. Francis Fukuyama, the man who proclaimed the end of history after the fall of the Berlin Wall, has deftly analysed the phenomenon, pointing to a strand of what he calls techno-libertarianism in the American psyche. Many of Wall Street's traders, for example, regard the government as a parasite standing in the way of "value creators" who generate the world's wealth. Because technology and capital know no national boundaries, such people felt, in the more optimistic world we all inhabited before the 11 September terrorist attacks in New York and Washington, that the nation state was on the way out – a view oddly similar to that of many anti-globalization protesters.

But for techno-libertarians the state appeared too strong, not too weak. And they drew very different conclusions from those of the globaphobes. Fukuyama tells of his sense of shock when a portfolio manager friend of this persuasion announced that he was considering renouncing his American citizenship and moving to the Bahamas to avoid paying US taxes. For capitalist fundamentalists like him, democracy offered a less efficient means of satisfying individual preferences than the exercise of free choice in markets.[9]

This peculiarly upmarket form of civic disengagement can also be found in Silicon Valley. There is an egoistical and amoral strand in

---

[8] This was pointed out to me by David Creed, a former head of Britain's Association of Corporate Treasurers. For a more detailed explanation of the events that led to the bankruptcy, see the very readable *What Went Wrong at Enron*, by Peter C. Fusaro and Ross M. Miller, John Wiley & Sons, 2002.

[9] *Financial Times*, 15 September 2001.

such attitudes that harks back to the narcissism of Oscar Wilde's Dorian Gray. And it echoes very precisely the anti-government mindset of Kenneth Lay and his minions at Enron, who were messianic in their advocacy of deregulation. They wanted government to get out of their way and were prepared to bribe politicians with campaign finance and heavy lobbying expenditure on Capitol Hill to ensure that lawmakers did just that. The terrorist attacks on New York's twin towers admittedly gave some of these rabid libertarians pause for thought, as they observed low-paid government bureaucrats – firefighters and police – sacrificing their lives in the attempt to rescue millionaire investment bankers in the World Trade Center. Yet, as with Enron, the derivatives trading culture on Wall Street and in London is Manichean in its capacity for both good and ill.

Paul Volcker, the former Chairman of the US Federal Reserve who tried to rescue Andersen from collapse, worries about the complexities of derivatives trading and the convolutions of financial engineering. His concern is precisely that so much trading is now directed at circumventing regulations, tax and accounting conventions. Nobody knows how much of the financial engineering is subversive and how much directed at hedging normal risks. But there is no doubt that convolutions are happening.

I first became aware of this when visiting a derivatives firm, O'Connor Associates, in Chicago in 1994. The firm, which has since been absorbed into what is now UBS, had a thriving line of business with Canadian pension fund-managers across the border who were constrained by regulatory ceilings on the amount they could invest in foreign securities. Through the use of equity swaps the derivative traders at O'Connor were able to give Canadian fund-managers a virtual portfolio of foreign securities known as synthetic equities.[10] No Canadian money left the country. So when confronted with governmental constraints on globalization, the investment

---

[10] Equity swaps are contractual agreements whereby one party receives the appreciation or pays the depreciation on an equity investment in return for paying another rate, which is usually based on equity index movements or interest rates.

bankers invented virtual globalization. Regulation crumbled in the face of financial innovation.

This is among the more innocent things in the investment bankers' box of tricks. It is perfectly legal and provides the beneficiaries of pension funds with a "virtual" opportunity to spread their risks internationally, which is nowadays regarded as more prudent than keeping all your money at home. That said, such business is often recorded in the bank's books in other financial centres around the world to take advantage of lower tax rates. Nor has all such derivatives activity been legal. When Japan's Financial Supervision Agency sent its investigators into CSFB's derivatives trading offshoot in Tokyo in 1999, it found that CSFB had been marketing trading strategies to help Japanese banks conceal their losses.

CSFB's efforts were the tip of a very large iceberg. Further investigation pointed to the systematic selling of window-dressing devices by other investment banks. Such activity helped perpetuate Japan's long-running banking crisis. By keeping financial zombies in being, it ensured that more healthy banks were at risk of contagion as inadequately capitalized competitors continued to do business on an unfair basis. And since the weak banks were already close to bankruptcy, they had little to lose by behaving imprudently. As we have seen in earlier chapters, investment bankers have also helped banks in developing countries evade regulatory constraints on foreign currency dealing. Because the extent of foreign exchange exposure was concealed, financial crises in countries from Mexico to Thailand were exacerbated.

Inventive investment bankers have also devised ways for their investment clients around the world to avoid capital gains tax by using equity swaps. Where pension funds and insurance companies are prohibited by law from speculating in currencies, derivatives can be used to create an instrument that is legally a bond, or IOU, but which nonetheless permits the investment banks' customers to take huge risks in currency speculation. And some bankers regard the democratic process as ripe for manipulation. Frank Partnoy, a former derivatives trader at Morgan Stanley, has recorded how a rival investment bank helped San Diego County in California restructure a $700m derivatives portfolio in a way that postponed the disclosure of derivatives trading losses until after an election.[11] This is more subversive of democracy than the crude approach of Enron or Andersen in buying the politicians with campaign finance because it is not open to the public gaze.

Invisible trillions

Much of the trouble with this derivatives-trading is that it is so opaque that we cannot know how big a threat it poses to the state's power to regulate and tax, to the integrity of corporate accounts or to the democratic process. Recent estimates of the visible part of this trade, which takes place on formal, regulated exchanges, put the notional value of outstanding contracts at around $14 trillion. The comparable figure at end-2000 for unregulated, over-the-counter trading taking place on the phone or online between banks and their clients was $95 trillion.[12] The trade is worryingly concentrated. J.P. Morgan Chase alone does more than half the business, with the rest being handled by no more than a handful of giant banks. The mind-boggling notional values, incidentally, are not necessarily the actual value of the contracts being traded, but the value of the underlying securities or paper on which people are hedging, betting or making swaps. They nonetheless constitute a vast black hole in the financial system very similar to the black hole that results from the operations of offshore financial centres, which are now the subject of a concentrated international effort to increase transparency and prevent abuse.

The arguments offered by the International Monetary Fund for this effort, terrorism apart, include the risk that the activities of offshore centres can erode the soundness of banks and contribute to the volatility of international capital flows and exchange rates, while

---

[11] F.I.A.S.C.O. – *Blood in the Water on Wall Street*, Profile Books, 1997.

[12] Figures are from testimony given by Frank Partnoy, now a law professor at San Diego School of Law, to the Senate Committee on Governmental Affairs, 24 January 2002.

the Organization for Economic Corporation and Development points out that the offshore centres' role in facilitating tax evasion can distort trade and investment, erode national tax bases and undermine the fairness of national tax systems. Much the same could be said of the trade in derivatives. Yet such is the power of the brand names of banks like Goldman Sachs, Morgan Stanley and CSFB that they largely escape criticism and investigation on this score in the US.

All this casts a fascinating light on the debate about corporate power. Anti-globalization protesters are convinced that large corporations are now so dominant in the global economy that they can ride roughshod over nation states and the rights of individuals. Yet the Enron saga is in one sense a story about the limits of corporate influence. Yes, the company bought politicians and bought itself the favourable opinion of auditors, analysts, lawyers and bankers on Wall Street. But when it ran into trouble, all its money and lobbying efforts proved to be of no avail. The US Treasury refused to come to the rescue. So, too, with the professional services giant Andersen. All the money earmarked for the politicians provided no protection from the US Justice Department for Andersen when the chips were down.

The more subversive threat to the power of the nation state appears to come from the financial community, of which Enron was an un-official, unregulated member. The growth in derivatives-trading clearly does have the potential to erode the tax base of countries, to subvert government regulation and to make a nonsense of the picture of economic events produced by generally accepted accounting principles. And that applies even to the great majority who are not involved in doing the illegal things that Enron did. Financial engineering with derivatives can be thoroughly subversive without being illegal. Because of its opacity, we have no means of assessing the extent of the subversion.

Malodorous values

The public may not appreciate the finer points about the workings of corporate and financial power. But it does have a sense of smell and a feel for values. The smell from Enron was not pleasant. And an intriguing postscript on the company is to be found in a statement in its last published annual report entitled *Our Values*. It reads:

Communications
We have an obligation to communicate. Here, we take the time to talk with one another ... and to listen. We believe that information is meant to move and that information moves people.

Respect
We treat others as we would like to be treated ourselves. We do not tolerate abusive or disrespectful treatment.

Integrity
We work with customers and prospects openly, honestly and sincerely. When we say we will do something, we will do it; when we say we cannot or will not do something, then we won't do it.

Excellence
We are satisfied with nothing less than the very best in everything we do. We will continue to raise the bar for everyone. The great fun here will be for all of us to discover just how good we can really be.

Appropriately enough, this statement was tucked away at the back of the report. But the scale of the hypocrisy is impressive. As far as communication is concerned, the Enron management was in reality committed to keeping things opaque and moving information off the balance sheet. Kenneth Lay and his minions could not have treated the employees and their pension aspirations with greater disrespect. The top ranks of the company were evidently devoid of integrity. And the management's idea of raising the bar was to conceal the ineptness of its handling of its business. It is a salutary warning against the potential glibness of statements of corporate values. And it nastily devalues those that are genuine and decent.

Ordinary people have detected that the impatient, individualistic and greedy individuals who ran Enron reflected a wider corporate malaise. The inescapable conclusion is that there is indeed a crisis of legitimacy in modern capitalism, not least because the American way of business has been hijacked by the values of a financial community that is so preoccupied with trading and deal-making that it has lost sight of the purpose of its own existence. It is a point that applies with equal force to the other English-speaking countries. After Enron, advocates of the Anglo-American capital market model can hardly claim that it is a clean machine worthy of adoption by all-comers around the world. The big and only question is how the integrity of markets and their public legitimacy can be restored.

Part 3

The Limits
of Convergence

8

Apocalypse later

In 1945 the pension systems of Continental Europe were largely in ruins. In Germany, the capital funds of the state system had been used to finance Hitler's war. In other countries capital had simply been wiped out, leaving the funded element of pension systems bankrupt. Since capital markets were shattered it was difficult to look to stock market investment to provide the chief means of financing retirement. So in the immediate aftermath of the war, with large numbers looking for employment and low levels of private saving, European governments confronted seemingly intractable problems in looking after the elderly. Necessity proved to be the mother of financial invention. They found a solution in state pay-as-you-go pensions, whereby the pension contributions of employed workers were used to pay the pensions of the retired population. This followed on a much grander scale the model established by Bismarck, the 19th century German chancellor who saw state welfare as a means of placating a potentially troublesome labour force when the Marxist tide was on the rise. It also led Continental Europe toward a very different kind of capitalism to the model that prevailed in the English-speaking countries.

The pay-as-you-go approach worked superbly when the labour force was growing and the retired population was relatively small. The arithmetic was such that early contributors to a state pension scheme saw a very generous return on a fairly modest investment. This was, in effect, a politician's dream. Governments were able to promise generous pensions for which the burden fell on future generations – though in fairness it should be said that pensions policy in the immediate post-war period was not consciously cynical. It probably did not occur to politicians at that time to think what might happen if population growth eventually slowed. Meantime the administration costs of pay-as-you-go were low and because their coverage was usually wider than in the Anglo-American world there was less inequality in the incomes of the retired population. In effect, people who suffered the miseries of the 1939–45 war enjoyed a peace dividend in retirement. But in the 21st century this approach to pensions, which allowed the development of the Continental European system of capitalism without capital, has come under threat because of the ageing of the European population. The resulting demographic problem is a consequence not only of the post-war baby boom generation moving through the age structure, but of people living longer and reproducing less. The impact on health care budgets as well as pensions is potentially enormous.

Investment bankers have made excellent use of this scare story, the so-called demographic time bomb, in selling the merits of the Anglo-American capital market model in Continental Europe. In essence their argument asserts that if Europeans are to avoid huge increases in taxation and growing pressure on public debt, more of the burden of pension provision will have to fall on the private sector. Provided private occupational pensions are funded, with workers' pension contributions being invested in advance to provide for retirement, savings should increase. That in turn will finance higher investment, so enhancing productivity and offsetting the restraint imposed on economic growth by the decline in workforce numbers. Thanks to globalization, runs the argument, European pension money can also be invested in developing countries where the returns on capital are higher. The investment income on these overseas assets could then be expected to boost living standards in Europe, just as it had done in Europe before 1914.[1]

---

[1] See Andrew Dyson, Nick Miller Smith and Andrew Burchill in *Leading Change for Pension Reform*, Policy Network, 2001 for an outline of this argument. The authors are senior executives of Merrill Lynch. Also Paul Wallace who offers an elegant statement of the liberal case in "Time to Grow up", a survey in *The Economist*, 16 February, 2002.

It's the people, stupid

A big shift toward pre-funded pensions would, of course, provide a bonanza for professional investment managers in investment banks and elsewhere. Yet, while the argument may be self-serving, the underlying diagnosis about demography is hard to refute. Post-war baby-boomers and those who come after them do indeed face a less comfortable retirement than they might have hoped. Most forecasters expect the working age population of the eurozone to start shrinking after 2010, with the World Bank suggesting a decline of half a per cent a year between 2010 and 2020. Population shrinkage is then expected to accelerate to 1.1 per cent a year in the decade to 2030 and to 1.3 per cent in the decade after. The estimate for the 2040s is for shrinkage at a 0.7 per cent annual rate.[2]

This is dismal news for Continental Europeans because living standards are bound to slow if the output of a given number of workers has to be shared among a greater total population. In fact the percentage of the European Union's non-working population that depends on the working population – the dependency ratio – is expected to rise from 49 per cent in the late 1990s to 78 per cent by 2050, with the big jump in the elderly population coming after 2010. Worse still for the Europeans is that their dependency ratio is much greater than that of the US. According to an Organization for Economic Cooperation and Development (OECD) study, the change in the respective ratios could lead to a fall in the level of gross domestic product per head of 18 per cent in the European Union by 2050, compared with a fall for the US of just 10 per cent. EU living standards could be damped by half a per cent a year between 2020 and 2040. If the UK is excluded the European trend is worse, because the British went through the ageing process earlier than the Continentals and are also more fertile.[3]

[2] Taken from the World Bank's World Development Indicators, 2001.
[3] Dave Turner, Claude Giorno, Alain De Serres, Ann Vourc'h and Pete Richardson, *The Macroeconomic Implications of Ageing in a Global Context*, OECD Economics Department Working Paper No. 193, 1998.

Whether the deterioration happens like that depends to a large extent on Europe's policy response. Inward migration, later retirement, lower unemployment, increased rates of workforce participation or higher productivity could all help compensate for the demographic handicap. But in practical terms there is no escaping the fact that on unchanged policies a smaller working population will be asked to pay more to finance the pensions of an enlarged retired population. A shift to pre-funding, whereby these same workers will accumulate assets in their own private occupational pension funds, means that they will be paying twice over for pensions. And the return they earn from the residual state pay-as-you-go pension systems will be dismal or negative. Young workers are unlikely to relish this prospect, as Meinhard Miegel, managing director of the Institut für Wirtschaft und Gesellschaft of Bonn, explains in the context of Germany's recent pension reform:

> When agriculture was collectivized in the Soviet Union in the 1920s the peasants were allowed to keep small residual holdings for their private use. After a while it emerged that more was being produced on these leftover acres than on the huge collective farms. Something similar will now happen in the area of old age security in Germany. In 8 to 10 years around 2010, the persons in dependent employment will hand over 20 per cent of their gross wages in contributions and another 10 per cent in taxes to the statutory pension scheme. At the same time, many will set aside 4 per cent of their income for private provision. And soon they will notice how this 4 per cent will grow and flourish with interest and compound interest while the 30 per cent they have to pay into the pay-as-you-go system will steadily lose value, ie, achieve a negative return. This holds for everyone who is 30 or younger today. They will get much less out of the statutory system in real terms than they paid in, and the elderly will have to be satisfied with mini-returns of at most 1 per cent real. The 4 per cent saved on the side, by contrast, will grow at least as strongly as the economy as a whole.
>
> Then it will be only a matter of time before more and more members of the statutory scheme press to learn why it is that seven-eighths of their contributions to old age provision are channelled into a system where they not only earn no interest but a negative return, and why they can only invest one-eighth in interest-bearing schemes. Whoever happens to be in government at the time will have difficulties answering this question ...[4]

---

[4] Speech to members of the management of Deutsche Bank recorded in Deutsche Bank Research's *Frankfurt Voice*, 26 October 2001.

If the state pension in countries like Germany does indeed turn out to be a fraud on younger workers, it raises the prospect of what demographers call inter-generational conflict, which leads to a potential nightmare scenario. If the older members of the population use their voting power to prevent any changes in policy designed to reduce the generosity of pensions, the young will have no conventional democratic outlet for their frustrations. They would have to vent them on the streets in civil strife. It follows that if the Anglo-American model offers a solution to this demographic nightmare Continental Europe would be wise to embrace it wholeheartedly. Yet it is far from clear that it does.

For a start, simply changing the way in which pensions are financed cannot change the demographic reality whereby old people are making bigger claims on current production of goods and services. Nor should it be forgotten that private-funded pensions can also be vulnerable to demographic pressure. There are huge pension fund deficits in mature industries in the English-speaking world, where a diminishing pool of workers contributes to pension schemes in which the majority of members are retired. In the UK our regulatory regime provides inadequate protection for pensions if the company goes bankrupt when the pension fund is in deficit. In the US the semi-public Pension Benefit Guarantee Corporation provides greater security for pensions. But in older industries such as steel, where many companies are in bankruptcy, healthcare promises are unlikely to be met. George W. Bush's administration has been reluctant to take over such private sector obligations despite the obvious hardship inflicted on retirees.

The real question is whether pre-funding pensions can compensate for demographic pressure by encouraging increased saving, higher investment and greater productivity. In a paper in the mid-1970s the American economist Martin Feldstein claimed that the US pay-as-you-go social security system reduced personal saving by about 50 per cent and the country's capital stock by a further 38 per cent.[5] Yet

---

[5] Martin S. Feldstein, *Social Security, Induced Retirement and Aggregate Capital Accumulation*, Harvard Institute of Economic Research Discussion Paper No. 312, 1973.

this is scarcely convincing given that the US and Britain, both of which rely heavily on pre-funded pensions and much less on state pay-as-you-go, had the lowest rates of household savings in the Group of Seven industrialized countries when they were building up their private pension systems. In contrast, households in Germany, France and Italy, which were heavily dependent on state pay-as-you-go, were much more thrifty.

What that suggests is that, if people are required to make mandatory savings via occupational pensions, they may run down their voluntary saving, especially if they see that the stock market value of their pension has increased their wealth significantly. And there is no guarantee that higher saving will necessarily find its way into productive investment. In the jargon of the capital markets much capital spending in the 1990s' information technology and communications bubble destroyed value. Raising productivity is also more difficult in ageing societies because older workers are less mobile, less flexible in their choice of jobs and less up to date in terms of knowledge than younger workers. So the relationship between pre-funding and economic growth is complex and cannot be distilled into a simple assertion that the two go hand in hand.

When looked at in global terms it is nonetheless hard to believe that a higher level of saving via private pension schemes does not have the potential to enhance economic growth in the developing world. After all, so little capital now flows to the emerging market economies in which a majority of the world's labour force is to be found (see Chapter 2) that it would not be difficult to make a significant difference. For another aspect of the demographic story is that there has been a very rapid increase in the working age populations of emerging countries over the past 20 years or so, with potential that cries out to be exploited. If capital can be harnessed to the task of improving labour productivity in these countries, there is a big and mutually beneficial prize to be won.

Will the Chinese finance your pension?

Yet the idea that bigger capital flows to the developing world can solve the demographic problems of the more mature countries runs into a whole series of obstacles, which concern the need for some sense of common values and interests to underpin the global relationships established via the capital markets. It is essentially an issue of trust, which can best be understood by looking at financial interdependence from the perspective of people in the developing world. China makes an ideal starting point, for the People's Republic of China is not only one of the greatest foreign policy challenges confronting the West in the 21st century, it could also soon be the world's largest economy. Indeed, China accounts for such a big chunk of the developing world's economy that it provides the litmus test of how far global economic integration can go. What follows is not intended as any kind of verdict on the political and economic prospect for this hugely important actor on the global stage. Nor does it engage in the debate on the liberalization of capital flows. It merely seeks to test the assumption of so many economic liberals that emerging market economies will, in their own interest, help finance developed world pensions.

There is certainly a possibility that China will develop some of the world's biggest and most active capital markets. The Chinese have an undeniable talent for financial market activity, and the leadership in Beijing believes that well-functioning capital markets could play a vital part in increasing investment efficiency, raising productivity and underpinning fast economic growth. The global investment banking community is also putting money on the rapid growth of an Anglo-American-style financial system. Investment bankers at Goldman Sachs, for example, forecast in May 2001 that the value of China's domestic stock market would reach $2 trillion, equivalent of 65 per cent of its gross domestic product, by 2010.[6] Yet, before concluding that China will play a constructive role in financing the

---

[6] Fred Hu, *Das Kapital: Capital Markets Are Transforming China*, Goldman Sachs, Global Economics Paper No. 61.

pensions of the developed world, it is worth putting the country's capital market aspirations into a longer context. For China's history has for centuries militated against easy participation in global exchange.

In the first half of the last millennium its economic performance was vastly superior to that of Europe. The Middle Kingdom was technologically more advanced, its agriculture was more efficient and its unitary state was administered with a degree of bureaucratic professionalism unknown elsewhere in the world. While Europe overtook China in technological ability and economic performance between the 16th and 18th centuries, the Chinese economy was still the world's biggest when Europe embarked on the industrial revolution at the end of the 18th century. Yet between 1820 and 1952, while the world economy advanced as never before, China's output per head actually fell, while its share of gross world product showed a catastrophic decline from one-third to one-twentieth. Chinese income per head fell from parity with the world level to a quarter of the world average.[7]

This woeful performance was in part due to internal disorder and foreign colonial intrusion. Yet it also seems clear that the insularity of the Chinese bureaucratic elite played a significant part. The mandarin bureaucracy failed to respond to the challenges of the Western renaissance and enlightenment. Its education system and culture were inimical to Western-style scientific enquiry. Where European states were outward-looking, intensely competitive and open to trade, China showed complete indifference to developments outside its borders. The bureaucracy prevented skills in shipbuilding and navigation from being used to expand international trade. It was not much interested in extending its power and influence in foreign parts.

That history makes the reform period that began under the com-

---

[7] These figures are from Angus Maddison, *Chinese Economic Performance in the Long Run*, OECD 1998 – a superb overview of Chinese economic history on which I have drawn extensively in this chapter.

munist regime in 1978 all the more remarkable. Following the example of the other Asian tigers on its doorstep China seized the opportunity that trade provides to specialize in the production of basic goods, where it enjoyed a comparative advantage. In the 1990s the impetus provided by exposure to international trade was supplemented by a growing flow of foreign direct investment by expatriate Chinese business people and multinational companies from the US, Japan and Europe. This led to the absorption of foreign technology and a much more efficient allocation of physical and human capital.

Some question whether the outcome is reliably captured by Chinese official statistics, which point to exceptionally high rates of economic growth since 1978. But the internationally respected economic historian Angus Maddison has made careful estimates suggesting that growth in income per head increased by 6 per cent a year between 1978 and 1995. This was faster than any other country in Asia apart from Korea and was six times as fast as the world average. And if the purchasing power of the Chinese people is measured on a comparable basis to that of other countries, China has displaced Japan as the second largest economy in the world after the US since the early 1990s. On this basis, the world's top five economies are, respectively, the US, China, Japan, India and Germany. Maddison calculates that if China manages to continue growing at a rate of $5\frac{1}{2}$ per cent it would reach US levels of gross domestic product by 2015 and would account for 17 per cent of gross world product.

The joys of globalization

For China's political elite, such growth is a means of reasserting the country's power and influence in the world. It also offers them a superb opportunity for enriching their families through corrupt patronage. For the Chinese people, whose per capita incomes in 1995 were still only 11 per cent of those in the US, 13 per cent of Japan's and 20 per cent of Taiwan's, it represents a highly attractive alternative to poverty. For whatever anti-globalization protesters may believe, industrialization and economic integration have never been more appealing, by the standards of history, for the poor of the earth. This can be seen by making a comparison with the plight of the Luddites, true antecedents of today's anti-globalizers, as they came under threat from the introduction of modern machinery in Britain at the start of the 19th century.

Between 1820 and 1870 growth in per capita income was a mere 1.2 per cent. At that rate, it took 58 years for UK living standards to double. Bear in mind, too, that in 1820 the average British life expectancy for both sexes at birth was 39 years. So weavers, wool-finishers and small artisans, if they had been endowed with perfect foresight, would have known that embracing capitalism's creative destruction would have entailed a self-sacrificing inter-generational transfer of income. Industrialization would be a boon chiefly to their descendents.

The Chinese, in contrast, are looking, on Maddison's estimate, at potential growth per head of 4.5 per cent a year. On that basis it will take less than 16 years for living standards to double in a country where longevity is now on a par with the West. So capitalism is a saleable proposition for the current generation. The visible evidence of the impact of high growth is such that people willingly put up with the turmoil of large-scale migration from the country to the cities. They are prepared to tolerate big interruptions in income and lifestyle in the knowledge that their own future as well as their children's will be materially enhanced.

All this helps explain why the Chinese pursued such a relentless diplomacy to obtain access to the World Trade Organization (WTO), despite the fact that trade liberalization will create losers as well as winners in China. A World Bank paper has estimated that accession could increase global income by $56bn by 2005, of which half would accrue directly to China and a quarter to countries in the OECD developed world club.[8] Interestingly, other developing coun-

---

[8] E. Ianchovichina and W. Martin, *Trade Liberalisation in China's Accession to the WTO*, World Bank, 2001.

tries are not among those who complain loudest about trade liberalization, even though some of them are net losers from China's accession to the WTO where the removal of quotas on Chinese exports will make those exports more competitive internationally. Politicians in these countries know that trade and capital are the key to future growth. If they have a beef about the US-led global system, it is simply that they have been under-represented in its workings and their concerns have been inadequately reflected on the trade and investment agenda.

Yet there is no guarantee that the process of integrating China more fully into the global trading system will be a smooth process or that Angus Maddison's projections will be realized. This is partly because the country will be an uncomfortable bedfellow. China's exports to countries in the OECD area in 2000 were only marginally more than Belgium's. But export volume generally increases at around twice the rate of growth in gross domestic product. So if Maddison's cautious growth forecast is right, China's exports will expand at 11 per cent a year, turning the country into a dominant player in international trade and bringing even more intense competition to industries in the developed world. In flexible economies like the US, businesses will adapt and seize the opportunities for increased exports to China, together with the chance to invest directly. The less flexible Europeans will find the going tougher. Global competition imposes structural adjustment in older industries. For employees it is singularly unpleasant to be structurally adjusted, and in Europe this is bound to swell the anti-globalization chorus.

A huge question mark also hangs over China's political regime, which derives its legitimacy exclusively from very rapid economic growth. The ruling elite has been relying on the private sector to outgrow the grossly inefficient public sector, which employs more than half all urban workers. Yet, to maintain growth, the government has been forced in recent years to pump-prime the economy through more investment spending by state enterprises. The result is that the private sector is squeezed by unfair competition. And a banking crisis has been perpetuated by a build-up of bad debts in the state-owned sector, which means that less finance is available for private businesses. Problems are thus piling up for the future.

A further problem for Western investors is that Chinese governments have little tradition of dealing with rules-based organizations like the WTO where sovereignty is pooled on a treaty basis. Nor has the Chinese political elite ever fully grasped the importance of providing secure property rights to ensure that high levels of inward investment can be sustained. As Maddison puts it:

> In the course of the reform period, there have been huge changes in the Chinese economy, with a lessened role for the state, increased use of market forces, and new opportunities for individual initiative and entrepreneurship. However, the basic system of property rights is ambiguous. Peasants control their land and can lease it, but they cannot buy or sell it. The lower levels of government are engaged in both administration and entrepreneurship. The legal system and property rights are much more fuzzy than in Western countries. This situation has been inevitable, because the reform process has been legitimised as a modification of socialism rather than an embrace of capitalism.[9]

That judgement raises serious doubts over the potential returns on foreign capital in China. Will foreign investors be immune from the kind of government intervention and arbitrary taxation that has been the bureaucratic norm in China over several hundred years?

From a Chinese perspective a free flow of portfolio capital across its borders is in one important sense unnecessary. The country has a spectacularly high household savings rate of close to 40 per cent of gross domestic product. These savings go mainly into the state-owned banking system, which pours them into the black hole of China's loss-making state-owned enterprises. They also provide the government with an invaluable offset to declining tax revenues. So, until China addresses its intractable and debilitating problems with public sector enterprise, it cannot afford to allow people to export their savings abroad. Nor, with such a high savings rate, is it in any need of foreign portfolio capital. In 2000 savings exceeded investment by

---

[9] Figures once again from Angus Maddison, *Chinese Economic Performance in the Long Run*, OECD 1998.

over $20bn, which was reflected in a current account surplus on the Chinese balance of payments of the same amount. If foreign capital holds out any attraction for the Chinese elite, then, it probably lies in its potential contribution to the development of more sophisticated capital markets and a funded private pension system. The pace of such development will, of course, be decided by the ruling elite.

Such grotesque governance

The stock market is small in relation to the domestic economy, with a value at the end of 2000 of 8.5 per cent of gross domestic product.[10] Only a small part of the market, on which there were 1,100 listed companies in mid-2001, is open to foreign investors and the government in the 1990s cynically regarded capital markets as a source of cheap finance for inefficient state enterprise. Standards of corporate governance were egregiously poor and there were numerous instances of fraud and malpractice. More recently the government has moved, via the China Securities Regulatory Commission, to clean up the markets. And as less pension and welfare provision is handled by shrinking state enterprises, it seems likely that China's capital markets will play a growing part in financing retirement incomes.

Yet the ownership of companies in China is so opaque that it is extraordinarily difficult for outside shareholders or even auditors to establish whether transactions are genuine or taking place with companies related to the controlling shareholders of the quoted company.

According to Professor Larry Lang of the Chinese University of Hong Kong, a great deal of outside shareholders' money is used by controlling owners for stock market manipulation and insider-dealing rather than genuine investment in plant and machinery. But they are exceptionally clever in concealing the chicanery. This is symptomatic of a wider breakdown of public morality in China, which has led to

---

[10] Figures calculated from data in *The International Economics Analyst*, March/April 2002 (Goldman Sachs).

systemic corruption in a society where trust is deficient. Tax evasion, bribery and corruption are rife in both private and publicly owned enterprise.

It is also questionable whether China's equity and bond markets will be capable of absorbing Western pension fund money on a scale that would help the West handle its demographic problem. The universe of quoted companies would have to expand to a degree that now seems implausible. The weight of foreign capital would anyway cause asset prices to soar, which would reduce the return on foreign investors' capital. Western pension funds can, of course, obtain exposure to China's economic growth through their investment in multinational companies. But a great deal of the development of the Chinese economy is being conducted by the Chinese business diaspora – the expatriate entrepreneurs in the Asian tiger economies who maintain ties with their home villages and towns in mainland China. Their family-dominated model of corporate enterprise is not particularly friendly to outside capital. And the Chinese state still maintains controlling interests in large numbers of quoted companies. With weak corporate governance, the return on foreign capital is thus very much at the discretion of family management and the Chinese bureaucracy.

There is an important and largely overlooked question, too, concerning China's political and economic interests in the integration of global capital markets. For, while economists argue that trade is a positive sum game overall, it is not clear that the same is true of capital markets. One of the difficulties I have never seen mentioned in the economic literature is that the globalization of capital resembles a game of pass the parcel. The ageing of the population, whether in a given country, region or across the globe, is bound to impose downward pressure on asset prices as more retired people stop investing and draw on their savings. It follows that if ageing Europeans try to escape the consequences of a decline in asset prices by encouraging developing countries to pre-finance their pensions in a global capital market, they pass a very problematic parcel.

In the investment bankers' view of the world, the elderly in the developed countries will draw on their savings outside Europe, while the savings of younger countries will protect them from falling asset prices. The snag here is that China and many other developing countries are ageing much more rapidly than Europe has done because of the diffusion of medical knowledge and changes in lifestyle. Life expectancy in China – 69 years for men, 73 for women – is the highest in the developing world. Not only has the population experienced one of the fastest industrial revolutions in history, it may now also experience the fastest ageing process in history. So ageing in China and many other developing countries is largely simultaneous with Europe and Japan, even if it is happening at a much lower level of per capita income. This means that much of the population of the developing world would, if pensions were pre-funded, want to draw on its investments at the same time as people in the developed world. The Chinese might reasonably respond to those who see the globalization of capital as the answer to demographic pressure by asking where they are supposed to invest to deal with their problems. The only young continent left by the middle of the 21st century will be Africa, where the political and economic prospects remain difficult. And poor Africans might reasonably ask in turn to whom they are supposed to pass the investment parcel, if they are to avoid playing host to an apocalyptic, demographically induced endgame: the greatest capital market boom and bust in financial history.[11]

It is, then, hard to escape the conclusion that the notion of full global capital market integration is a politically naive and Utopian dream. Countries like China and India, which account for not far short of half the developing world's gross domestic product, can obtain enough of the fruits of globalization from trade and foreign direct investment without feeling any need to regard the liberalization of portfolio capital as an equally pressing imperative. China has, after all, pulled off one of the most rapid industrializations in the history of the world without a significant inflow of foreign portfolio capital. For

---

[11] For data on ageing in the developing world, see *Averting the Old Age Crisis*, World Bank/OUP, 1994.

their part, the ageing Europeans would be taking an unconscionable political risk in putting much of their pension fund nest egg into this potentially vast economy. Financial interdependence sits ill with a low-trust economic environment and a political regime of questionable legitimacy. Instead they will probably address their demographic problems not only through more pre-funding of pensions, but by a variety of other means including swelling the supply of labour. More women will be drawn into the workforce, while ways will be found to make continuing work more attractive to old people. And both Europeans and Asians will, I suspect, continue to look to the US as the global capital importer of last resort, the pre-eminent home for pension fund money. This is not completely crazy: the US is, after all, a younger and more robust economy than Europe, a net recipient of immigrants, a healthy democracy and the home of the biggest capital market in the world. The risk if portfolio capital is trapped in the developed world in this way is that it may end up contributing to further stock market bubbles and wasteful investment in the US when the balance of economic activity in the world shifts further to Asia.

No doubt the world will find a way of muddling through in the face of the demographic challenge. Reform in Europe will continue to be slow and insufficient because the nature of demographic pressure is that it is a slow-burn affair that never produces a crisis. There is no early shock to provide the impetus for politicians to convince electorates of the need to accept higher pension contributions, lower retirement benefits or other reforms. And it may be that the scope for addressing the challenge by means other than pre-funding pensions is such that the demographic time bomb may prove to be less frightening than has been suggested by people with a powerful vested interest in increased private pension provision. But of one thing there can be no doubt at all. As any realistic consideration of the case of China demonstrates, the elegant global solution proposed by economic liberals is simply not going to happen. On demography they are offering a false prospectus.

9

The semi-detached samurai

On 12 July 2001 Hiroshi Okuda, Chairman of Toyota Motor Corporation, gave the keynote speech at a dinner for representatives of some of the world's most powerful investment institutions. They were members of the International Corporate Governance Network, a private sector group that aims to promote good corporate governance across the world. Between them these money moguls spoke for some $10 trillion of portfolio capital – a sum equivalent to more than two and a half times Japan's gross domestic product (GDP). The dinner, at Happo-en, one of Tokyo's finer traditional restaurants, was the high point of the network's annual conference. No more powerful Japanese industrialist could have been found to address this gathering. As well as being chairman of Nikkeiren, the Japan Federation of Employers' Associations, Okuda was a member of Prime Minister Junichiro Koizumi's main economic policy-making body, the Council on Economic and Fiscal Policy, which was charged with implementing Koizumi's slogan of "no economic recovery without structural reform".

Yet this scion of the Japanese industrial establishment took the opportunity to deliver what the non-Japanese diners could only interpret as an extraordinarily patronizing snub. His message was that it would be irresponsible to run Japanese companies in the interests of shareholders. And he conveyed it by explaining what Japanese junior high school textbooks said about corporate social responsibility. Under Japanese law shareholders are the owners of the corporation. But if corporations are run exclusively in the interests of shareholders,

Japanese children are taught, short-term profit will take precedence over considerations such as research and development or employment. To be sustainable, runs the argument, companies need to look after their relationships with stakeholders such as employees, suppliers and local communities. So, whatever the legal position, the textbooks insist, companies do not belong to their owners.

Japanese textbooks have a certain notoriety, most notably in relation to their inaccurate historical accounts of the behaviour of the Japanese military in China in the 1930s and 1940s. On this evidence they also appear to be deficient on corporate behaviour too. There is an extensive economic literature, for example, showing that stock markets respond favourably to higher research and development spending and take a long-term view of it. And the 1990s' US stock market bubble was an illustration of how the Anglo-American model was just as capable as the Japanese one of taking long-termism to extremes, since investors were wildly overexcited about profits that would take aeons to materialize, just as they were in the earlier Japanese bubble.

Interestingly, all reference to junior high school textbooks in Okuda's speech was expunged from the official record of the conference prepared by the Japanese hosting committee, which suggests that the hosts recognized that his homily was potentially embarrassing.[1] Yet the Chairman of Toyota was at least being realistic about the extent of Japanese exceptionalism on the questions of what companies are for and whose interests they serve. Most Japanese industrialists have no wish to converge on the Anglo-American shareholder value model and regard shareholders as an irritating irrelevance. They are strongly attached to a model that Brian Reading, one of the most perceptive outside observers of the Japanese economy, calls corporate communism.[2] It is a model that delivers returns on capital well below global standards. But how, it might be asked, has the country achieved

---

[1] The account here is from my own notes taken at the dinner.

[2] See his *Japan: The Coming Collapse*, Weidenfeld and Nicolson, 1992, which remains the most perceptive account of the Japanese bubble and its consequences.

such extraordinary economic success over the past half-century if
there is no accountability to shareholders and no respect for the
capital interest?

Pre-bubble bliss

For much of the post-war period Japanese quoted equity shares were
held mainly by companies and by financial institutions such as
insurers and banks. These were largely cross-shareholdings designed
to cement relationships within *keiretsu* groups, loose-knit quasi-
conglomerates in which the participating companies had mutually
supportive trading links and a long-term connection with a main
bank. These loyalties extended to the employees, who drank the
beer or bought the cars produced by companies in their own *keiretsu*.
Cross-holdings also served the purpose of keeping predators at bay.
Loyal corporate members of any *keiretsu* could be relied on to spurn
unwelcome bids from outsiders for fellow *keiretsu* members, which is
why hostile takeovers are virtually non-existent in Japan. Foreign
corporate raiders such as the Texan T. Boone Pickens have failed
to penetrate these samurai defences. Yet despite the apparent cosiness
of this system *keiretsu* groups competed fiercely against each other. In
areas such as motors and consumer electronics they were phenomenally competitive in world markets.

Returns on capital and dividends in Japan have always been low as
companies have obsessively invested in new productive capacity and
pursued market share. Those shareholders who were interested in
achieving a decent return took it in the form of capital gains on an
ever-rising stock market. Or, if they were foreigners, they took it
through an appreciating yen as well. Yet most Japanese people preferred to put their savings into the safe and heavily regulated banks.
The banks, whose lending priorities were influenced by government
bureaucrats, were happy to extend credit on the collateral of company
property that always seemed to go up in value. Companies in the
keiretsu groups were equally happy to borrow because their main
bank would support long-term investment plans, which in turn

permitted lifetime employment. And employees throughout the economy did well. In the three and a half decades to the mid-1990s unemployment did not exceed 3 per cent.

Accountability to shareholders was deemed unnecessary in this relationship-based system because the consensualism that prevailed in hierarchically organized companies provided a strong internal discipline, while the banks acted as external guardians, monitoring the companies within their *keiretsu*. If a company ran into trouble the main bank would step in and sort out the management. Since the bank had access to privileged financial information and employees provided a check on management from within, the need for a strong external audit function was not as great as in the US and UK systems. But then came the 1980s Japanese bubble, which collapsed in the early 1990s. Since then the Japanese economy has stagnated. By December 2001 unemployment had risen to its highest level since 1945 at 5.6 per cent.

Welfare penury

This was a catastrophe in Japan, which lacks an adequate welfare system to handle the financial strains experienced by the unemployed. In the past, the inefficient service sectors of the economy provided a private welfare safety net by employing far more people than they needed. Large companies in the more competitive sectors of the economy also offered a welfare cocoon since their employees were scarcely ever sacked. The erosion of the safety net has had profound implications. For, in a workaholic country where self-definition and self-respect were very much tied to employment, to be fired was a greater psychological disaster than in the US or even Europe. Early in the new millennium there was growing governmental concern over an alarming rise in the suicide rate. The banking system, meantime, had long been in a state of turmoil and all attempts to reform the economic structure were blocked at every turn by powerful vested interests.

In some respects the Japanese bubble was not unlike the subsequent

US bubble of the late 1990s. For a period the stock market rode so high that capital was extraordinarily cheap. Interest rates were low. So Japanese companies overinvested in low-return projects of marginal viability. Newly deregulated banks plunged heavily into property lending. And there were scandals galore, involving criminality on a scale that makes the Enron saga look tame by comparison. Yet the misallocation of capital was worse than in the subsequent US bubble because the banks had no experience of estimating or managing credit risk. Their loans had always been steered to whatever tasks the government's powerful bureaucrats wished them to undertake. Unlike US banks they were also vulnerable to any fall in the stock market because of their large cross-shareholdings. When the market went into a tailspin these holdings collapsed in value, causing the banks' capital to shrink. At the lowest point since 1990 the Japanese equity market stood at a quarter of its bubble era peak. And when the property market embarked on a 10-year decline, which continued into the new millennium, the banks' bad debts spiralled.

As with the US after the 1929 Wall Street crash, the Japanese have been left with a huge burden of debt, along with assets that have greatly diminished in value. In the corporate sector Toyota is unusual in the strength of its balance sheet. Other companies are stretched. In the case of Toyota's troubled rival Nissan, a foreign owner Renault has taken management control in a move that would have been unthinkable in such a nationalistic country a decade ago. Yet the market in corporate control remains confined to distressed companies, ensuring that Japan is imperfectly integrated into the global capital markets. And Japan's problem has been compounded by a difficulty that did not affect the US between the wars, in the shape of unhelpful demographics. Ageing is occurring faster in Japan than in any other large developed country. Economists have estimated that the ratio of dependent people to those in work could rise from a level of 44 per cent in the late 1990s to 65 per cent by 2020. Continuing deterioration in the ratio suggests that per capita gross domestic product could fall by 23 per cent by 2050, compared with 10 per cent for the US and 18 per cent for the

European Union.[3] Yet the current peculiarity of Japan is that it has an extraordinarily large number of people in the age groups that are busy saving for retirement, while relatively few who are actually retired. Also striking is the small number of young people in the economy, which means that the workforce is expected to shrink at a rate of just over half a per cent a year for the first 20 years of the century.

Thrift and super-thrift

The result is that Japan saves much more than it invests. Its national savings rate is higher than that of any other country in the Organization for Economic Cooperation and Development rich nations' club apart from Korea. Because the ageing process has taken place ahead of most other countries, Japan, unlike China, is in a privileged position where globalization does have the potential to provide part of the solution to demographic strain. It would make sense for the country to run an even larger current account surplus on its balance of payments than it does at present, while exporting more surplus capital to the rest of the world. Then in due course, as the retired population increases, savings will run down and it could draw on its overseas investments. Yet there is a monumental difficulty in getting from here to there, not least because this excess of savings, together with the legacy of private sector debt accumulated during and after the bubble, causes the economy to suffer from a shortage of demand. Early in 2002 prices were falling at a rate of about 2 per cent a year in the first potentially serious deflation the developed world had seen since the slump of the 1930s.

Part of the problem is that while Japan is now a mature economy it has not yet adjusted to that reality. While the rate at which it invests in plant and machinery has fallen, its business people nonetheless managed, in the depressed Japanese economy of the late 1990s, to invest even more than Americans did in the course of their contemporaneous wild and wasteful investment boom. Put another

---

[3] *The Macroeconomic Implications of Ageing in a Global Context*, OECD Economics Department Working Paper No. 193, 1998.

way, Japan has continued to invest at the kind of rates more normally seen in developing economies despite there being fewer profitable investment opportunities now that the country has caught up with the West. The result is that much capital in recent years has been going into inefficient investment where the returns are well below global standards. And much more of Japanese business investment has been financed by short-term debt than is normal in the English-speaking economies where greater reliance is placed on equity financing. With falling prices the value of this debt is increasing, while the value of the assets financed by the debt is falling. The plight of the banking system has worsened as its customers have been squeezed. And with interest rates at record low levels, retirement incomes appear depressed. There is thus an overwhelming need to raise the return on capital in Japan closer to global levels while bringing down the level of investment.[4]

The trouble is that no corporate governance mechanism exists to secure this change. As the banking crisis has grown worse, the banks have been selling off their cross-shareholdings, causing the *keiretsu* links to weaken. They no longer have an incentive to monitor company performance so closely. Insurance companies, trust banks, pension funds and other professional investors have no tradition of calling management to account. In the Japanese model of capitalism that was never expected of them. At the same time accountancy and auditing in Japan are weak. Japanese accounting firms were often themselves part of the *keiretsu* group whose companies they audited. They could scarcely be called independent and, despite establishing affiliations with the big five global accountancy firms, their standards were poor. Indeed, a leading figure in the American Chamber of Commerce in Tokyo, lawyer Anthony Zaloom, declares bluntly that auditing practices are terrible. As a result capital inflows into Japan

---

[4] The economic analysis in this chapter draws on a succession of research papers by Andrew Smithers of Smithers & Co. and Brian Reading of Lombard Street Research. It has also been informed by interviews at the Japanese Ministry of Finance and the Bank of Japan over a decade and a half, and my conversations with Ariyoshi Okumura.

are seriously impeded because foreign direct investors are nervous about taking over Japanese companies. Under US pressure, the Japanese government is forcing the banks to improve their accountancy practices. But Japanese business is not going to write down the value of its assets to realistic levels, least of all when the real value of its debts is increasing thanks to deflation. Nor will industrialists lightly abandon their long-standing habit of excessive and inefficient investment.

There is, in fact, a nascent corporate governance movement in Japan that is trying hard to promote shareholder value. A few leading industrialists have broken ranks with the establishment to push for greater external accountability for boards that are usually steered by over-dominant bosses. And the country even has a shareholder activist in the shape of Yoshiaki Murakami, an engaging former bureaucrat at the Ministry of International Trade and Industry, who brings a missionary fervour to corporate governance. He has been prepared to flout the tradition of corporate consensualism and wage proxy battles against underperforming companies that engage in wasteful investment. His biggest battle to date has been at Tokyo Style, an apparel-maker that in 2002 had $950m of cash and securities sitting idle in its balance sheet yielding a minimal return. Its dividend policy was absurdly ungenerous, and the company was proposing to move into property development, an area in which it had no expertise.

Murakami's company M & A Consulting put proxy resolutions at the annual meeting for the company to buy back shares and increase the dividend. It also proposed the appointment to the board of an independent non-executive director, in the shape of Ariyoshi Okumura, a former director of the Industrial Bank of Japan (now part of the Mizuho banking group) and a leading light of the corporate governance movement. Though this rebel initiative failed, Murakami's proposals attracted a surprisingly high protest vote. They also exposed cronyism among the big banks, insurers and other cross-shareholders in Tokyo Style. Despite the poor profitability and financial weakness of some of these institutions, they rejected the opportunity to vote for a much increased dividend. So they blatantly failed to observe their fiduciary duty to their own shareholders and beneficiaries to secure the best return.

For all that, Yoshiaki Murakami remains a singular figure in a country where individualism is not admired. And, despite the reformist rhetoric of Junichiro Koizumi and his government, there is no real consensus for radical reform. Koizumi's efforts have been hampered at every turn by the barons of his own Liberal Democratic Party. Meantime the Ministry of Justice's recent proposals for the revision of the commercial code have been flabby. While advancing a number of significant corporate governance reforms, such as calling for more non-executive directors, it has declined to make them mandatory. The fact remains that a majority of industrialists share the view of Toyota's Hiroshi Okuda about the responsibilities of companies to stakeholders other than shareholders. And as a senior member of the business community has pointed out to me, for most Japanese industrialists the phrase corporate governance is an unpleasantly alien import that they associate with the so-called Black Ships – the American force led by Commodore Perry in 1853–4 that put an end to the policy of national seclusion pursued by Japan since the 17th century under the Tokugawa shoguns.

There is, then, a corporate governance vacuum in Japan and no immediate likelihood that the country will move closer to the Anglo-American capital market model except at snail's pace. Whatever the flaws of that model, it has to be acknowledged that the plight of the Japanese highlights its greatest strength: flexibility in confronting the need for change. In the absence of a hostile takeover discipline the Japanese have no satisfactory mechanism for creative destruction. Capital is reallocated slowly within large companies or *keiretsu* groups in a way that is highly respectful of the workers. This paternalistic corporatism is attractively humane when compared with the more brutal Anglo-American way of treating workers. But it is not well designed to handle new challenges and shocks. And it should be noted in passing that the Japanese also suffer from a fundamental disadvantage relative to the US in adopting newer technologies in the information area. Japanese character writing is not easy to adapt for keyboards and the use of Japanese on computers is complex.

The illusion of riches

There is one sense, oddly enough, in which this inflexibility is helpful. Anglo-American-style shock treatment now would simply increase the deflationary pressure in the economy as more people became unemployed in the short term. Yet in the long run there remains a problem. Assuming Japan does somehow make the transition to economic maturity with a lower level of investment and lower savings, creative destruction will be both possible and desirable. In the interim the Japanese people will continue to find themselves in a rather odd financial relationship with the rest of the world. On the face of it, they are incredibly rich. Their net wealth at the start of the millennium amounted to 723 per cent of their disposable income, compared with a comparable figure for Americans of only 637 per cent.[5] Yet the official statisticians' numbers describe a cloud cuckoo land. The wives, who do all the saving and investing in Japanese households, invest heavily in Japanese banks and insurance companies. As we have seen, the banks' assets have plunged in value since the bursting of the bubble, although they had not been written down to remotely realistic values at the start of 2000. And many insurance companies are in deep trouble. They are not generating a sufficient return on their assets to meet existing pension obligations, but, like the banks, they have not adopted realistic accounting. This has led to an extraordinary situation where independent estimates of the value of the assets and liabilities of the life assurance industry in one of the world biggest economies suggest that the industry is hopelessly insolvent.[6] What is

---

[5] These figures in the OECD Economic Outlook are provided by Japan's Economic Planning Agency.

[6] *Japanese Life Insurance: Waiting for Inflation*, Smithers & Co. Report No. 172 by Andrew Smithers, 31 January, 2002. The report, compiled with help from consulting actuaries Tillinghast, estimated the industry's liabilities at then current interest rates to be Y247 trillion, while assets had a book value of only Y183 trillion.

clear is that Japanese household wealth is significantly overstated if allowance is made for the losses incurred over the past decade.

The other big outlet for Japanese housewives' cash is the postal savings and life insurance system. This money is managed by the Ministry of Finance's Trust Fund Bureau and goes into a special government budget called *Zaito*. It is used to make loans to public corporations for infrastructure developments, public works, home loans and small business loans, operating like a public sector banking system. And this is partly how the government has tried to address the problem of excess savings in the Japanese economy. In the 1990s it vastly increased public spending, with the result that gross government debt rose from 65 per cent of GDP in 1990 to a disturbingly high 123 per cent in 2000, which is expected by most forecasters to rise to 150 per cent by mid-decade. But if the assets of the social security system and the investments and loans made by the Trust Fund Bureau are deducted from the government's liabilities, the outstanding debt in 1990 falls to 51 per cent.

Unfortunately public sector accounting in Japan is as wayward as private sector accounting. The Bureau's lending and investing operations have been subject to pork-barrel political influence [funds to win votes], with the result that huge losses have been incurred on the politicians' pet schemes, probably amounting to more than half the value of the original investments and loans. Japan is littered with magnificent, but underused road schemes, bridges and other expensive infrastructure projects. As a Ministry of Finance official once said to me half-humorously, half in despair, he was tired of financing bridges that would be used chiefly by badgers and bears. Yet the Ministry of Finance has been reluctant to acknowledge publicly the full extent of the losses on these dubious projects financed via the *Zaito*.

Meantime the Trust Fund Bureau also invests postal savings in Japanese government bonds. In fact the public sector is the biggest buyer of new government bonds. It provides the mechanism whereby the country's excessive savings depress the yield on these IOUs to an exceptionally low level by international standards. At the start of 2002 Italy, which had gross government debt of 111 per cent of

GDP in 2000, rather less than Japan, was paying 5.2 per cent interest on government 10-year bonds, compared with 1.4 for Japanese government bonds of similar duration. In fact the Japanese government's bill for debt interest was lower than that of any other country in the Group of Seven industrialised countries, despite its outstanding debt being the highest in the G7. As for the return on bank deposits, short-term interest rates at the start of 2002 were zero.

Corporate zombies

This highlights another inflexible aspect of Japan's corporatist model. After the bubble, loose fiscal policy should have provided a window of opportunity. For with the government committed to debt-financed pump-priming of the economy, the human cost of reshaping the banking system and dealing with excess capacity in industry and commerce would have been lessened. But not only did the country lack a governance mechanism capable of raising the return on capital, low or zero short-term interest rates also meant that over-indebted companies continued in business because little cash was needed to service the debt. The persistence of the corporate living dead, known as zombie companies, meant that excess capacity became endemic in some industrial sectors, so that hitherto healthy companies were weakened.

Meantime the limited restructuring that did take place put the fear of unemployment into the hearts of Japanese workers, making them less willing to spend, thereby exacerbating the deflationary forces in the economy. And, because the banks were not required to acknowledge the real losses on their loans, they too were able to soldier on – very dangerously for the global financial system. In attempting to trade their way out of trouble in the 1990s, many took high risks in the hope of generating high profits, especially in the Asian tiger economies. They thus made a thoroughly malign contribution to the stock market and property bubbles that led to the Asian crisis of 1997–98.

This is not how globalization is meant to work. And Japan remains out of line with the rest of the world in terms of the value of its assets and the returns those assets generate. Even allowing for the fact that in the Japanese deflationary environment cash that pays no nominal interest actually has a positive real return because it is going up in value thanks to the fall in the price level, that real return has been low by global standards. So, too, has been the return on government bonds. Hence the fact that non-resident investors held only 5.6 per cent of outstanding Japanese government bonds in 2001, compared with 21.6 per cent for the US. The percentage of listed equities held by foreigners stood at 18.8 per cent at that time, which was much closer to the norms for other industrialized countries with large stock markets.[7] But this arguably represented a triumph of foreign hope over experience. Throughout the 1990s foreign investors were the marginal buyers of Japanese equities, absorbing the stock that Japanese institutions shed as they unwound their cross-shareholdings. The return on this foreign investment was usually negative.

Debts and defaults

There is now a big question of whether Japan can service its large public sector debts, which would double if the present value of its unfunded pensions liabilities were taken into account. In 2001 the Japanese economy shrank, while the burden of debt increased in real terms by 1.5 to 2 per cent. Most historical precedents suggest that it is difficult to cope with such a high level of debt, unless economic growth – and thus the ability to service debt – is running at a much higher level than demographically stressed Japan is going to deliver in the next two decades.

---

[7] Figures from the Ministry of Finance website, quoted by Professor Sahoko Kaji of Keio University in *Japan's Lost Decade, the Koizumi Reforms and Prospects for the Future*, a discussion paper for the French Institute of International Relations (IFRI), December 2001.

To stabilize the debt, it would be necessary either for Japan's economic growth rate to exceed interest rates on the debt; or, if growth fell short, for the public sector to run a budget surplus before interest – a "primary" budget surplus – sufficient to offset the amount by which interest rates exceeded the growth rate. Lombard Street Research's Brian Reading points out that Japan would have needed a primary surplus of 4 per cent of GDP in 2001 to keep the debt-to-GDP ratio from rising. Instead it had a deficit of 5 per cent. On that basis it would require a huge improvement of 9 per cent of GDP for Japan to reverse the slide into a debt trap. The problem of achieving such a turnround is compounded by a double bind. Tightening the budget when the economy is weak might add to the deflationary pressures in the economy and knock recovery on the head.

Most developed countries, when confronted with the problem of a mountainous public sector debt burden, have found it too difficult. They have either formally repudiated the debt, as Italy did between the wars under Mussolini through debt conversions, or they have defaulted less explicitly through inflation, which erodes the real value of the outstanding debt, as the UK did in the 1970s. That said, the ability to service public sector debt is extremely sensitive to the rate of economic growth. And it is just possible that Japan could find its way out of the debt trap without a catastrophic inflation that would destroy the savings of the ageing Japanese people. If the country's excess savings were diverted from financing public expenditure at home, to investment overseas, the resulting capital outflow would weaken the yen and create a modest inflation that would restore some value to Japanese assets and reduce the burden of the liabilities in the public and corporate sectors.

Yet this would be a politically tricky course. The US might tolerate a weaker yen against the dollar on the basis that continuing capital inflows from Japan would make an uncomfortably rapid, belt-tightening reduction of the US current account deficit less likely. But the rest of the world including China might not take kindly to the increased Japanese export competitiveness that would result from a yen depreciation. Back at home, there are practical obstacles.

Japan's experience of hyper-inflation after the war and 20 per cent-plus inflation in the mid-1970s means that it is hard to persuade an older generation of policy-makers to see inflation as a solution rather than a problem. Such a policy is also very risky because it requires a shock-free economic environment if domestic confidence in the value of the currency is not to crack.

The Japanese government has long been adamant that inflation is not on the agenda and that public sector debts will be honoured in real as well as nominal terms. Politicians and officials deeply resent decisions by the international rating agencies to downgrade the country's credit rating to the level of Botswana when it remains a big international creditor. The government's debts are owed chiefly to the Japanese, not to foreigners. Yet there remains a risk in the current decade that Japanese investors and savers may conclude that there is not a ghost's chance that either the government or the corporate sector will honour their outstanding debts in real terms. In the event of a panic, there would be an exodus from the government bond market. The resulting collapse in bond prices would further damage the banks, which invest heavily in government IOUs. And money would look for outlets overseas. Panic-induced capital flight would almost certainly force the government into a dramatic retreat from globalization because it would feel obliged to introduce capital controls to limit the financial damage. The question then would be whether the shock would be sufficient to provide a platform for renewed growth or whether it might be thoroughly destabilizing.

It is dangerous to underestimate Japan's capacity to respond dramatically to shocks. Before the Meiji restoration of 1868 this was a feudal society incapable of defending itself against a foreign invasion. By 1905, after the fastest industrialization in history until then, it was a great power capable of humbling Russia in a full-scale war. Looked at in historic context, the risk is that the political strains resulting from a huge loss of Japanese people's savings would lead to a backlash taking the form of a return to right-wing nationalism. Europe, where the Weimar hyperinflation paved the way for the rise of Adolf Hitler, provides an unnerving precedent. It is doubly unnerving given that an extreme nationalist politician, Shintaro Ishihara, the populist right-wing Governor of Tokyo, stands ready in the wings to exploit any opportunity.

On the other hand, an unexpected inflation might just provide the beneficial shock necessary to turn the country's samurai instincts toward making the overdue adjustment to economic maturity. It might then be able to embrace a process of creative destruction without precipitating renewed deflationary pressure. One does not have to be an uncritical fan of Anglo-American capital discipline to see that Japan will need more of that discipline in due course if restructuring is to happen. Until then Japan, despite being the developed world's biggest creditor country, will remain imperfectly integrated into the global capital market. Its form of capitalism has been phenomenally successful, but it was designed for a smaller, more dynamic economy that was still in the catch-up phase. Today the model has become a luxury that only cash-rich giants like Toyota can still afford. As with the zombie companies, it is a model that lives on borrowed time. If Japan cannot bring itself to give capital its due reward it will condemn itself to continuing economic stagnation or worse.

Part 4

Beyond Shareholder Value

10

The legitimacy crisis

With hindsight, George W. Bush's arrival in the White House was a watershed for globalization. In foreign policy his administration's commitment to multilateral solutions was strictly á la carte. So, too, with trade, where the shift toward a protectionist stance on steel imports and farm subsidies in 2002 looked an ominous pointer for the world. As for capital, the picture was more complex. This was not an administration that was ever going to look for grand global solutions to the problem of financial instability, any more than it would willingly engage in nation-building in Afghanistan. It seems unlikely, though, that the administration would have found much support outside the US for ambitious global initiatives. The political will across the world for economic policy coordination on a grand scale simply does not exist.

That said, the new American flirtation with trade barriers is unlikely to extend to financial protection in the shape of constraints on private capital flows. The US, with its huge foreign direct investments, vast financing requirement for its payments deficit and its dominant position in global investment banking, has an important interest in giving capital as free an international rein as possible. Yet the collapse of Enron, the fiasco of the high-tech bubble, the demise of numerous telecoms companies and the many accountancy frauds have combined to turn the US capital market model into a more problematic export. Corporate scandals and stock market crashes are admittedly part of the counterpoint of the capitalist system.

Bankruptcy is essential to its dynamic. But, just as Robert Maxwell's looting of pension funds in the UK set back the cause of independent funding of pension schemes in Continental Europe for years, there is a possibility that Enron, WorldCom and all the other scandals will have a similar demonstration effect on a global basis.

Admittedly, the notion that globalization could ever push the world toward an Anglo-American capitalist straitjacket was always far-fetched. As long as there are different legal systems, different national cultures and, for that matter, different appetites for given levels of economic growth, capital will behave according to a wide variety of rules. But the desire for convergence on what, since Enron, is widely perceived to be a flawed US capital market model is waning. The model has, moreover, turned out to be much closer to the crony capitalist models of Asia than previously assumed.

Yet it would be wrong to pass too harsh a verdict on the workings of American-dominated global capital markets over the past decade. Without the globalization of capital flows, the Japanese economy might have sunk into a deep depression because its excess savings would have had a profoundly deflationary impact if Japan had been a closed economy. The country would have been condemned to relive the experience of the 1930s' Slump. Instead the economy merely stagnated and its surplus savings helped finance the American current account deficit, thereby encouraging the US to act as the spender of last resort in the global economy. The ability of the US to run such a colossal deficit was likewise crucial in preventing the Asian crisis from turning into a more protracted disaster. And with both Japan and Continental Europe over-dependent on export-led growth, the world still badly needs this US growth locomotive.

Moreover, despite the evaporation of the high-tech euphoria, the US did not suffer a quick-fire stock market crash followed by a slump of the kind that afflicted the country after 1929. The recession of 2001 was mild thanks to the sharp reflexes of the US Federal Reserve, which slashed interest rates again and again that year. So while the stock market bubble may not have been the smooth capital recycling process trumpeted by the great and good in Washington, it still ensured that e-commerce developed very rapidly. Whether that would or could have happened in Europe or Japan is moot. And whatever may have gone wrong, the Anglo-American model does not have problems of the kind that confront the German or Japanese systems, which sit uneasily with globalization. The model that evolved in the English-speaking countries has, in contrast, been remarkably flexible in addressing the strains of globalization.

Festering imbalance

Yet to suggest that the flow of cross-border capital has facilitated higher global growth and saved some countries from economic disaster is not the same as saying that the Anglo-American capital market model has worked perfectly. There has been a downside. To recap, the story of the economic cycle in the English-speaking countries in the 1990s was one of economies becoming increasingly hostage to the movements of their highly developed stock markets. As stock market values soared into historically outlandish territory from the mid-1990s, the consequent rise in household wealth was associated with a decline in savings. And because a rise in equity prices causes the cost of capital to fall, companies embarked on an excessive and wasteful investment binge. With savings in the US falling to near-zero as a percentage of household income, the boom had to be financed by foreigners, with the result that by 2000 the US was sucking in $1.2bn a day from the rest of the world just to keep its current account stable. These so-called imbalances, which also afflicted the UK and other English-speaking countries, were not a problem for the bank-dominated systems of Continental Europe. Because equity holdings were a much smaller proportion of their household wealth, the rise in stock markets did not lead to a comparable decline in savings.

The US bubble nonetheless had global consequences in a way that the Japanese bubble of the 1980s did not, because Americans borrowed and consumed on such a huge scale. And the world economy's new sensitivity in the 1990s to stock market wealth effects posed an exceptionally difficult challenge to policy-makers. The response of Alan Greenspan's Federal Reserve, as we saw in Chapter 3, was to let the markets rule on the way up, but to put a safety net under equity prices whenever a financial crisis threatened to bring the market down. Then, when the bubble burst, the Fed responded much more rapidly than the Bank of Japan did a decade earlier in the attempt to put the economic show back on the road. The result was that the global economic cycle was extended and an immediate deflation in the US was averted.

On the face of it, the US had pulled off a remarkable trick. It appeared to have defied historical precedent by experiencing a bubble that was not followed by a devastating financial crisis. Yet any verdict on this huge experiment in economic management has to be provisional because little attempt had been made by mid-2002 to address the imbalances that accumulated in the economy over the 1990s. Companies and households remained over-borrowed, the government had moved from surplus to deficit and the current account of the balance of payments remained stubbornly vast.

Economists usually discuss the impact of a falling stock market on the economy in terms of its impact on the wealth of households and the consequent effect on household spending and saving. They also focus on the way a falling market causes companies' cost of capital to rise. Yet the striking feature of the market slide that began in 2000 was that it left companies much more vulnerable than in previous market downturns. They were prey to a novel kind of negative wealth effect. Such was the growth in the size of company pension funds over the previous two decades that they had become an important factor for corporate profitability and even solvency.

Pension fund glasnost

In previous bear markets nobody worried too much if pension funds sank into deficit because actuaries smoothed the numbers when they valued pension funds. This rendered market fluctuations relatively harmless. Little information about the solvency of pension funds appeared in company accounts. But in the 1990s accounting for company pension costs became more transparent. So the bear market had an impact not unlike that of glasnost in the old Soviet Union. It exposed an economic reality that people had previously been no more than faintly aware of. One aspect of this economic reality was that many large companies in mature industries were dwarfed by their own pension schemes. In 2001 in the US, for example, General Motor's pension assets of $74bn were worth 271 per cent of the company's stock market capitalization, while US Steel's pension assets of $8.6bn were worth as much as 531 per cent of its market capitalization. Many companies in the UK were in a comparable position. In 2002 the equity holdings of British Airways' pension fund were worth more than three times the company's value in the stock market.

This creates enormous corporate vulnerability to the gyrations of equity prices, especially in mature sectors of the economy where defined benefit pension schemes predominate. Although defined benefit pension funds may be legally separate from their sponsoring company, the company cannot escape the underlying economic reality, which is that the pension fund is an investment subsidiary. Its pension obligations are similar to long-term debt in the company balance sheet. Trying to meet such obligations by investing in equities is dangerous, because the assets and liabilities are poorly matched. When equities go down, the pension liabilities remain stubbornly the same. Or they may even go up because of increased longevity among pension scheme members. The implication is that where the fund is very large in relation to the company, corporate appearances are deceptive. British Airways, for example, could reasonably be characterized as a hedge fund with a sideline in air transport. Its viability is even more dependent on the mood swings of the equity market than on the fortunes of the airline business.

A falling stock market affects companies via their pension funds in a number of ways. Cash flow is hit because contributions into the fund have to go up to cope with widening pension fund deficits.

Credit-rating agencies have started to worry about such deficits and increasingly take them into account in assessing companies' credit-worthiness. Investors are also becoming more conscious of the risks inherent in pensions. And companies themselves respond to the negative wealth effect in their pension fund by acting more cautiously. General Motors was one of many companies in 2002 that felt obliged to place heavy emphasis on tidying up its balance sheet. Such retrenchment, however desirable in the circumstances, can take the focus away from the development of the operating businesses while leading to cuts in capital spending. And there was a psychological reaction in boardrooms across the English-speaking economies. The newly cautious instincts of directors whose stock options were already down in value, or completely worthless, were made more cautious by bad news emanating from the pension fund.

Actuarial hokum

Companies' vulnerability was compounded because actuaries had often employed flawed methodologies in valuing pension funds during the boom. In the UK many of them had adopted a curious valuation basis, lacking in any theoretical economic justification, whereby a higher exposure to equities led to lower company contributions into the pension fund. So managers working under the intense pressure for short-term performance imposed by the capital markets had an overwhelming incentive to invest in equities despite the higher risks involved relative to investing in bonds. Similarly dubious techniques were used in America, but with the further complication that the US generally accepted accounting principles allowed companies to vary the pension costs they charged in their profit-and-loss account according to their assumptions about future investment returns.[1] Not surprisingly, some companies raised their

---

[1] See my article "Bubble, bubble default trouble", in the *Financial Times*, 4 October, 2002, for a more detailed exploration of actuarial hokum.

estimates of expected returns progressively as the equity market rose throughout the 1990s, which conveniently boosted profits. Yet this was illogical, for the more expensive equity prices became the lower future returns were likely to be.

By 2002, when the bear market was well under way, the investment bank UBS Warburg found that about 60 per cent of the companies in the S&P 500 index were assuming a return on assets of 9–10 per cent, while 20 per cent were assuming more than 10 per cent. Given that most funds had part of their portfolio in bonds, which return less than equities, the assumed equity return was even higher – and well above the long-run historical average growth in real terms of 6–7 per cent.[2]

To return to the larger picture, both the US economy and the world economy remained vulnerable to an over-rapid adjustment of the imbalances. One risk was that rising inflation and a collapsing dollar would prompt an upward move in long-term interest rates, causing a synchronized plunge in the value of equities, bonds and housing, which would produce a painful negative wealth effect for the economy and a return to recession. Another, perhaps more likely, was that a straightforward move by companies and households to rebuild their savings would push the economy into a deflation of the kind that followed the Japanese bubble. For just as people borrow and spend more as their wealth increases, they pull in their horns and rebuild savings when wealth shrinks. And since the Fed had reduced short-term interest rates to a mere $1\frac{1}{4}$ per cent by the end of 2002, its ability to stave off a deflation by cutting rates further was severely restricted.

It is also worth noting that the financing of the US current account at the turn of the millennium was heavily dependent on gullible Europeans and Japanese buying into the stock market bubble at the top. With the bursting of the bubble and the collapse of the invest-ment boom, foreigners in the first half of the new decade were being invited to finance private and public sector consumption, as Americans continued to spend and the US government plunged

---

[2] Figures taken from UBS Warburg's *Pensions: S & P 500 Update*, 19 September 2002.

into deficit. This was scarcely an attractive investment prospect. In effect, foreigners had to decide whether to continue taking a depressed view of prospects in the rest of the world, or whether to stage an evacuation from the dollar that would force a post-bubble adjustment on the world's biggest economy.

It's the poor who pay

Equally important is that global capital flows have not been uniformly efficient. While they have helped make global economic growth more stable, they have often made national growth less stable, as the constant financial crises in the developing world have demonstrated. Indeed the behaviour of these flows can often be downright perverse. As the American economist Joseph Stiglitz has put it:

> One might have thought that money would flow from rich countries to the poor countries; but year after year, exactly the opposite occurs. One might have thought that the rich countries, being far more capable of bearing the risks of volatility in interest rates and exchange rates, would largely bear those risks when they lend money to the poor nations. Yet the poor are left to bear the burdens. Of course, no one expected that the world market economy would be fair; but at least we were taught that it was efficient. Yet these and other tendencies suggest that it is neither.[3]

Stiglitz also points out that the US has been one of the strongest advocates of globalization and capital market liberalization. This has made developing countries more vulnerable to the volatility of international markets. So they have been obliged to set aside more money in their official reserves, which they use to protect their currencies from extreme fluctuations. The outcome is an unhappy example of American double standards. For while Washington lectures developing countries on the need for good fiscal and financial housekeeping, the US lives beyond its means year in year out, spending more on imports of foreign goods and services than it earns from its own

---

[3] From Stiglitz's review of *On Globalisation* by George Soros in *The New York Review of Books*.

exports. The developing countries then help the US plug the spending gap by investing their reserves in US Treasury bonds, which yield much lower returns than their money would earn back at home. So the world's poorer countries have ended up subsidizing the richest economy in the world. It may not be an intentional conspiracy, but it is still shockingly absurd.

The turbulence of this financial world underlines once again that the shared vision in Washington, New York and London of global convergence on a superior Anglo-American capital market model was a triumphalist canard. Yet, despite the more jaundiced view that policy-makers in Continental Europe and Asia now take of that model, there are powerful economic and regulatory forces at work that make some further convergence inescapable. On the economic front it seems likely that as ageing populations outside the English-speaking world increase their investment in securities, albeit slowly, to finance their retirement, they too will find that their household wealth is more hostage to swings in the value of the assets they hold. The risk is of a much bigger synchronized boom-and-bust cycle across the world as the structure of economies becomes more similar on this score. Yet the whole world cannot run down its savings and run a current account deficit simultaneously. Someone will have to run surpluses to match the deficits. The best guess is that while saving and spending in Continental Europe becomes more sensitive to market gyrations, Asia, where China and Japan will remain imperfectly integrated into the global capital market system, will continue to run a current account surplus for some time.

Another important economic impulse for countries to move closer to the Anglo-American approach while maintaining many of the distinctive features of their individual models of capitalism arises because Anglo-American corporate governance standards have become the de facto norm of international capital markets. It follows that anyone who wants access to global capital on attractive terms will have to observe certain basic tenets. These include such things as transparency, accountability and fair treatment for non-controlling shareholders. If companies choose to place the interests of stakeholders such as employees above those of shareholders, nothing will prevent them doing so if this is legally permissible in their home country. But if the result is a return on capital that falls below global standards, their access to global capital will be impaired.

Opting out and backing out

On the legal and regulatory front there are two further substantial forces for convergence, of which the first is permissive and European. Since the European Union summit at Nice in 2000, member states of the EU are committed to introduce legislation by October 2004 to make a new form of European company available for use by business. Its significance is that it will permit companies to opt out of their home country's model of capitalism and shop around the jurisdictions of the EU in search of their preferred legal framework. The irony here is that the original intention was to create a European jurisdiction in company law with a uniform legislative base to encourage cross-border restructuring in Europe's internal market. Yet, after 25 years of horse-trading, much of the proposed uniform structure of corporate govern-ance, complete with two-tier boards and employee participation, has been lost in the compromise EU law that has emerged. The new European company format to which this legislation has given birth will take its legal character mainly from the law in its country of registration. So there will be as many kinds of this new European company as there are member states.

All the members of the EU are obliged, under the compromise, to change their own company law to permit an alternative form of governance. The outcome will be a huge legislative upheaval. Coun-tries like Britain and Ireland have unitary company boards, with no distinction between supervisory directors and manager-directors. They will have to pass laws to permit two-tier boards in the new European company format. In Germany and other countries where two-tier boards are the norm, an equal and opposite legislative exercise will be necessary to permit unitary boards. In practice, member states may decide to give freedom of choice on board structure to all their domestic public companies as well. While there remain considerable uncertainties about how this regime will work, it seems likely that corporate Europe will be working in a legal framework that comes much closer to that of the US. Jonathan Rickford, who acted as project director for the UK's Company Law Review, sums it up in these terms:

> The new regime clearly enables a public company to opt out of its domestic law and choose one of the other 14 available. This could be the basis of European jurisdictional competition, or a market, in corporate law, on US lines – a "race for the bottom" in providing weak regulation, or perhaps, more optimistically, "for the top", in developing efficient rules attractive to company controllers.[4]

A legislative proposal originally designed to foster European integration will thus almost certainly end up encouraging legislative arbitrage. Given the not insignificant number of Continental European business people who yearn for more flexible labour market practice, it seems plausible that many will seek to operate under the new European corporate format in a jurisdiction that relieves them from the more onerous requirements of employee participation. The traffic from Britain in the other direction, in contrast, is likely to be scant, since most top British executives have a visceral antipathy for the two-tier board structure and for meaningful employee involvement.

The other powerful legal force for convergence on the Anglo-American capital market model is less permissive and more intrusive. It is the extraterritorial reach of US securities law and, more specifically, the Sarbanes-Oxley act passed in July 2002. This legislation was the first, hurried response to the string of corporate scandals that began with Enron. And its provisions, which range across corporate governance, accountancy and audit, apply to foreign companies listed on US stock exchanges. The act also gave US regulators powers to discipline auditors outside the US who conducted audits either of

---

[4] This is taken from Jonathan Rickford's Unilever Professorship Inaugural Lecture at the University of Leiden, given in September 2002.

foreign companies listed in the US, or subsidiaries of US companies abroad.

To the extent that the Securities and Exchange Commission (SEC) has discretion in the way it implements its new mandate, there is some scope for compromise on extraterritoriality. Yet at the time of writing it remains unclear how many of the Sarbanes-Oxley legislative measures that are firmly rooted in American corporate governance practice will allow for exemptions. Requirements, for example, that audit committees of the company board should consist of independent non-executive directors pose huge problems for German companies because employees and bankers who sit on supervisory boards cannot be regarded as independent in the American sense. Japan, where boards are largely ceremonial and outside directors are still a rarity, is caught in a similar dilemma. The Sarbanes-Oxley act is potentially subversive of these models of capitalism. Yet its form of extraterritoriality is not inescapably brutal. If they feel that the compromises offered by the SEC fall short of the tolerable, foreign companies can delist from American stock exchanges to avoid the American legislative steamroller, but only at the cost of denying themselves access to the world's biggest pool of portfolio capital. The decision by US lawmakers not to exempt foreign companies from provisions that conflicted sharply with their own domestic legislation reflected a similar attitude to that of George W. Bush after the atrocities of 11 September, 2001. The politicians on Capitol Hill were saying to foreigners, in effect, that they were either for American capitalism or against it.

So where does this leave countries like Germany and Japan, where the old corporate governance systems are already under strain? Given the flaws in the Anglo-American model demonstrated during the bubble, their unreconstructed governance arrangements emerge from any comparison looking less bad than before, but under siege from hostile economic and regulatory forces. Yet in the end the importance of corporate governance for a country's economic performance should not be overestimated. A far more powerful and effective discipline comes anyway from product markets. The reason so many countries have done well despite being tainted with the label of crony capitalism is that they have exposed their economies to the competitive pressures of international trade. That explains the robustness of many Asian economies in recovering from the savage deflation of the 1997–98 crisis. It also explains the success of the smaller economies of Western Europe such as Switzerland, Denmark and Norway, which are richer than the US in terms of gross domestic product per head. The fact that outside shareholders in Continental European countries have sometimes had a raw deal does not mean that the companies themselves are inefficient. The accountability in these systems is just different.

The capital market pressure cooker

An interesting question here is the precise nature of the model to which the non-English-speaking countries are moving closer. The shareholder value revolution in the 1980s and 1990s had the beneficial effect of reducing managerial self-aggrandizement and increasing management's focus on earning a return over the cost of capital. Yet in the second half of the 1990s the fate of companies, like that of the wider economy, became hostage to share prices and to the mood swings of capital markets, analysts and credit-rating agencies. Enron existed to maximize its stock price, while the proximate cause of its bankruptcy was the downgrading of its bonds to junk status. Despite its aspiration to be at the cutting edge of financial engineering, its treasury management – the handling of its liabilities – was so inept that this single change in credit-rating caused it to blow up. Such vulnerability to market movements and credit-ratings is more widely shared by the general run of companies thanks to the pension fund problem explored earlier.

Meantime the impact of increased competition through globalization has caused companies to become much more meritocratic. Chief executives are highly motivated and focused. In some companies, General Electric being the best known, managers who fall into the bottom 10 per cent bracket in the annual performance assessment are routinely fired in a process known as "rank and yank". (It was entirely characteristic of Enron that its performance assessment was six-monthly, while the number fired was as high as 15 per cent.) Such a fiercely meritocratic approach to business makes it all the more important that capital market incentives and penalties steer the formidable business energy of top managers in a sensible direction. Yet the definition of shareholder value has become perverted, as have the capital market sticks and carrots.

Thanks to a demented system of accountability that puts managers into a financial pressure cooker, the managers have had to redefine their role. They have turned themselves into what the British economist John Kay calls meta-fund-managers, who see their task as being to buy and sell companies on a portfolio basis for the shareholders, instead of concentrating exclusively on the performance of the underlying businesses. The demand from the capital markets to transform large, complex organizations over ridiculously short time periods drives chief executives into the hands of the investment bankers who advise them on potentially transforming takeovers that too often transform for the worse. And thanks to a stock option and bonus culture that provides chief executives with handsome rewards for failure, their interests are poorly aligned with those of outside shareholders.

In many respects, the capital market system has become unhelpfully like the political system. Not only has the timescale of business moved closer to the short-term electoral horizons of politics, top managers, like politicians, have also become more remote, notably from their customers and employees. Takeovers are now a central feature of the workings of the system. And the ethos of the Anglo-American model requires information about takeovers to be confined to a tiny group of people at the top for fear of insider-dealing or the creation of false markets. So management has moved from benign paternalism to a more brutal and remote elitism. Even very senior employees at companies like Marconi knew nothing of the deals that were to transform and wreck their employer until the day they were publicly announced.

The ultimate beneficiaries of the capital market system – chiefly pension scheme members – are also victims of exclusion. Those in defined benefit pension schemes have no direct stake in industry and commerce. The pension fund assets are simply there to provide collateral for the company's promise to pay the workers' pensions. The money is, in effect, controlled by management, and much of the fruits of superior investment performance in the 1990s found its way back into the profits of the company through reduced corporate pension contributions. Pension beneficiaries or, for that matter, investors in mutual funds, have rarely been told how the fund-managers or trustees have exercised their control rights in big takeovers or proxy battles. Like the voters in Western democracies who no longer bother to turn up at the polling booths, they have been passive observers of an increasingly closed system.

Among the more dangerous things about the short tenure afforded to chief executives is that they now have a powerful incentive to sweep under the carpet any difficult issues that might distract them from the overwhelming priority of pushing up the share price. This applies particularly to externalities such as environmental costs that fall on people outside the company, or to product flaws that pose a threat to customer safety. Yet for managers to adopt a cavalier attitude to externalities is not in the interests of the giant institutional investors who dominate global equity markets or of their beneficiaries, because many of these costs are simply being shunted from one company to another in the same giant long-term portfolio. As for customer safety, the more enlightened managers see it in terms of reputational risk to the company. Yet it is also a moral issue that turns on responsibility to fellow human beings. In the greedy climate of the bubble too many managers and employees simply shed their morals when they walked through the company's doors.

Corporate graveyards

These distorted incentives have caused the capital market model to swing away from genuine shareholder value back toward the older "philosopher king" model of executive behaviour, but with the novel dimension that the managers are now in an unholy alliance with the investment bankers. In a world of turbocharged dealmaking and rewards for managerial failure, the principal-agent problem is simply with us in another guise. The result is that the system fails to fulfil its potential for creative destruction.

On the creative side of the equation, the venture capital market, as indicated in Chapter 1, saw a hugely wasteful misallocation of resources in the high-tech sector during the boom, as the venture capitalists abandoned conventional appraisals of business plans. The useful innovation that did emerge took place at an exceptionally high cost, delivering poor returns to investors. On the destruction side, meantime, the takeover splurge that lined the pockets of the investment bankers in the 1990s left corporate winners as well as corporate losers. Unilever, for example, emerged handsomely from the sale of its speciality chemicals business to ICI. Yet much merger-and-acquisition activity produced a hugely wasteful misallocation of resources, while inflicting a needlessly high level of transaction costs on those economies where the dealmaking was hyperactive. From an investor perspective it also caused enormous loss of value at individual companies, reflected in astonishingly large charges against corporate profits in 2001 and 2002 to write down the acquisition costs incurred during the boom to realistic levels.

The biggest came from the ill-judged merger between AOL and Time Warner, which led to a scarcely believable loss of $54bn in the first quarter of 2002 after the biggest write-down in corporate history at this, the world's largest Internet and media company. But there were huge overpayments for acquisitions at other corporate giants such as WorldCom, Vivendi Universal and Vodafone. From being a playground for ego-tripping big businessmen, the market in corporate control turned into a corporate graveyard. And as the fallout multiplied, it also became clear that the Anglo-American system was lacking in those features of transparency, fairness and responsibility that were supposed to be its trademarks. By 2002 investors were losing confidence in the reliability of reported corporate profits, thanks to the questionable accounting at Enron, WorldCom,

Xerox and the rest. This was the kind of uncertainty that initiates not the savage and instantaneous downward adjustment experienced in the stock market crash of 1987, but a long and insidious bear market.

Investors were also traumatized by the way in which the plethora of potential conflicts of interest in the American approach to investment banking proved to have been systematically abused. Under the integrated model of investment banking, banks advise companies on the issue of securities while simultaneously advising the investment institutions on whether to buy them. They conduct trading activities on their own account in competition with the investors for whom they act as market-makers and brokers. They advise companies on mergers and acquisitions where they take big fees without taking any responsibility for the success or failure that results from their advice. And they do private client-broking business with the directors of companies where they act, or hope to act, as corporate finance advisers.

After the collapse of the bubble, the thrust of the regulatory response, whether from Congress, the SEC or the New York State Attorney General Eliot Spitzer, was directed mainly at the most politically charged areas. These included the peddling of deliberately misleading company research to support the marketing of securities to private investors, or the grant of stock in "hot" initial public offerings to directors of companies from which the investment banks hoped to win corporate finance fees. Yet far greater economic damage was inflicted by the high level of transaction costs and the wasteful investment that resulted from the unsuccessful takeover activity urged on company clients by bonus-driven bankers.

It is hard to see the logic, from a shareholder perspective, in much of the financial conglomeration that prevails on Wall Street. Investment bankers like to have a fund management arm because it helps smooth profits when highly cyclical corporate finance business dries up. But that pre-empts a portfolio decision that more properly belongs to shareholders, who ought to be able to decide for themselves whether to invest in the business of asset management. Nor can there be much synergy between investment banking and asset management in a modern financial world that frowns on using investment clients' money to rig the market in support of the takeover activity of corporate clients of the investment bank. If the firewalls imposed by the regulators are effective, synergy between investment banking and asset management is largely ruled out.

As the downturn in the equity market in 2002 became more severe, the financial conglomerates that incorporated everything from insurance, commercial banking, investment banking and fund management also began to look increasingly shaky. In particular, the advantages of combining insurance and banking appeared to be outweighed by the risks to overall solvency. With the equity market plunging, insurers needed emergency capital injections just when the commercial banks were suffering from increasing bad debts as a result of the telecoms disaster. Putting these two problems together in a single financial conglomerate was a toxic combination. The stock prices of banking and insurance-based conglomerates such as Citigroup in the US, Lloyds TSB in the UK and Credit Suisse in Switzerland seriously underperformed for much of 2002 as a result. So not only was this universal model of banking in trouble with the regulators, it was also out of favour with investors. Having gone back to a conglomerate model of universal banking that had originally been banned by the Glass-Steagall Act of 1933, such Wall Street giants as Citigroup were forced to think again about the merits of trying to be the ultimate one-stop shop. In future they are likely to face increasing pressure from investors and regulators to ring-fence more of the activities that give rise to conflicts of interest and cross-subsidies within the group.

The ethics deficit

Public confidence in the system was further eroded by spiralling boardroom pay bearing no relation to directors' performance. The magazine *Business Week*, whose writers scarcely fall into the category of closet-Marxists, complained that in 2001 Joseph Nacchio, then CEO of Qwest Communications International, received a $1.5m bonus, $24m in cash, $74m in exercised options and new options that could be worth up to $194.2m, while the company posted a $4bn loss and fired employees. The magazine's editorial writers also worried about the unfairness in CEO compensation going from 42 times that of the average worker in 1980 to 531 times in 2000.[5] And they were surely right to do so. This is irresponsible capitalism, given that boardroom pay inflation has not been subject to proper checks and balances. Far from being a market process, boardroom rewards are decided by committees on the basis of advice from unregulated and often self-interested consultants appointed by the CEO. The extreme example is Disney, which is notorious for the size of the pay awards made to CEO Michael Eisner and for the cronyism that infects its board compensation committee. The economists Martin Conyou and Kevin Murphy have calculated that Eisner earned more than the aggregate paychecks of the top 500 British CEOs when he exercised stock options worth more than $500m in the single year of 1997. As well as Eisner's personal attorney, the compensation committee's members include an actor under contract to one of Disney's studios and the head of a school once attended by his children.

John Kenneth Galbraith captured the nature of the scam in a characteristically pithy aphorism:

> The salary of the chief executive of the large corporation is not a market award for achievement. It is frequently in the nature of a warm personal gesture by the individual to himself.

Certainly the achievement during the bubble period did not live up to its New Economy billing. In the period of maximum escalation in the 1990s more of the improvement in corporate profitability came from declining interest rates and taxes than from managerial effort, as we saw in Chapter 3. Indeed, the indiscriminate use of stock options by American and British executives is reminiscent of the behaviour of the Russian oligarchs who misappropriated the assets of the Russian state with the connivance of Boris Yeltsin. The US shareholder activist Robert Monks accuses the stock option oligarchy of

---

[5] "No wonder CEOs are so unloved", *Business Week*, 22 April, 2002.

perpetrating the greatest non-violent transfer of wealth from one class to another that history has ever seen.

The professional fund-managers who did nothing to prevent this wealth transfer usually excuse themselves by saying that they are not in the business of identifying or preventing excessive awards. A common refrain is that they like to see people being well paid for doing a good job. Yet no less a person than William McDonough, President and CEO of the Federal Reserve Bank of New York, has a different take on the widening gap between CEO pay and the pay of the average employee. Speaking at Trinity Church in New York's financial district on the anniversary of the twin towers attack, he argued not only that the disparity was unjustified by CEO performance, but that it was "terribly bad social policy and perhaps even bad morals."

It is hard to disagree. In the 1990s the ethos in US business became increasingly individualistic. Somehow people in the business and financial community lost touch with the civic instincts and public spirit that Alexis De Tocqueville identified in the 19th century as one of America's most impressive strengths.[6] By the end of the 20th century there was, in effect, an ethical deficit at the heart of capitalism. And because of the bubble the rewards for unethical behaviour were vastly magnified to the point where the temptation was too great for the majority of CEOs to resist. The greed, as Fed Chairman Alan Greenspan has rightly observed, was infectious. CEOs are by nature highly competitive people. So when one CEO obtains an outsize

---

[6] A flavour of De Tocqueville's argument is the following: "The free institutions which the inhabitants of the United States possess, and the political rights of which they make so much use, remind every citizen, and in a thousand ways, that he lives in society. They every instant impress upon his mind the notion that it is the duty as well as the interest of men to make themselves useful to their fellow creatures; and as he sees no particular ground of animosity to them, since he is never either their master or their slave, his heart readily leans to the side of kindness. Men attend to the interests of the public, first by necessity, afterwards by choice; what was intentional becomes an instinct, and by dint of working for the good of one's fellow citizens, the habit and the taste for serving them are at length acquired." *Democracy in America*, Part 2, Chapter 4, Everyman's Library, 1994.

award, the others want their compensation committee to ensure that they do not fall behind. The result is that a whole generation of top managers turned themselves into robber-barons. For their part, the auditors observed the vast sums being made by fellow professionals in the investment banks and the law firms. They allowed themselves to become increasingly enmeshed in conflicts of interest as the lure of moneymaking got the better of sturdy professional values. It goes without saying that honesty and integrity are absolutely fundamental to the task of the auditor because the auditors are the guardians of the capitalist system and the guarantors of the financial information on which the capital markets depend.

These issues are not exclusively a matter of morality, because ethics have important economic implications. In crude terms, ethical conduct is a low-cost substitute for internal controls within a company and external regulation without. Joshua Ronen, a professor of accounting at New York University's Stern School of Business, argues:

> Suppose the board of directors believes management and other employees rank low on the ethical scale. It would then direct the investment of some corporate resources in improving the internal control and audit systems to avert the higher potential costs of fraud, chicanery, embezzlement, and other detrimental self-interested behaviour on the part of its officers and employees. High ethical standards would result in net savings to the corporation, which would require less internal control and audit services. If more managers of corporations are known to be ethical, auditors would need to invest less effort, reducing audit fees and the total social cost of ensuring such credibility of financial statements as would allow proper functioning of the capital markets. Were the market to realize that a given corporation has become more ethical, such as by ridding itself of the unethical and hiring the ethical, the value of the corporation would increase by the amount of anticipated savings in the consumption of control and audit services. In this sense accounting controls and ethical conduct can be viewed as economic substitutes.

Looked at from another perspective, ethics create trust. And trust reduces transaction costs in the economy, while a lack of trust increases them. Consider, for example, what happens if a stock market is plagued with insider-dealing. The market-makers who deal in stock will feel obliged to widen their spreads – the margin between buying and selling prices – to protect themselves from being on the wrong side of a deal where the insider gains at their expense. By the same token investors will insist on paying less for new issues of securities because they have to be compensated for the risk of being exploited by insiders.[7] And in a low-trust system, expensive litigation becomes a substitute for behavioural constraint.

No system can rely on ethical self-restraint alone. It cannot be ignored that self-interest is a vital motivating force for wealth creation. The need is to ensure that the incentive structure encourages ethical behaviour and channels self-interest in a constructive direction. Instead, in both the US and UK in the 1990s, it provided directors with an open door to push at a set of rewards that were conveniently inflated by the bubble. If there was a transatlantic difference it was that Americans were corrupt as well as greedy, while the British were more incompetent than corrupt. Directors' pay was not, incidentally, the only morally contentious area. There was a time when the world's leading banks would have refrained from lending money to off-balance sheet partnerships of a company like Enron and where decent lawyers, accountants and auditors would have wanted nothing to do with such business. Because they guarded their reputations jealously, they would have shied away from actions that, despite being legal, were unethical. But that ethos evaporated with the increasingly intense competition that resulted from deregulation and globalization, together with the shift to a more transactional culture in finance. And once an ethos of self-constraint goes, it is extraordinarily difficult to rebuild.

A wider consequence of the lack of restraint in the boardroom is that employees have been demoralized, while the public has been left feeling that business is now as much tainted by sleaze as politics. Enron was at the intersection where business sleaze and political

---

[7] Utpal Bhattacharya and Hazem Daouk of Kelley School of Business at Indiana University have shown that where insider-dealing is effectively policed the cost of equity decreases significantly. See the results of their research in "The world price of insider trading", *Journal of Finance*, Vol. 57, Issue 1, 2002.

sleaze overlapped. And by now there is growing public alienation, as business people appear more remote and unprincipled to the citizens, much as politicians do. Even before the collapse of the bubble, public confidence in the system was not high. Unaccountable non-government organizations such as Greenpeace or Friends of the Earth enjoyed far greater respect than the management of some of the best companies in America and the UK. The sight of so many directors extracting huge rewards for failure has exacerbated this problem of perception. The combination of economic inefficiency and manifest unfairness strengthens the hand of those who argue for protectionism and an end to globalization. So much so that Henry Paulson of Goldman Sachs was moved to acknowledge in mid-2002 that there was truth in the allegation that something was rotten in the workings of business. "In my lifetime American business has never been under such scrutiny," he said. "To be blunt, much of it is deserved."[8] Even business people, it seems, are beginning to recognize that the legitimacy of corporate activity, no less than that of politics, is in urgent need of repair.

---

[8] Speech to the National Press Club, June 2002.

11

Putting the world to rights

The stock market euphoria of the late 1990s was one of the greatest bubbles in history, comparable with the British railway mania in the 19th century or the period before the 1929 Crash on Wall Street. So it is hardly surprising that policy-makers in Washington and financiers on Wall Street should have convinced themselves that there was something uniquely efficient about their model of capitalism. Bubbles and hubris go hand in hand. By the same token it is difficult when nemesis comes and the bubble bursts to distinguish between transient problems and genuine systemic flaws.

What seems indisputable is that the capital markets of the Anglo-American world are not fulfilling their potential for allocating capital efficiently. Huge losses have been incurred in the information technology and telecoms industries, and much investment across the wider economy has been wasteful. It is also clear that the instability of private capital flows has inflicted disproportionate losses of output and employment on developing countries, which were not exclusively caused by these countries' flawed budgetary policies, exchange rate regimes and weak banking systems.

Within the Anglo-American world the structure of capital market incentives has pushed managers into manic efforts to raise the price of their stock in the short term at the expense of genuine shareholder value. This was epitomized by Bernie Ebbers' singular approach to investor relations during the bubble, which consisted of pointing to a chart of the soaring WorldCom share price and bluntly asking: "Any questions?" At the same time the transactional ethos that now pervades the whole system has led to a plethora of inefficient takeovers, along with much frenetic and costly trading activity that distracts attention from the real purpose of the financial system.

The bizarre irony here is that the shareholder value movement has ended up replicating the errors of socialist planners in the old Soviet Union who imposed targets on industrial managers that were frequently met by fiddling the figures or doing damage to some other aspect of the business. By fixing on a single managerial incentive – the share price – the Anglo-American system has encouraged management to maximize short-term profits at the expense of longer term growth. When managers found that they could not generate enough short-term profit to satisfy investors and stock market analysts in the bubble period, they resorted to takeovers as a means of keeping one step ahead of the baying hounds of the financial community. And when takeovers became difficult to pull off in the depressed stock market conditions that followed the bubble, they took to window-dressing the figures either within the rules or fraudulently as at WorldCom.

That is not to say that this capital market model is broken in the way that caused the Soviet model to come to grief. For while the capital market signals are distorted, the price signals in the real-world markets for goods and services are not. That has been the saving grace of the Anglo-American system, as it has been of other flawed models of capitalism. None of the models is perfect. And the best complexion that an enthusiast for the Anglo-American approach could put on it is that the model is less bad than most in coping with the wrenching adjustments imposed by rapid technological change and the pressures of globalization. The snag is that people need to feel confident about the integrity and efficiency of the system. This does not come easily when workers are having to cope with the extraordinarily intense competition that results from globalization and the integration of countries such as China into the world's trading system. Nor is it easy to sell the merits of a system to ordinary people on the negative sounding basis that it is less bad than the others, especially against a background of corporate scandals and collapsing stock markets. The task is made all the harder when big business is deeply involved in the financing of political parties and electoral campaigns. A solution to the problems of political funding lies beyond the scope of this book, but as a matter of observation it seems unlikely that full confidence in the integrity of any model of capitalism can be restored where politicians are systematically bought by business interests, as they have been in the US.

Unless private capital can be made to work more efficiently and more fairly, the legitimacy problem is destined to become more acute. The danger is that if policy-makers fail to put a more persuasive case for the capital market model and fail to restore trust in corporate behaviour, workers will vote for the wrong kind of safety net. They will look to protectionism to cushion them from capitalism's creative destruction, thereby inflicting lower living standards on the world in exchange for what they hope will be less insecurity and instability. The Bush administration's lurch in a protectionist direction in 2002, whose effects included subsidizing some of the world's richest farmers and cushioning inefficient steel producers that had failed to restructure in response to global competition, was a loud wake-up call on the need to confront this challenge.

For Europe the legitimacy problem is less pressing. The genius of the post-war Continental European models of capitalism lay precisely in their emphasis on orderly, cooperative behaviour in social partnership and on the taming of the red-in-tooth-and-claw quality of market capitalism. While these models have lost much of their potency, Europe has moved in a more liberal economic direction, but with the novel stabilizing influence of a single currency. That said, a generation of new investors in Continental European equity has been severely burned by the plunge in share prices since 2000. The resulting disillusionment has cast a cloud over the development of the region's capital markets. And at a broader level Europe's economic and monetary union remains a halfway house experiment. The single currency has been introduced into a region where labour markets remain inflexible. The coordination of fiscal policy, which is essential for managing a successful single currency, is already giving rise to friction between states that are having difficulty curbing their deficits and that face growing demographic pressure. Such difficulties will increase with enlargement, as the European Union embraces more of Eastern Europe.

In economics any move to stabilize one part of the system often results in the destabilization of another. Europe has undergone a huge deregulatory shock not only as a result of the single currency but a raft of legislation designed to liberalize its financial markets. Such liberalization frequently leads to financial crises. Managing a systemic crisis on a cross-border basis will be an exceptionally demanding task for Europe's central banks and European finance ministries, given the existence of national rivalries, different languages and conflicts of interest.[1] And in a supranational regional entity like the European Union, where the political and bureaucratic elite appears remote from the European electorate, there are wider problems of democratic legitimacy.

Supranational policy-making on this scale across a whole continent is a unique historical development, and the introduction of a single currency is a notable achievement. Whether the innate inflexibility of the European Union's political processes in the face of fast-changing economic and financial circumstances proves to be a serious systemic handicap remains to be seen. The combination of unfavourable demography and half-hearted economic reform does not point to the kind of robust economic growth that would help Europeans cope better with the stresses of global competition and population ageing. There is a risk that the eurozone could experience a regional version of the break-up of the Bretton Woods exchange rate system if fiscal and monetary strains prove intolerable for Germany or if other, heavily indebted countries have to be thrown out of the monetary club to preserve its integrity. Nor for the foreseeable future does Europe's continent-wide model have export potential. The rest of the

---

[1] See my article "Crisis in the making", *Financial Times*, 12 April 1999 for an analysis of the problems of last resort lending by the European Central Bank.

world will have to find other ways of achieving economic and financial stability in the face of vólatile private capital flows.

Elusive magic bullets

In essence, the world faces two separate but overlapping economic policy challenges in relation to private capital. One is to ensure that the globalization of capital works more efficiently. The other is to address the weaknesses in Anglo-American corporate governance that were exposed after the bubble. Where the first is concerned, especially in relation to the developing world, the temptation is to look to governments and demand a menu of dramatic growth-enhancing initiatives. Yet if a key to improving the lot of the world's poorer countries lies in encouraging trade, increasing the flow of private capital and fostering technology transfer, there are limits to what governments and international financial institutions can do, because governments cannot build private businesses. Indeed, one reason the record of the IMF and the World Bank in dealing with the emerging market economies has been mixed is precisely that these institutions were designed for a post-war world in which most cross-border capital flows were between governments, not multinational companies and private financial institutions.

In response to the privatization of capital, the International Monetary Fund (IMF) has created a new role for itself in policing capital flows and acting as a cheerleader for liberalization. Yet this impressive job re-creation project has produced policy prescriptions that no longer command uniform respect, even in the markets. The Asian crisis and the disastrous experience in Argentina have seen to that. As for the World Bank, its President James Wolfensohn has sought to redefine its role in the light of the globalization of private capital flows. Yet he has had difficulty in dragging this giant bureaucracy into line with his vision for a "knowledge" bank. Unpalatable though it may seem, it is much easier for bureaucrats to apply

themselves to the task of lending money to corrupt governments than
to engage in the more subtle business of influencing the behaviour of
private capital.

The greatest contribution that the governments of the US, Europe
and Japan can make to economic development is to avoid making big
mistakes in their own economic policies, so ensuring wider stability in
the global economy. With the IMF and the World Bank they can also
try to boost official flows to the poorer countries and make them more
efficient. Government funds can clearly play a part in building
infrastructure. But where private capital is concerned there is no
simple cookbook of policy remedies, because the new game is about
improving the investment climate in individual developing countries
and – less often recognized – removing barriers in the developed world
that make it harder for pension funds, mutual funds and other collective investment vehicles to invest effectively in the emerging markets.
The rules of engagement observed by these giant financial institutions
were not framed with any regard to their potential impact in the
developing world and they have often been harmful.

To their credit the IMF and World Bank already provide advice to
emerging market economies on the design and functioning of financial systems, though the advice is sometimes controversial. The
various initiatives and standards that they have promoted since the
Asian crisis to improve the financial architecture of the developing
countries have, on balance, made a positive contribution. The IMF is
also providing a new bankruptcy procedure for sovereign debt.
Another constructive initiative to come out of the Asian experience
is the joint Organization for Economic Cooperation and Development
(OECD)–World Bank body, the Global Corporate Governance
Forum. With input from a private sector advisory group led by the
eminent New York lawyer and governance expert Ira Millstein, the
forum works in cooperation with developing country governments
and private sector representatives to improve their corporate governance. Millstein's mantra is that "capital doesn't come to dangerous
neighbourhoods; it comes where there is a climate conducive to investment." The forum's aim is thus to pave the way, through dialogue

with emerging market countries, for them to obtain cheaper and more flexible access to foreign capital.

Damn bankers (again)

Among the overwhelming priorities on this score should also be to ensure a more stable mix of flows to the developing world. That means less bank finance, which is highly volatile, more equity and bond finance, and more foreign direct investment, which is the most stable and potentially constructive flow. Yet since bank finance will continue to be needed, it is important that it should behave in a more stable fashion. Sadly, the revised international capital regime for banks known as Basle II, which will be the crucial influence on the behaviour of cross-border bank lending, is a looming disaster. As Avinash Persaud of State Street Bank argues:

> Basle II will lead to more amplified cycles and more instability ... this cyclicality will impose its greatest burdens on risky borrowers, small companies and developing countries. The cyclicality of lending will lead to a volatility of returns that would dampen the long-run average flow of capital. In the boom time developing countries will receive more capital than they have capacity for, initially leading to high returns and then leading to bad investment decisions and in the crunch, the flows will stop and defaults will rise as these borrowers are less able to fall back on retained savings. There is already an unhealthy feast and famine in the flow of lending to developing countries and the use of pro-cyclical bank assessments will only accentuate this.[2]

By now it is unrealistic to look for radical changes to Basle II. Too much capital has been invested in the project by too many important bankers for these flaws to be fully and properly addressed. We will have to wait for a Basle III for a better opportunity to make bank lending to the developing world more stable. And one of the non-technical priorities here should be to ensure better representation of

---

[2] Extracted from Avinash Persaud's inaugural lecture as visiting professor at Gresham College, London on 3 October 2002.

the developing countries in the whole process, because they have tended to be the losers in the trade-offs that have taken place in the course of the debate.

The Basle committee under William McDonough of the New York Federal Reserve was well aware, for example, that its proposed capital regime had the potential to exaggerate business cycles. But it argued that the benefits of the capital framework it proposed outweighed this concern. For the developed world's larger banks that may well be true. But financial crises are connected to the business cycle and many developing countries are more vulnerable to its fluctuations because their chief means of catching up with developed countries is through industrialization. Their economies are thus disproportionately weighted toward manufacturing, which is highly cyclical. They lack the large service sectors that help cushion more mature economies in the downturn. It follows that any trade-off in the capital regime that exaggerates the business cycle is likely to be at their expense.

In this instance the interests of the developed countries and of their big banks are not at one. For it is not in the interest of the developed world for developing countries to be saddled with more frequent or more severe financial crises. Since the Asian crisis, to take an obvious example, many Asian economies have ceased to be a source of demand in a world economy that is over-dependent on the locomotive power of the US. There is thus a mutual interest in more stable growth in the developing countries and in better representation for them in deliberations over the regulation of global capital flows. This would lend legitimacy to any future capital regime.

Backing fast and fickle horses

The inadequacies of the Basle process doubly underscore the importance of ensuring that the other components of capital flows to emerging markets work in a more stable fashion. With foreign direct investment (FDI) the issues are less technical, but no less difficult, because FDI seems extraordinarily bad at rewarding countries that are improving policy and extraordinarily good at flooding into those where the investment climate is seriously flawed. Among the half dozen countries that have been taking the lion's share of FDI, for example, are Argentina and China, as indicated in Chapter 2. The one is an economic disaster zone, while the other has poorly defined property rights and a dismal human rights record. With Argentina much foreign business was simply investing in support of the conventional wisdom of the Washington consensus. In the case of China many companies in the 1990s took the view that they could not afford to be out of a market the size of China – though they seemed curiously reluctant to apply the same logic to India, where the record on property rights and human rights is better.

To some extent, this problem of excessive concentration in FDI will be self-correcting. Companies are on a learning curve with cross-border investment, which has only recently overtaken trade as the chief engine of globalization, while country risk management is a relatively new discipline in corporations. The accident rate in China, for example, will probably be disproportionately high, especially among the less powerful foreign companies, as they encounter corrupt local governments and corrupt joint venture partners in an unhelpful political and legal environment. Some argue, too, that current methodologies of assessing political risk are a source of bias against lower income countries in foreign direct investment. If this is true, it helps explain why so many are pursuing inferior investments in the privileged group of developing countries that grabs a disproportionate amount of the available flows.[3] Experience and improving methodology will help here, though optimism has to be tempered with the knowledge that al-Qaeda's terrorism has done lasting damage to the prospects of many Islamic countries for increased inward investment. Much of the investment that does take place there in future will be in highly protected ghettos that are ill-designed to spread technology and skills among the wider population.

---

[3] See, for example, Philipp Harms, *International Investment, Political Risk, and Growth*, Kluwer International, 2000.

Where equity and bond flows are concerned, there are, paradoxically, grounds for optimism in the collapse of investment interest in emerging markets after the Asian crisis. The earlier portfolio flows, like the comparable bank flows, were excessive in relation to the capacity of Asian economies and markets to absorb them. They were also being deployed by investment managers in an under-researched, Gadarene rush on the basis of a flawed understanding of those markets. When responding to surveys by McKinsey, fund-managers in the late 1990s extolled the benefits of good governance and said they were willing to pay over the odds for it. What they did in practice was entirely different. Too many allocated resources to emerging markets without any serious attempt to differentiate between political systems, government effectiveness and the corporate governance regimes of individual countries in the region. They failed to recognize the extraordinarily different protections and opportunities that these countries offered to equity investors.

With some, that remains the case in the new millennium. At a conference in November 2001 at the Royal Institute of International Affairs in London, I heard the head of the investment strategy unit of a leading global fund management group give a presentation on international portfolio diversification. His background was in mathematics and his approach was entirely theoretical. He made no reference at all to corporate governance. When I questioned him on this omission, he said without irony that he knew nothing about the subject. There are many others in emerging markets investment who share his background and approach. It amounts to a highly sophisticated form of tunnel vision, oddly lacking in professionalism.

Part of the key to more stable flows lies in better informed and more responsible trusteeship among the pension funds of the developed world, of which more later. But it is also important that these portfolio flows should be more professionally managed. Given the disparity in size between the pool of institutional money in the US and UK and the tiny scale of stock markets in the developing world, most of the lumbering giants of global investment would do better to eschew putting money directly into emerging markets. They lack the managerial and analytical resources to do the job properly. And the excessive reliance of some on pro-cyclical techniques such as global index-tracking, or in Calpers' (Californian Public Employees Retirement System) case on the crude corporate governance screening approach described in Chapter 2, is inherently destabilizing. The job needs delegating to smaller, specialist intermediaries capable of distinguishing between the multifarious varieties of capitalism in the emerging markets and rewarding good corporate governance on a long-term basis through carefully considered investment policies. To some extent this is already happening. Templeton is a well-known advocate of activist investment in emerging markets, to the point where its high-profile fund-manager Mark Mobius is prepared to join the boards of companies in which Templeton invests. The US fund-manager State Street runs Asian funds where the investment of new capital is conditional on compliance with specific corporate governance criteria. That is the constructive way of the future in emerging markets.

David takes on corrupt Goliath

Another ground for optimism on portfolio flows is that improvements in corporate governance are not taking place exclusively on the basis of external pressure. A growing number of corporate governance activists is applying pressure from within for change in emerging markets – and with a fair amount of success. Among the most impressive has been Hasung Jang, a professor at Korea University in Seoul, who has campaigned on behalf of a non-governmental organization, the People's Solidarity for Participatory Democracy. He believes passionately in improved corporate governance as a way of bringing wider political legitimacy to Korea's form of capitalism, as well as a means of promoting greater equity and economic efficiency. In a country where economic activity has been dominated by giant conglomerates, the *chaebols*, which have been noted both for corruption and the mistreatment of outside shareholders, Jang's task looked forlorn at the outset in 1997. Against the odds he has campaigned highly effectively through the Korean courts to win restitution for shareholders from corrupt directors who milked their companies. He has also successfully applied pressure for such things as greater independent representation on the boards of poorly governed companies.

Against the background of an even more hostile governance environment in Russia, a former securities watchdog Dmitry Vasiliev has embarked on a similar campaign. Having resigned in frustration at his inability to obtain support from the authorities and the courts in enforcing Russian securities laws, he decided to pursue the same objectives from outside the public sector. His aims include lobbying the government and the courts on behalf of investors to ensure laws are followed and fair treatment accorded to shareholders. His organization also provides collective representation in legal cases between investors and companies and tries to influence the composition of company boards on the investors' behalf.

In the case of David Webb, a former investment banker in Hong Kong, campaigning is conducted via the Internet. Webb-Site.com has become famous in the region for its forthright criticism of poor regulatory standards in relation to takeovers and in capital-raising by Chinese companies. Such has been the professionalism of his campaigning that the authorities in Hong Kong appointed him to the Hong Kong Securities and Futures Commission's Takeovers and Mergers Panel. It is salutary that these individual campaigners are making headway in corporate governance activism when many big institutional investors in the developed world have achieved so little. They deserve greater support from the global fund management community.

An essential final component of any agenda for more stable capital flows is better accounting, for accountancy plays a vital part in economic development. At its simplest, economic growth is the cost-conscious pursuit of productivity. Unglamorous accounting skills that are taken for granted in the West are hugely valuable in poorer countries because they provide the element of cost-consciousness in the growth process that drives up living standards. At the same time sound accountancy and audit offer reassurance to foreign capital. They provide the basis on which companies make investment decisions both within countries and across national borders.

In this respect the commercialization of the professional ethos in accountancy has been singularly unfortunate. The fact that the big accountancy firms franchised their brand names outside the US and Europe without maintaining the quality of their audits has contributed to corporate scandals in the emerging market and transition economies, so eroding investor confidence. Poor quality audits in the banking sector have also been a factor in prolonging and exacerbating financial crises in the developing world. Since Enron, the quality of audits has been brought into question more generally, but that scarcely mitigates the damage in emerging markets.

Government competition watchdogs around the world will need to look more critically at the big four accountancy networks. The audit committees of international companies should likewise bring a more sceptical eye to bear on the quality of audit service provided by the big four firms at foreign subsidiaries. At the same time the work of bodies like the International Accounting Standards Board will comprise a critical element in the plumbing of globalization. Under the guiding hands of former Fed Chairman Paul Volcker and Sir David Tweedie, late of the UK Accounting Standards Board, it looks set to play a powerful and constructive role. But it would be greatly helped if its funding base could be broadened to the point where its dependence on the big professional firms and large corporations was insignificant.

A hundred and one ways of missing the governance point

In the developed world corporate governance and the financial architecture are clearly in need of attention. Since Enron, they are receiving a great deal of it, notably in relation to the role of non-executive directors, auditors and stock market analysts. Worthy and laudable things are being done to improve the structure of boards, to mitigate conflicts of interest in investment banking and enhance the independence of non-executives and auditors. But much of this effort is missing the point by taking far too narrow a view of corporate governance. The focus is all on the external side of governance and on conflicts of interest. Yet it is clear that at companies like Enron, Global Crossing and WorldCom, internal governance mechanisms, which are about delegation and control from the board and the CEO to the employees, were devastatingly flawed. Social capital, the organizational guarantee of corporate integrity, was deficient in these companies.

Mark Goyder, who heads the Centre For Tomorrow's Company, a British think tank, powerfully argues that there is a need for a values-based approach to governance. Non-executive directors ought to look at a behavioural audit trail, he argues, as well as a financial one. At Enron this would have entailed asking what kind of behaviour won people bonuses and promotion in the company. It would have involved looking at the impact of Enron's warped performance review process on employees' motivation. And it would have led non-executives to consider the stated values of the business and explore the gap between what was preached and practised. "The truth," says Goyder, "is that purpose, values and relationships are the leading indicators that tell you something is wrong before it hits the bottom line. If you focus on financial indicators, you will be too late."

That said, there is a risk of overestimating what non-executive directors can hope to achieve. Human beings in boardrooms are no less fallible than human beings elsewhere. Yet they face an increasingly daunting task. The case for not pitching expectations too high has been forcefully put by the revered economist Henry Kaufman, looking back on his own experience on Wall Street:

> I first realized the enormity of the challenge of managing large financial institutions when I joined Salomon's board following our merger with Phibro in 1981. The outside members of the board brought diverse business backgrounds to the table. With the exception of Maurice "Hank" Greenberg, none had

strong first hand experience in a major financial institution. How, then, could they possibly understand, among other things: the magnitude of risk taking at Salomon, the dynamics of the matched book of securities lending, the true extent to which the firm was leveraging its capital, the credit risk in a large heterogeneous book of assets, the effectiveness of operation management in enforcing trading disciplines, or the amount of capital that was allocated to the various activities of the firm and the rates of return on this capital on a risk-adjusted basis? Compounding the problem, the formal reports prepared for the board were neither comprehensive enough nor detailed enough to educate the outside directors about the diversity and complexity of our operations.

Today, this problem is magnified as firms extend their global reach and their portfolio of activities. In recent years, quite a few major US financial institutions have become truly international in scope. They underwrite, trade currencies, stocks and bonds, and manage the portfolios and securities of industrial corporations and emerging nations. Some of the largest institutions contain in their holding company structures not only banks but mutual funds, insurance companies, securities firms, finance companies and real estate affiliates.

The outside directors on the boards of such firms are at a major disadvantage when trying to assess the institution's performance. They must rely heavily on the veracity and competency of senior managers, who in turn are responsible for overseeing a dazzling array of intricate risks undertaken by specialized, lower-level personnel working throughout the firm's wide-flung units. Indeed, the senior managers of large institutions are beholden to the veracity of middle managers, who themselves are highly motivated to take risks through a variety of profit compensation formulas. It is easy for gaps in management control to open up between these two groups.[4]

The complexity of modern financial institutions means that the non-executive director's job is more onerous than in many other sectors of the economy. Even so, Kaufman's strictures are an important warning. If people are to be persuaded to do the non-executive job it is essential that the penalties for failure should not be so harsh as to become a deterrent to sitting on boards of all but the least complex companies.

Raising the auditors' game is another area where the debate is going off-beam by focusing too heavily on the conflict of interest inherent in the big audit firms' consultancy businesses. This is a genuine dilemma, and the Sarbanes-Oxley act of 2002 rightly set out to prohibit auditors

---

[4] "The fallout from Enron: Lessons and consequences", address to the Boston Economic Club, April 2002.

from carrying out many of the non-audit services that have proved so lucrative for them in the past. Yet the legislation completely misses the more fundamental point about auditors' independence, which relates to their appointment and pay being a matter for the CEO or finance director. The incremental reform proposed by Sarbanes-Oxley is to put these functions into the hands of an audit committee of the board peopled exclusively by independent non-executive directors. But that runs up against the problem that the non-executives on a typical quoted company board are chosen by the CEO and are often reluctant to alienate the CEO and chief financial officer. Nor will this shuffling of responsibilities restore the professional ethos in big accountancy firms that have spent the past 30 years turning themselves into an aggressively commercial global service industry.

The audit is such a crucial safeguard within the capitalist system that the pressure for more radical medicine will almost certainly grow. The choice is between public sector and private sector solutions. Either auditing can be turned into an independent regulatory function conducted directly under the aegis of bodies like the Securities and Exchange Commission (SEC) in the US or the Financial Services Authority in the UK. Or a completely different approach to the independent validation of accounts could be adopted whereby the auditors' appointment and pay are put in the hands of third parties who have a financial incentive to encourage integrity in accountancy and audit. Joshua Ronen of New York University's Stern School of Business, for example, has advocated a system whereby the insurance industry insures the integrity of corporate accounts and handles the appointment and pay of the auditors in its own interest as underwriter.

Democratization and daylight

There is also a risk in the post-Enron climate that more fundamental factors, which are important for the allocation of capital, will be ignored – not least the structure of capital market incentives. Too little attention is paid to the sticks and carrots that influence human and corporate behaviour. This is true for everyone in the system, including the moguls who invest the money. The biggest chunk of money in the US and UK is in defined benefit pension schemes that are, in effect, controlled by the management and run largely according to management's requirements. Where investors do have a direct stake in the stock market, as in mutual funds, they have only a limited say in how their money is run. Meantime the elite of corporate managers and professional fund-managers who are in charge are only weakly accountable and their incentives are not well aligned with those of the ultimate investors.

An important consequence has been highlighted in the recent review of institutional investment for the UK Treasury by Paul Myners, a former chairman of the Gartmore fund management group. It is that many professional fund-managers are more concerned with managing their own business risk than those of the ultimate investors. They pursue relative rather than absolute returns on a short-term basis because it is their performance relative to their competitors that determines whether they retain their pension fund clients. Such behaviour, as indicated in Chapter 3, contributed to the stock market bubble. And because the absolute returns generated by such professional investors have been unimpressive, the field has been left wide open for hedge funds that pursue absolute returns, but on an even more short-term basis. This is as true of the US as the UK, despite tougher legislative requirements on US fund-managers to observe their fiduciary obligations to pension scheme members. The concept of responsible ownership, meantime, is alien to hedge funds. Most have no interest in playing a role in corporate governance.

Corporate managers' incentives are likewise poorly aligned with those of the ultimate investors because they are incentivized through stock options on a short-term basis and rewarded for failure when ambushed for performing poorly. The lessons of Enron, World-Com and others are that genuine shareholder value has been sacrificed in favour of efforts to manipulate stock in the short term. The question is how to rearrange the sticks and carrots of the capital market system to align the interests of professional investors and managers more closely with those of the ultimate investors and of society at large.

The closed pension fund system badly needs to be democratized and made more transparent. It makes sense, for example, to oblige fund-managers to disclose to their clients and ultimate beneficiaries how they have exercised their voting rights. In an unexpected fit of reformist zeal in 2002 Harvey Pitt, the then head of the SEC, introduced just such a disclosure requirement. The UK Company Law Review, in its final report in 2001, was also keen to see greater disclosure of how fund-managers exercised their voting rights, not least because of the potential to help legitimize the workings of capital. But government ministers, under heavy lobbying pressure from the fund management business, decided that there were practical difficulties in implementing the recommendation. In the light of the SEC's action, this British government sell-out to the fund-managers looks craven.

Meantime the Institutional Shareholders Committee, a UK umbrella organization that represents the main categories of institutional investors, has responded to Paul Myners' report by publishing a code of best practice whose recommendations include a requirement for fund-managers to disclose their policy on activism to institutional clients. This modest step could usefully be taken further by requiring fund-managers to disclose the worst performing shares in the client portfolios and to explain what action has been taken to address any managerial failure in the companies concerned. Whether it will prompt a more rigorous exercise of fiduciary duties to the ultimate pension scheme beneficiaries remains to be seen.

There is also a pressing need to change the wider investment culture in pension funds. In defined benefit schemes heavy reliance on equities to meet fixed pension liabilities has exposed some of the largest companies in the Anglo-American world to excessive risk. The fluctuations in the solvency of pension funds now colours decision-making in the boardroom in an unhelpful way for the wider economy. Pension scheme members are also inadequately protected in the UK. They have been severely short-changed on their retirement expectations where companies have fallen into bankruptcy or the pension scheme has simply been closed down by the employer. Taxpayers have also had to meet large bills where, as in the US, government offers a guarantee of employee pension rights via bodies such as the Pension Benefit Guarantee Corporation.

Death of the equity cult

There is bound to be a big shift, in the light of the stock market decline after 2000, away from the cult of the equity toward pension fund investment in bonds. Boots, the UK retail group whose pension fund sold all its equities in 2000 in a brilliantly timed moved, was a pioneer in this respect. Yet it needs to be asked whether the paternalistic defined benefit approach to pension funds makes sense either for companies or employees in a modern context. Most companies that run such schemes are turning themselves into unacknowledged conglomerates. They are running a financial services business alongside their core business. This flies in the face of current management thinking on the importance of focus on the core.

It can also be inefficient in terms both of managing balance sheet risks and tax liabilities. If management and trustees believe that they could increase returns to shareholders or offer more generous defined pension benefits to employees by investing in equities, there is nothing to stop them doing it in the company rather than in the pension fund. A debt-financed portfolio of equities at the company level in the US, for example, can yield as much as $150m in tax savings for every $1bn of assets in equities.[5] And if the investment is on the balance sheet, rather than in the pension fund, the risks are transparent and thus more likely to be prudently managed.

Now that the stock market bubble is history, the case for shifting from defined benefit to defined contribution pensions is also more

---

[5] These figures come from a *Financial Times* article "Risk and transparency in pensions" by Peter Hancock and Roberto Mendoza, partners of HMDM, a specialist investment banking firm, on 20 March 2002. Hancock was formerly Chief Financial Officer and Mendoza Vice Chairman of J.P. Morgan.

compelling. In a defined benefit scheme the members have little or no stake in the economy, merely a company promise of a pension. In a defined contribution scheme, their pension depends on the level of stock market returns. Over a lifetime's employment, the risks of stock market investment are acceptable, with the caveat that the quality of trusteeship needs to improve considerably – a point addressed in the UK by the Myners report.

Cutting companies loose from their pension funds, or shifting from defined benefit to defined contribution schemes will not do anything to address the problems of conflicts of interest that inhibit fund-managers from holding company management properly to account. But there are other grounds for optimism here. It does not take many corporate activists to change the investment climate. And the number of activist funds has been increasing both in the US and UK. Part of the benefit of this trend is that it helps shift the culture of institutional investment away from the current, narrowly theo-logical discipline, dominated by actuaries and consultants, toward one that focuses more directly on business reality and how managers run the companies in which the institutions invest. It could and should mark the beginning of a retreat from the crude thought process whereby fund-managers and trustees look for heroic qualities in every CEO and identify the prospects of companies too closely with the talents of a single individual.

That would be helpful, too, in short-circuiting the game of ambush, whereby supposedly heroic CEOs are given a minimal time span in which to make their mark, or bail out. Of paramount importance is also to attack the "rewards for failure" culture, which takes the pain out of the CEOs' absurdly short average tenure and provides an incentive to excessive and short-termist risk-taking in the takeover market. This is partly a matter of compensation packages. The meth-odologies and accountability of the compensation consultants are among the least scrutinized areas of capital market discipline. Yet the task of designing pay structures for large multinational companies operating in very different environments all around the world can be nightmarish in its complexity. The consultants are also heavily conflicted, since their appointment and pay are in the gift of chief executives who often explain very forcefully their requirements for their own compensation packages. They nonetheless have a vitally important influence on executive behaviour because they design the sticks and carrots.

Robert Monks and Allen Sykes argue that the right to appoint these people should be taken away from the CEO and placed in the hands of independent directors on the compensation committee of the board.[6] This would undoubtedly be better than what happens at present in dealing with the underlying conflict of interest, but it still runs into the problem that non-executives tend to be friendly to the CEOs. So it would need to be buttressed by other measures. One useful measure would be to give American shareholders the right, which their UK counterparts already have, to vote on compensation packages and stock option schemes. While the issue of incentive stock options in the US must be approved by shareholders, non-qualified stock options, which are more widely used, only require approval by the board of directors.

This would also help align executive directors' interests more closely with those of outside shareholders by shifting the emphasis of compensation at quoted companies from stock options to plain equity, so that directors share the pain when the stock goes down. Directors also need to be locked into equity incentives for much longer periods, with no opportunity to cash in early in the event of loss of office or the company being taken over. A better solution would be to prohibit stock options in quoted companies and encourage the issue of restricted shares that vest after several years, subject to a performance target. Better still would be to go back to a much greater emphasis on basic pay, with awards of equity being used only at the margin for truly exceptional performance.

---

[6] *Capitalism without Owners Will Fail*, Centre for the Study of Financial Innovation, 2002.

Squeezing the shareholder

The debate about stock options gives rise to a wider question about the shareholder function and the role of equity in global capital markets. This turns on the future of the Anglo-American model and whether it will prove as well suited to changes in the pattern of economic activity and technological development in the decades ahead as it was to the turbulent business environment of the 1990s. For there are grounds for thinking that a system that glorifies the role of the shareholder may be less well suited to the world we are moving toward. Indeed, the controversy over stock options may reflect the difficulty of adapting a 19th century company law and corporate governance framework to a 21st century business structure.

Symptomatic of this is the way outside shareholders such as mutual funds and pension funds are quite literally being squeezed out of their ownership rights in the information technology sector. If the very generous grant of stock options to directors and employees of high-tech companies had been accounted for as an employment cost, it would have been apparent that in many cases most of the profits were being removed by insiders. Microsoft provides the most obvious case in point. This giant of the computer industry has no need for external capital. Its balance sheet is awash with cash. Nor does it pay a dividend to its shareholders. But it does issue lavish amounts of equity to its directors and employees in the form of stock options, which under current US accounting principles are not charged against profits.

Had they been charged, according to the London-based research firm of Smithers & Co., employee costs paid in the form of options at Microsoft would have come to an estimated $11bn or so in the year to end-June 2000. On that basis these employee costs would have absorbed 77 per cent of the published pre-tax profit. The comparable figure for the whole information technology sector was 73 per cent. This compared with a figure of just under 20 per cent for the survey sample of 325 of the largest US listed companies. What emerges strikingly from the numbers is the contrast between high-tech companies in which human capital is vital and low-tech industries such as utilities, where the cost of employee stock options is minimal.[7]

On one view, the huge transfer of resources from shareholders to directors and employees in the information technology sector amounted to a colossal failure of ownership. The institutional shareholders could have used their power to prevent this misappropriation of value, but chose not to do so. It should also be noted in passing that the size of the transfer of resources has shrunk thanks to falling stock prices, though the transfer will continue with the grant of more options at a lower level of the market. Yet it could equally and more plausibly be argued that in a business where so much competitive advantage derives from human capital and there is no continuing need for outside equity, giving the shareholder the ultimate right to the profits of the business is unrealistic and unfair. In the 19th century the directors' duties were owed exclusively to shareholders for the good reason that risk capital was scarce, while labour – "hands" in the literal expression of the day – was cheap and plentiful. Even in industries where knowledge was important, such as chemicals, intellectual capital was not, in itself, the key to success. Knowledge of organic chemistry was widespread. But only those few companies capable of crystallizing the knowledge in huge investments in physical assets were able to profit from it. So the notion of the shareholder as the risk-taker of the system, with a right to the residual profits after workers and other claimants had been paid, was both logical and inherently legitimate.

Today, requirements for capital and labour fluctuate. But the developed world is not short of savings. Human capital, which consists of skills acquired through education or experience at work, is more scarce than financial capital, which is now a mere commodity. This

---

[7] Estimates by Derry Pickford in *Employee Stock Options – A Closer Look*, Smithers & Co. Report No. 175, March 2002. The figures are for the cost of issuing options, which is determined by the number issued, the price of the related shares and the life of the options. The methodology is the standard Black–Scholes valuation model. For a full explanation see the earlier Report No. 170 by Derry Pickford and Andrew Smithers, *Employee Stock Options – The Results for 2000 and the Ongoing Debate*.

intangible capital belongs to the individual members of the workforce. Human capital may need the support of financial capital to be productive, as in the case of currency-traders in investment banks who cannot deploy their skills to best effect unless they are backed by much larger capital sums than they can hope to accumulate as individuals. The value of human capital can also be enhanced by cooperation. Sharing knowledge in science-based pharmaceutical companies creates value that is tantamount to social capital, which consultants McKinsey define as the internal and external relationships that collectively link together individual talents and translate them into organizational competitiveness. Some forms of human capital may be specific to a single company, as in skills relating to software developed for a specific project. Others, such as derivatives-dealing skills, are transferable. It follows that it is increasingly difficult to measure the value of the inputs of managers and employees as against outside shareholders. The boundaries are fuzzy and property rights become indistinct. But we do know that the shareholder is not the ultimate risk-taker in this kind of world. The value of the shareholders' input, especially if the company is large and has no need of external capital, is not conspicuously great.

In this fuzzy environment it is wrong to ignore or disguise the real cost of employee stock options. But it is not clear on what basis the revenues should be shared between shareholders and employees when it is not possible to identify a specific market value for individual employees or where the employees have made investments in skills that are specific to the firm. What is certain is that the rougher corporate governance disciplines such as hostile takeovers are more likely to destroy value in such firms than enhance value. Knowledge-workers are footloose and can take value elsewhere if a new and unwelcome ownership is imposed on them. And if they live with the threat of hostile takeover, they will be more reluctant to make investments that are specific to their company or to share knowledge with fellow employees. Such people are, of course, owners of capital via mutual funds, pension funds and other collective investment vehicles. But their behaviour at the company is more likely to be influenced by their concerns as knowledge-workers, happiest in a high-trust environment where they can identify with the goals of the organization, than as shareholders.

In short, shareholder primacy sits oddly with the knowledge-intensive world. And intangible assets are becoming increasingly important all across modern industry and commerce. Margaret Blair and Thomas Kochan at the Brookings Institution point out that in 1978 roughly 83 per cent of the value of the debt and equity of non-financial quoted companies was represented by the book value of their tangible assets. By 1998 tangible assets had fallen to 31 per cent of the value of these companies' capital.[8] While some of the remaining 69 per cent may represent unrecorded increases in the value of physical assets, most consists of intangible assets such as intellectual capital, copyrights, patents, trade secrets, customer lists, know-how, research in progress, market knowledge, employees' contact lists and the synergies of a functioning team.

The stakeholder comeback

It follows that thinking about companies in terms of the old categories of capital and labour, with a layer of management to mediate between the two, no longer makes sense. Having gone off the rails with an old model of capitalism, the challenge now is to find a new set of rails to enable knowledge-managers and workers to be incorporated into the corporate governance process. That points more in the direction of something akin to the currently unfashionable insider, or stakeholder, systems of capitalism, in which accountability is imposed by informed insiders rather than outside shareholders working through independent non-executive directors and a hostile takeover discipline.

The trouble with this diagnosis is that measuring realistically the inputs of managers and employees against those of shareholders is

---

[8] *The New Relationship: Human Capital in the American Corporation*, Brookings Institution, 2001, quoted by James DeLong in *The Stock Options Controversy and the New Economy*, Competitive Enterprise Institute, June 2002.

simply not possible in the present state of the accountancy art. Much effort, for example, has been put into establishing methodologies for valuing brands. Yet the numbers produced by brand valuation consultants have carried little credibility in stock markets. As with other intangible assets, judgements about brand values, however dressed up with fancy valuation models, are too subjective to be very helpful. The likelihood is, then, that the English-speaking countries will continue to muddle along with a corporate governance model based on shareholder primacy. Yet it needs to be made more sensitive to the interests of stakeholders both on grounds of the importance of human capital and the imperative of addressing externalities such as the environment.

A pragmatic way forward has been provided by the UK Company Law Review, which forms the basis of forthcoming legislation by the Blair government. The review redefines the duties of directors, suggesting that they should act in the ways most likely to promote the success of the company for the benefits of its members, the shareholders, while taking into account wider stakeholder interests. These would include the company's need to foster its business relationships including those with employees, suppliers and customers and its need to have regard to the impact of its operations on the communities affected and on the environment. The review then advocates wider disclosure of human capital and stakeholder relationships in a statutory operating and financial review in the annual report. Where there is a conflict between the narrow interests of shareholders against employees, as for example when the viability of a manufacturing plant is in question, the shareholders' interest would trump that of the other stakeholders. But the disclosure requirements act as a crude proxy for stakeholder accountability.[9]

Even with directors' legal duties defined in this inclusive way, it is inevitable that directors of knowledge-intensive companies will con-

---

[9] *Modern Company Law for a Competitive Economy*, Final Report of the Company Law Review Steering Group, Department of Trade and Industry, July 2001. I declare an interest, having been a member of the steering group.

tinue to enjoy a high degree of discretion over the division of spoils within the company and between insiders and outside shareholders. Or they will come into conflict with outside shareholders. In many cases the outcome will be messy and unfair. By the same token, the rating of high-tech shares, where the value of managers' and employees' stock options is high, should arguably reflect a corporate governance discount in much the same way that a Korean conglomerate does if the insiders are, in effect, extracting private benefits of control. This mirrors the more basic concern about the reliability of the numbers produced by conventional accountancy.

There is another sense in which the primacy of the shareholder is open to challenge, which relates to the role of equity capital in the systems of the English-speaking countries. Part of the purpose of equity is to provide a cushion against risk and against the kinds of shock that cannot be easily predicted. Yet the dramatic advances in financial innovation over the past three decades are eroding the importance and value of this function. In theory, banks should be able to live with a more slender wedge of equity capital than in the past because they now take out specific insurance against volatility in the price of their assets through swaps, futures, options and all the other paraphernalia of the derivatives markets. Bankers should not need the comfort of a big cushion of equity capital when they can resort to such sophisticated financial insurance or, in the case of the very largest, the knowledge that they are too big for the government to allow them to fail.

Much the same is becoming true in non-financial markets. Energy producers can use derivatives to insure against the cost of big fluctuations in demand for electricity or gas. Manufacturers can hedge against fluctuations in the price of metals, raw materials or the weather. As more and more of the risks of doing any kind of business are identified and disaggregated, they will be specifically insured in the new derivatives markets rather than by insurers, or by a buffer of equity capital in the company's own balance sheet. In due course only the most obscure and difficult risks will be underwritten by the insurance industry, which will continue to have a need for equity capital as a safety cushion, while the most toxic risks arising from such things as terrorism will continue to be shouldered by governments.

That, at least, is the logic of where recent trends in financial innovation are taking us. Yet there is an issue of timing. So, many are the flaws in the current methodologies of risk management that it is hard to believe that equity will be redundant for a while yet. This is certainly the view of the world's central bankers. For it is striking that, while derivatives have been bringing extraordinary sophistication to the management of individual financial risks, the chief priority of the supervisory authorities in commercial banking over the past decade and a half has been to raise the amount of capital banks are required to hold to support a given level of business. In other words, the people who regulate the world's biggest banks are not convinced that all the new derivatives-based techniques of managing risk are doing enough to mitigate the possibility of a financial meltdown.

Envoi

What seems clear, at the very least, is that capital markets are in a period of extraordinary transition, which helps explain the great financial dislocation that took place around the turn of the millennium. After such an extreme experience of creative destruction, tainted with so much corporate scandal, it would be easy to conclude by passing a verdict on the Anglo-American model similar to the one passed by Keynes in the interwar period on capitalism itself:

> I think that Capitalism, wisely managed, can probably be made more efficient for attaining economic ends than any alternative system yet in sight, but that in itself it is in many ways extremely objectionable.[10]

Certainly the choices the developed world now faces are not that different from those it confronted in the 1930s when Keynes

---

[10] J. M. Keynes, *Essays in Biography*, 1933, published for the Royal Economic Society by Macmillan and Cambridge University Press, 1972.

penned that jaundiced remark. In crude terms, one option would be to embrace the further globalization of capital and trade, while trying to make sure that the world's savings are channelled more efficiently toward their most productive uses. This would be advantageous for global welfare, but creative destruction would throw up losers as well as winners. In the course of the century, on this scenario, the balance of economic power in the world would probably shift back to the pattern that prevailed in the 18th century before the industrialization process began. China would be the biggest economy, measured in terms of gross domestic product, followed by India in second place. With more developing countries opting into the global trading and capital market system to exploit the industrial window of opportunity, their share of the world economy would move closer to their weight in the world's population. The change in the balance of economic power, with China and India shooting, not without interruptions, to the top of the league table, would present an awesome political challenge. But on the principle in Shakespeare's *Julius Caesar* of "let me have men about me that are fat", it may be easier to live with two rich nuclear powers than two poor ones.

The alternative option would be to retreat into the defensive posture of the interwar years, which can now be seen as a hiatus in the long sweep of globalization that started to gather momentum in the 19th century. This would be more likely to take the form of increased trade protection than the reintroduction of capital controls for the reasons explained in Chapter 10, except possibly in the unusual circumstances of Japan. Global welfare would be less than in a liberal trade and capital regime and the world would probably split into regional trading blocks dominated by North America, Europe and Asia, with Africa and the Middle East once again falling miserably by the wayside.

In practice, the question is about the balance that will be struck between these two extremes and how far the world moves away from the first toward the second in response to recent financial and corporate shocks. The outcome will depend substantially on the US, for, despite the protectionist instincts of many in Continental Europe, the thrust of EU policy is still moving firmly in a liberal direction even if the impetus is flagging. American instincts, by contrast, have un-doubtedly turned protectionist since George W. Bush moved into the White House.

Yet it would be surprising if the fallout from the bubble, along with Enron, WorldCom and all the other scandals, were to produce the kind of rabid populist anti-business sentiment that created pressure for the sweeping protectionist measures and capital controls of the 1930s. After the 1929 Crash the US lost nearly 30 per cent of its output in the slump and the financial system collapsed. Modern bubbles, in contrast, appear to leave a less painful aftermath. It is often forgotten, for example, that in Japan's so-called lost decade, the post-bubble economy still achieved per capita growth in gross domestic product of just under 1 per cent. And it seems unlikely that the US would exacerbate its economic problems by repeating the extreme policy mistakes of the 1930s. Moreover, the notion that the country that pioneered the information technology revolution and most actively promoted the globalization of capital might now retreat into eco-nomic parochialism seems too paradoxical to be credible.

It is striking how often in history bubbles have been associated with awkward economic and financial transitions. At the time of the 1929 Crash the US was having difficulty taking on the hegemonic role in the global monetary and financial system previously filled by the UK. Japan in the 1980s' bubble was still reliant on an export-led model of growth that was perfectly designed for the task of catching up with the West, but wholly inappropriate for the developed world's second largest economy. It is still in transition, struggling to find a model that fits its current circumstances.

The recent US bubble can also be seen as symptomatic of yet another awkward transition. Changes in the relative scarcity of human and financial capital along with advances in financial innova-tion have created tensions and instabilities in a system that was designed for a very different world. Company law, corporate govern-ance and accountancy have been stretched beyond the limits by this upheaval. The legitimacy of the Anglo-American model of capitalism is thus an issue that runs far deeper than the mere matter of corporate scandals.

In effect, the bubble has been a rite of passage. And that, in the end, is the best argument for optimism about the workings of private capital. Having lived through a period in which some of the world's most intelligent economists and financiers swallowed the gloriously simple notion that impatient capital could be a magic bullet for the world, we are now back to capitalism as usual, clearing up after the party and muddling through. It will take a long time to reassemble a capital market model that better fits the new circumstances. The legitimacy problem will linger. And the risk of deflation is real enough to be a matter of some concern. But, unlike the old Soviet Union or modern Japan, the US has a remarkable capacity for rapid policy responses, which is shared to a considerable degree by the other English-speaking countries. So while capitalism, to echo Keynes, has not been wisely managed of late, it will be better managed in the Anglo-American world as a result of the bubble. Until, of course, the next bubble comes along.

Index

Adelphia 170
AEI 122
African Development Bank (ADB)
    25–6
Albert, Michel: *Capitalisme contre
    Capitalisme* 4
Alcatel 122
Alstom 124
ambush game 148–51
Amoco 152
Andersen 19, 139, 141, 165, 176, 179
Anglo-American capital market model
    8, 10–11, 12, 13, 47, 114, 115
    crisis of legitimacy 21
    convergence on 22, 23
    in Europe 90–1, 92–3, 102, 104
AngloGold 47
anti-globalization protests 4, 23
AOL 127, 234
AOL Time Warner 133
Argentina 18, 45
Asia
    crony capitalism 33
    financial crisis 32–3, 35, 37, 41, 57,
        120, 212
Asian Miracle, The 27
Astra 121

AstraZeneca 121
audit 139–41
Augar, Philip 173
Australia, GDP in 17

BAE Systems 124, 126
Bagehot, Walter 66
bailouts, theory of 66
Balladur, Edouard 81
Banca di Roma 93
Bank for International Settlements 61,
    66
Bank of Italy 93
Bank of Japan 222
Bankers Trust 86
Barnes, David 119
Basle Capital Accord 40, 41
    Basle II 249
Basle Capital Adequacy Regime (1988)
    76
Bell South 124
Berle, Adolph 114, 148
Berlin Wall, fall of 26
Berlusconi, Silvio 83, 95
Bevin, Ernest 84
Billiton 47

Bismarck 12, 185
Black Ships 209
Blair, Margaret 266
Blair, Tony 83, 268
"blank cheque" preferred stock 109
Bleichroeder 78
Blodget, Henry 20, 167
boom-and-bust cycle 72
Boots 261
Bové, José 92
BP 152
Brady, Nicholas 112
Bretton Woods 54–5, 246
British Aerospace 124
British Airways 223
British Telecommunications 123, 124, 147
Bubble Act (1824) 55
Buffett, Warren 154
Bush, George, Snr 112
Bush, George W. 3, 4, 8, 19, 77, 83, 161, 162, 165, 189, 219, 230, 245, 271
Business Round Table 154
buy-backs 153–4

Cadbury, Sir Adrian 147
Calpers (California Public Employees Retirement System) 45, 48, 146, 164, 252
chaebols 253
China 190–200, 271
    accident rate 251
    corporate governance 197–200
    economic history 191–2
    exports 194–5
    foreign capital 196–7
    per capita income 193–4
    rate of GDP 14
    Securities Regulatory Commission 197

since 1978 192–3
    trade liberalization 194–5
Chirac, Jacques 29
Chung Wu 166
Cisco 7, 16, 125, 134
Citicorp 70
Citigroup 67, 111, 172, 236
Clapman, Peter 114
Clearfield, Andrew 152
Clinton, Bill 8, 36, 74, 112, 161
Clore, Charles 115
Coca-Cola 114
Cold War 3, 4
command-and-control model of management 7–8
Commodity Futures Modernization Act (2000) (USA) 162
Commodity Futures Trading Commission 162
Company Law Review (UK) 268
Congress of South African Trade Unions (COSATU) 47
Conyou, Martin 237
Coopers & Lybrand Deloitte 140
Costa Rica 39
Crédit Lyonnais 100
Credit Suisse 236
Credit Suisse First Boston (CSFB) 166, 177, 179
Crockett, Andrew 58, 60
crony capitalism
    Asia 33
    Europe 88–91

De Tocqueville, Alexis 238
Deloitte & Touche 140
DeLong, Bradford 116–17
Deutsche Bank 86
Dimension Data 47
Disney 237

dotcom bubble 16, 22, 83
Drexel Burnham 68
Drucker, Peter 152
Dutch tulip mania 128
Dye, Tony 63

Ebbers, Bernie 19, 21, 149–50, 152, 167, 170, 243
economic liberalism 8–9
Eisner, Michael 237
Electric Storage Battery 115
Elf 89
English Electric 122
Eni Eramet 89
Enron 4, 18–19, 21, 22, 45–6, 77, 82, 104, 138, 139, 141, 159, 161–81, 219, 220, 235, 240, 256, 271
    Our Values 180
Ernst & Young 140
euro 84, 100–1, 104
Europe 81–105
    Anglo-American capital market model in 90–1, 92–3, 102, 104
    corporate governance 86
    crony capitalism 88–91
    labour market inflexibility 98–9
    poison pills 94–100
    privatization 87
    relations with SA 100–5
    stock markets 11–12
    unemployment 82
European Central Bank 98, 103
European Commission 94
European Monetary Union (EMU) 83, 84, 86, 91
European Union 83–4, 92, 97, 98, 105, 187, 228–31
    pension directive 100
    takeover directive 93–4
Exchange Stabilization Fund 112

Fastow, Andrew 18, 164
Federal Reserve 8, 36, 53, 66, 67, 75, 103, 220
Feldstein, Martin 189
Financial Accounting Standards Board 154, 168
Financial Services Authority 147, 258
Fisher, Peter 162
Ford Motor 93
Fore Systems 125, 126, 128, 129
Foreign Corrupt Practices Act (USA) 135
foreign direct investment (FDI) 49–51, 250–1
France, shareholder activism 89–90
France Télécom 90, 100
Friends of the Earth 241
FTSE 100 47
Fukuyama, Francis 27, 175

Galbraith, John Kenneth 237
Gartmore 149
General Electric 20, 122, 130, 134, 144, 231
General Electric Company 121, 122–6, 150
General Motors 7, 223, 224
Generali 89
Gent, Sir Christopher 21
Germany
    bank domination 85, 86
    long-termism in 7
    successful economy 5
    takeovers 93
    taxation 88–9
Glass-Steagall Act (1933) 171, 172, 236
Glaxo 133
Global Corporate Governance Forum 36, 248
Global Crossing 4, 19, 173, 256

global index-tracking 252
globalization of capital flows 9
gold standard 35, 58
Goldman Sachs 48, 67, 109–10, 113,
    120, 135, 136, 166, 179, 191
Goyder, Mark 256
Gramm, Phil 161
Gramm, Wendy 161
Grant, James 72
Gray, John 31–2, 33
Greenberg, Maurice 'Hank' 256
Greenpeace 241
Greenspan, Alan 10, 15, 38–9, 54, 55,
    68, 69–70, 71, 73, 74, 76–8, 222,
    238
Groupe André 90
Grubman, Jack 20, 167
Gucci 89, 94

Hampel, Sir Ronnie 119, 135
Hanson, Lord 118, 130, 131
Hasung Jung 253
Hawley, Michael 156
hedge funds 64–5
Henderson, Sir Denys 118, 119
Hermes 147
Hitler, Adolf 95, 215
Hollywood 114
Hong Kong Securities and Futures
    Commission's Takeovers and
    Mergers Panel 254
Hotpoint 122
Hurn, Sir Roger 123, 124, 126

IBM 7, 20
Imperial Chemical Industries (ICI)
    118–21, 125–7, 129–36, 234
Ina 89
Indonesia 36, 45

Institutional Shareholder Services (ISS)
    146, 147
International Accounting Standards
    Board 255
International Corporate Governance
    Network 201
International Finance Corporation 27
International Institute of Finance 51
International Monetary Fund (IMF) 31,
    33–6, 56, 178, 247, 248
International Nickel (INCO) 115
Investec 47
Investor Responsibility Research Center
    140
irrational exuberance 54
Ishihara, Shintaro 216
Istituto per la Ricostruzione Industriale
    (IRI) 87

Jager, Durk 155, 156
Jang, Hasung 253
Japan 201–16, 220
    1980s bubble 14, 15–16, 73, 76,
        204–5, 220, 221–2, 225–6
    corporate governance 207–10
    deflation 97–8
    Financial Supervision Agency 177
    investment 206–7
    GDP 201, 214
    government bonds 211–12, 213
    inflation 215–16
    keiretsu 203–4, 207
    life insurance 210–11
    long-termism in 7
    Ministry of International Trade and
        Industry (MITI) 14
    model of capitalism 170–2
    public sector debts 213–16
    savings rate 206
    shareholding in 12–13

successful economy 5
Trust Fund Bureau (Japanese
    Ministry of Finance) 211
Jeune Afrique 26
Jospin, Lionel 81, 90, 92, 99

Kaufman, Henry 256, 257
Kay, John 131, 132, 232
keiretsu 12, 170, 203
Keynes, John Maynard 51, 270, 273
    Economic Consequences of Peace 27–8
Khrushchev, Nikita 4
Kidder Peabody 134
Kindleberger, Charles 54
knowledge-workers 266
Kochan, Thomas 266
Koizumi, Junichiro 201, 209
Komansky, David 68
Korea banking systems 44
KPMG 121, 140

labour market
    mobility 29
    regulations, Europe 98–9
Lafley, Alan 155
Lang, Professor Larry 197
Latin American crisis 30, 36
Lay, Kenneth 18, 163, 166, 169, 175,
    180
Lazard Frères 88
Le Pen, Jean-Marie 29
least developed countries 49–50
Legrand 90
Lens fund 147
leverage 35
Levitt, Arthur 165
Lloyds TSB 236
Long-Term Capital Management
    (LTCM) hedge fund, collapse of
    42, 57, 65–70, 162

Lucent 125
LVMH 89, 94

M&A Consulting 208
Maastricht Treaty 84
Maddison, Angus 193, 194, 195
Malaysia 36, 45
Mannesmann 88, 93, 101
Marconi 121, 124–9, 133–5, 149, 232
Marron, Donald 68
Marx, Karl 61
Maxwell, Robert 140, 166, 220
Mayer, Martin 41
Mayo, John 119, 123, 125, 128, 129,
    135
M'Baye, Sanou 25–6, 52
McDonald's 92, 101, 114, 141
McDonough, William 67, 238, 249
McGinn, Richard 156
McKinsey 104, 120, 252, 266
McKinsey Global Institute 17
Means, Gardiner 114, 148
Mediobanca 88
Mencken, H.L. 23
Meriwether, John 65, 67, 68, 69
Merrill Lynch 48, 167
    Asset Management 149
Merton, Robert 65
Messier, Jean-Marie 91, 99
meta-fund-managers 232
Mexico 57
Microsoft 7, 16, 64, 264
Miegel, Meinhard 188
Milken, Michael 68
Miller Smith, Charles 119–20, 121, 136
Millstein, Ira 44, 248
Minc, Alain 82
Ministry of Defence 123
Ministry of International Trade and
    Industry (MITI) (Japan) 14

Mobius, Mark 253
Monde Diplomatique, Le 26
Monks, Robert 138, 145, 146, 147, 237, 263
Morgan Chase, J.P. 111, 172, 178
Morgan Stanley 48, 179
  Capital International Index 32
Morrison, Dale 156
Mugabe, Robert 47
Mullins, David 68
Murakami, Yoshiaki 208, 209
Murphy, Kevin 237
Mussolini, Benito 87, 214
Myners, Paul 259, 260, 262

Nacchio, Joseph 236
NASDAQ 13, 64
National Front 29
National Starch 120
Neuer Markt 17, 90
new paradigm 15
New York Federal Reserve 67–8, 162
New York Stock Exchange 64
Nissan 205
Nixon 55
Nokia 132
non-audit fees 139–40
Nortel 63, 125
Nouveau Marché 90
Nuovo Mercato 90

O'Connor Associates 176
OECD 36, 178, 206, 248
OECD–World Bank Global Corporate
  Governance Forum 44
Okuda, Hiroshi 201, 202, 209
Okumura, Ariyoshi 208
Old Mutual 47
Olivetti 89
Ollila, Jorma 132

Olsen, Mancur 103, 145
O'Neill, Paul 162
option-pricing, theory of 59
Oxford Analytica 45

Partnoy, Frank 177
Paulson, Henry 'Hank' 109, 241
Pax Britannica 58
PDFM 63, 149
Pension Benefit Guarantee Corporation 260
pension rights 260
Pensions & Investment Research
  Consultants (PIRC) 147
pensions 142–3, 144–5, 185–90, 233
  funds 42, 222–4
  pay-as-you-go 11–12, 185, 188, 189–90
People's Bank of China 77
People's Solidarity for Participatory
  Democracy 253
Perry, Commodore 209
Persaud, Avinash 57, 249
Persson, Goeran 99
Phibro 256
Philippines 45
Pickens, T. Boone 203
Pirelli 94
Pitt, Harvey 260
Post Office 147
Powers, William 163
PricewaterhouseCoopers 140
principal-agent problem 115
privatisation 87
process-oriented regulation 60
Procter & Gamble (P&G) 155
Provera, Marco Tronchetti 95
Prudential 149

Qwest Communications 19, 120

Railtrack 173
rank and yank 232
Reading, Brian 202, 214
Reed, John 67
Regan, Donald 112
Reltec 125, 126, 128, 129
Renault 205
Reuters 132–3
'Rhenish' (Rhineland) capitalism 84
Rickford, Jonathan 229
Rigas family 170
Rogowski, Michael 97
Roll, Eric 9
Ronen, Joshua 239, 258
Roosevelt, Franklin D. 112
Rousseau, Jean-Jacques 116
Royal Dutch Shell 63
Rubin, Robert 34, 112, 162

S&P 500 index 63
Salomon Smith Barney 166, 167
San Paolo-IMI 93
Sappi 47
Sarbanes-Oxley Act (July 2002) 23,
    229, 230, 257
Schneider 90
Scholes, Myron 65
Schroders 149
Schroeder, Gerhard 88, 92–3
Schumpeter, Joseph 10, 62, 72, 158
Securities and Exchange Commission
    (SEC) 230, 258
Senegal 39
September 11, 2001, terrorist attack 3,
    26, 31, 51, 52, 70, 76
Shiller, Robert J.: Irrational Exuberance
    62, 79
Siemens 122, 124
Silicon Valley 29

Simon, Bill 112
Simpson, Anne 32
Simpson, Lord George 123–4, 126
Singapore 36
Skilling, Jeffrey 18, 171
Smithers, Andrew 74, 154
Smithers & Co. 264
Soros, George 64
South Africa 46–7
South African Breweries 47
South Sea Bubble 55, 128
Soviet Union, demise of 3
special purpose entities 163, 164, 172
Spitzer, Eliot 20, 167, 235
Stiglitz, Joseph 34–5, 169, 226
    Globalization and its Discontents 34
Stoiber, Edmund 92
Strousberg, Bethel Henry 78
Sullivan, Scott 19
Summers, Lawrence 7–8, 14–15, 16, 60
supermajority provision 110
Swissair 173
Sykes, Allen 145, 158, 263
synthetic equities 176

Taiwan 36, 44
Takeover Panel (UK) 118
Telecom Italia 89, 94, 95
Templeton 253
Thailand 45
Thatcher, Margaret 87, 91, 102, 103
Thoman, Richard 156
TIAA-CREF 89–90, 146, 152
Time Warner 127, 130, 234
Tobin tax 92
Tokyo Style 208
TotalFina 89
Toynbee, Arnold 3
Toyota 205, 216

Trust Fund Bureau (Japanese Ministry
    of Finance) 211
Turner, Lynn 19
Tweedie, Sir David 255
Tyco 4, 21

UBS Paine Webber 166
UBS Warburg 135, 176, 225
UK
    Company Law Review 268
    productivity growth (1990s) 15
unemployment
    Europe 82
    USA 82–3
Unicredito for Banca Commerciale 93
Unilever 119–20, 234
United Nations 49
US Steel 223
USA
    Federal Reserve 8, 36, 53, 66, 67, 75,
        103, 220
    stock market bubble (1990s) 57–8,
        61–3, 71, 73, 221
    unemployment 82–3

value destruction 148
values gap, transatlantic 83
Vasiliev, Dmitry 254
venture capital market 117
in the USA 7, 13
Verité 45
Vietnam war 55
Vivendi Universal 91, 99, 234
Vodafone 21, 88, 101, 167, 234
Volcker, Paul 176, 255
Volkswagen 93

Wall Street crash (1929) 58, 73, 171,
    205, 220, 272
Wall Street Walk 144

Warburg, S,G, 119
Ward, Lloyd 156
Warner-Lambert 155
Webb, David 254
Webb-Site.com 254
Weinberg, Sidney 112
Weinstock, Lord Arnold 122–3, 150
Welch, Jack 143
Wellcome Foundation 133
Wellcome Trust 133
Welsh, Jack 134
White, Lord 118
Wilshire Associates 45
winner's curse 114
Winnick, Gary 169
Winter, Jaap 94
Wolfensohn, James 39, 40, 247
World Bank 8, 27, 31, 33, 36, 39–40,
    141, 187, 247, 248
World Trade Center terrorist attack see
    September 11 terrorist attack
World Trade Organization (WTO)
    194–5, 196
    riot in Seattle (1999) 4
WorldCom 4, 19, 21, 22, 127, 139, 149,
    152, 167, 220, 234, 235, 243, 244,
    256, 259, 271
Wright, Stephen 74, 154
Wriston, Walt 134
Wyser-Pratte, Guy 90

Xerox 235

Year 2000 (Y2K) computer problem 70
Yeltsin, Boris 237

Zaito 211
Zaloom, Anthony 207
Zeneca 119, 121, 120, 126, 129, 131
Zimbabwe 47